LEBANON
Improbable Nation
A STUDY IN POLITICAL DEVELOPMENT

Indiana University International Studies

LEBANON
Improbable Nation

A STUDY IN POLITICAL DEVELOPMENT

Leila M. T. Meo

INDIANA UNIVERSITY PRESS

BLOOMINGTON

*Publication of this book has been
assisted by Indiana University's Advisory
Committee on International Studies.*

To the People of Lebanon

PREFACE

In the fall of 1959 I went to Lebanon to try to find at first hand the causes of the five-month crisis and revolution that the country had sustained the previous year and that had brought it world attention when American marines were landed on its shores. I found myself immediately absorbed not only in a study of the events of 1958, but also of Lebanese history and political institutions—and, in fact, of the creation of the state itself. For as it turned out, the crisis was related to all these factors and it was impossible to know its real causes without knowing at the same time how modern Lebanon was created and how it has continued as a viable state. The following pages tell the story. It is the story of Lebanon in her domestic, regional, and international setting.

In my research I have relied on Arabic, English, and French sources for both the historical and the modern phase of this study. My main concern has been, of course, the creation of modern Lebanon and the establishment and maintenance of the balance of power among the various religious minorities which constitute her population. Thus I have limited my treatment of the historical phase to those social and political developments of the nineteenth century which laid the groundwork for Lebanon's confessional democracy, and which help explain certain characteristics of the modern period. I have also treated the development of Arab nationalism insofar as it related to the question of Lebanese viability.

In addition to academic sources, I have made wide use of the Lebanese and foreign press, especially with regard to the orisis of 1958, as well as of the writings of Lebanese journalists, politicians, and other public figures who have had something to say about Lebanon, her politics, and her people. During my year in Lebanon I also interviewed former leaders of the Opposition of 1958, spokesmen for the former regime of President Chamoun, third-party mediators, and informed observers of the crisis. To all these people I wish to express my gratitude for their courtesy and cooperation. I am also grateful to the American University of Beirut for allowing me unlimited access to its library, and to the University's Department of Political Science and Public Administration for use of its press clipping files.

This study was originally made under a grant from the Ford Foundation. It was later revised to include greater detail on the international aspects of the crisis. The writing of this final version has been made possible by a grant from the Carnegie Faculty Seminar on Political and Administrative Development, Department of Government, Indiana University.

I wish to extend my special thanks to Indiana University Professors P. J. Vatikiotis, who advised me on the original manuscript, and Edward H. Buehrig, whose encouragement and advice have resulted in the publication of this book. But though I acknowledge the kind help of many people, I take sole and full responsibility for its entire contents.

LEILA M. T. MEO

Washington, D. C.
January, 1965

CONTENTS

ix

x   *Contents*

MAPS

CHAPTER 1

The Introduction of Confessional Politics into Lebanese Society, 1830-1860

In 1958 the tiny Mediterranean Republic of Lebanon, independent since 1943, was seized with an internal crisis that split its population into two opposing and about equal halves over a complex political question, disrupted its prospering economy, and even caused its sovereignty to be an issue of international debate. The crisis, which had been growing beneath the surface for more than a year, erupted in May in the form of a small revolution, or more properly an armed resistance, against the regime of President Camille Chamoun. The President's term in office was due to expire in September, and his friends in the unicameral legislature had been about to introduce a constitutional amendment to permit him to succeed himself, when the revolution broke. The Opposition deputies in the legislature had long warned in the press and in public speeches against any move to permit the President to succeed himself. Now, the leaders of the revolution, including the legislative Opposition, declared that no less than his immediate resignation would be necessary to end the "general strike" that they had called. About half the population supported their demand. The President, however, refused to resign and let it be known that he would complete his legal term in office. He was backed by the other half of the population.

What were the issues behind these incompatible objectives? The leaders of the revolution contended that the President had deviated from Lebanon's traditional policy of neutrality in in-

3

ternational politics by concluding a military-political treaty with the United States, and that he had generally inclined toward the West, contrary to the interests of Lebanon and of its sister Arab states. In order to put an end to this harmful deviationist foreign policy, they argued, the President must resign immediately. Denying that he was following a deviationist foreign policy, and that his written understanding with the United States (which was based on the Eisenhower Doctrine) was a military-political treaty, Mr. Chamoun countered by blaming the United Arab Republic for instigating the revolution through "massive interference" in internal Lebanese affairs. In fact, he charged, the revolution was being directed and sustained with men, money, and materiel by the U.A.R. in order to undermine the independence of Lebanon because it was acting as a sovereign nation and not as a satellite of the U.A.R.

Nonsense, replied Chamoun's opponents, the revolution was not inspired by the U.A.R., it was a purely internal and spontaneous act of resistance. Cairo joined the debate by publicly repudiating the official Lebanese allegations, and on May 16 President Gamal Abdel Nasser declared that the U.A.R. supported and respected Lebanon's independence, did not interfere in its internal affairs, and would not accept any interference from any other source. Yet on July 15 the United States charged the U.A.R. with indirect aggression against Lebanon and, in response to a request from President Chamoun and in accordance with its commitment to Lebanon under the Eisenhower Doctrine, landed American marines there to protect Lebanese sovereignty and integrity.

The situation was full of contradictions. Who was right? Was the revolution a purely internal affair, as its leaders claimed, or was it instigated and abetted by the U.A.R., as the Chamoun regime maintained? Why was Lebanon's foreign policy so sharply attacked—and so strongly defended? After fifteen years of independence, why were Lebanon's sovereignty and integrity now

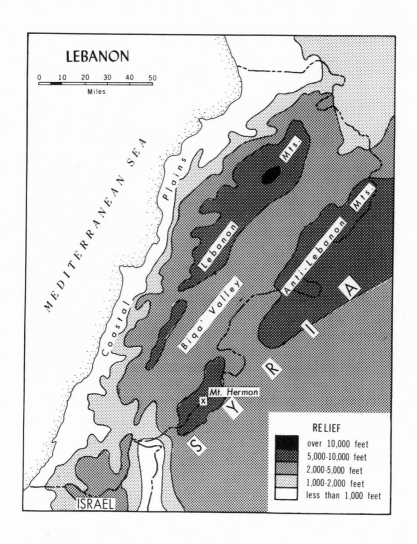

LEBANON

0 10 20 30 40 50
Miles

MEDITERRANEAN SEA

Plains

Coastal

Lebanon Mts.

Biqa' Valley

Anti-Lebanon Mts.

SYRIA

Mt. Hermon
x

ISRAEL

RELIEF

over 10,000 feet
5,000-10,000 feet
2,000-5,000 feet
1,000-2,000 feet
less than 1,000 feet

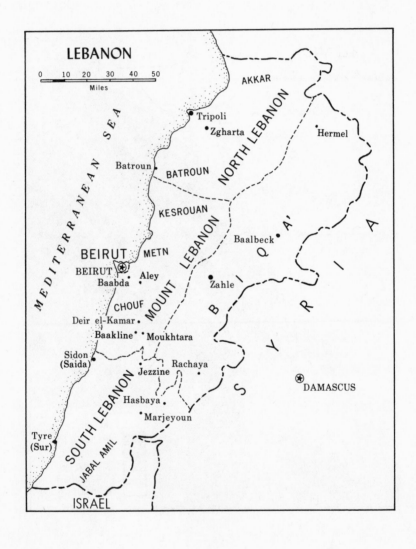

LEBANON

0   10   20   30   40   50
Miles

M E D I T E R R A N E A N   S E A

AKKAR

Tripoli

Zgharta

NORTH LEBANON

Hermel

Batroun

BATROUN

KESROUAN

MOUNT LEBANON

BEIRUT

METN

BEIRUT

Aley

Baabda

Baalbeck

B I Q A'

Zahle

CHOUF

Deir el-Kamar

Baakline

Moukhtara

S Y R I A

Sidon
(Saida)

Jezzine

Rachaya

DAMASCUS

Hasbaya

Marjeyoun

SOUTH LEBANON

Tyre
(Sur)

JABAL AMIL

ISRAEL

put into question? And just how was the United States committed to the protection of both under the Eisenhower Doctrine, its new Middle East policy? Amid all the confusion and babel of voices, one fact was clear. Not only were the Lebanese people divided into more or less equal camps over the issues involved, but they were divided along religious lines also. Most of those who supported the revolution and its objectives were members of the Muslim communities. Most of those who defended the Chamoun regime and concurred in its views belonged to the Christian communities. This was, then, a deadlock of Christians and Muslims. So part of the answer to the crisis must be sought in a study of these two major components of Lebanon's population, their historical relationships, and how they differed in their attitudes and aspirations for their homeland. The study will take us back to the creation of Greater Lebanon in 1920 under French mandate. Against the background of the emergence of Greater Lebanon, with its new geographical boundaries, we can then pursue the questions raised above with an examination of the Eisenhower Doctrine and its purposes, of its acceptance by the Chamoun regime and its rejection and condemnation by the revolutionary Opposition, and of the involvement of the doctrine in inter-Arab affairs. We shall show how the crisis was finally resolved and evaluate the usefulness of the doctrine as a vehicle for the achievement of American objectives in the Middle East.

But there are other pieces of the Lebanese puzzle that cannot be explained through an analysis of the obvious issues of the quarrel. Why, for instance, did certain Christian parliamentarians and public figures, as well as the spiritual head of the largest Christian community, publicly align themselves with the position taken by the leadership of the Muslim Opposition? Perhaps there was more to the crisis than a Muslim-Christian split over the questions of foreign policy and national integrity. Were private ambitions and individual frustrations involved? If so, how did they relate to the contentions on which both Government and Opposition chose to base their respective cases?

The logical place to start looking is within the political institutions of the country. Lebanon is a parliamentary democracy with a legislature consisting of the Chamber of Deputies and an executive composed of the President of the Republic and the Cabinet. Representation in both places is on a confessional basis, that is, candidates for these elective or appointive offices must belong to certain religious communities. There are six major sects in Lebanon, three Christian (Maronite, Greek Orthodox, and Greek Catholic), and three Muslim (Sunni, Shi'i, and Druze). All must be represented in the Chamber of Deputies according to a ratio that was fixed in 1943, when spokesmen for the six sects reached a compromise for the consolidation and maintenance of Lebanese independence. The ratio, which does not vary with population changes,[1] gives the Christians, including a few other minor sects, a slight edge over the Muslims in the Chamber, where the size of the membership must always be a multiple of eleven so as to allow the Christians six representatives for every five for the Muslims. The President of the Chamber, however, must always be a Shi'i Muslim. Within the executive, the compromise of 1943 permanently reserved the presidency of the Republic for the Maronite Christians, the largest community, and the premiership for the Sunni Muslims, the next largest community, and called for a balance of sectarian representation within the other Cabinet posts.

The compromise of 1943 is to be found neither in the state constitution nor in any of the state laws. It is a tacit understanding that enjoys the force of law because each religious community invokes it to protect its own position and interests within the state. The struggle for power among the politicians must therefore take place within the limiting boundaries of its confessional framework. And it is here that we must look to see whether any personal motives kindled the revolution of 1958. It is here also that we must try to find whether private ambitions and frustrations among the politicians attached themselves sub rosa to the larger issues of foreign policy and independence. If, indeed, the struggle for power among the politicians operated in 1958 under the umbrella of foreign policy and independence issues, we must seek the reasons for this joining of the battle. The clue again lies in the compromise of 1943, for before that date there had been no general agreement among the religious communities on the type of independence that Lebanon should seek from the mandatory power, France, and no general agreement on the geographical limits that the sovereign state should have. The reasons for this lack of consensus may be found in the history of Lebanon, which culturally and geographically forms part of the Arab world. Only a confessional balance of power within the governing institutions could bridge the gap of disagreement among the communities.

But confessional representation was not a new formula invented in 1943 to keep together the various parts of the newly independent nation. It had been evolving for approximately one hundred years, and its development created certain patterns of political accommodation which were manifested in the post-independence period, and the disruption of which could have also spurred the revolution of 1958. To place the events of that year in their proper perspective, we must therefore trace the evolution of confessionalism in Lebanese politics from its earliest times. Three pre-independence periods can be identified: 1830–1860, when the Sublime Porte, Lebanon's suzerain, first introduced confessional representation within the governing institutions of the time; 1861–1914, when confessionalism was established on a firmer foundation by the Sublime Porte and the Concert of Europe powers within the government of an autonomous Mount Lebanon; and 1920–1943, when confessionalism was reintroduced into Lebanon's political institutions by France in the interest of "sectarian equity."

As the history of confessionalism unfolds, it becomes increasingly clear that though it is a phenomenon of the Lebanese political scene, it is not an entirely home-grown product. From its earliest manifestations up until independence it was helped and encouraged by external influences, by the policies of other nations. In this study, we must therefore necessarily pursue the impact of regional and international politics on Lebanese confessionalism as well as the influence of this very confessionalism on Lebanon's regional and foreign policies. The interaction between the two phenomena becomes the story of Lebanon's political development up through the crisis of 1958, when the tangled threads of the charges and countercharges can be sorted out, the roles and objectives of the domestic and foreign protagonists identified, and the way indicated to permit this improbable but fascinating nation to continue as a viable entity.

FROM ACCOMMODATION TO COMMUNAL STRIFE

Occupying roughly the middle third of the eastern shore of the Mediterranean Sea, the small Republic of Lebanon owes much to both its geographical location and its topographical characteristics in the shaping of the long and significant history of its land and people. Lebanon has an area of only 4,062 square miles and a population officially placed at some 2,152,000 for 1963–1964, but from the beginning of recorded history this small country has been in constant interaction with much larger and more important nations.

Lebanon may properly be called a *carrefour*—a busy crossroads on the highways of the world. Its coastal plains and ports and its inland plain of the Biqa' made of it in the past a passageway for conquerors going east or west, north or south to occupy territory in Asia, Europe, or Africa. At other times its two mountain ranges, the Lebanon and Anti-Lebanon, with their almost unnegotiable towering peaks and deep valleys, served as a buffer against similar conquests.

Secure against sudden attack, these mountains and valleys became a ready refuge into which streamed various groups of heretic sects fleeing from persecution by orthodox religions in neighboring lands. Finding themselves all in the same plight, the settlers learned to live with each other as neighbors, and often joined forces to drive off a common aggressor from beyond their mountain strongholds. Though the Middle East was consecutively taken by Byzantine, Arab, Mameluk, and Ottoman conquerors and ruled directly by them, the Lebanese mountains remained effectively autonomous most of the time, thanks to their difficult terrain, the hardy character of the mountaineers, and the cunning leadership of their chieftains.

When the Ottoman Turks conquered the Middle East in 1516–1517 the Lebanese mountain ranges, the Lebanon and Anti-Lebanon, technically became part of the Arab region of the Ottoman Empire, but throughout the 400 years of Turkish rule the Ottomans were never able to acquire direct control of the Lebanons. By paying them the annual tribute due them as suzerains of the mountains, the feudal lords, the actual rulers of the Lebanons, kept them at bay. Money for the tribute was raised through local taxes collected by the fiefholders or, as they were known in Arabic, the *mukate'jis*.[2] At first, the *mukate'jis* held office by virtue of election or appointment by the top feudal prince, the Emir of the Mountain as he was called, who held sway over the lesser feudal lords. But in time the office became a hereditary one, although powerful Emirs from the Ma'an and later Chehab dynasty could and did replace one *mukate'ji* by another when it suited their purpose.

Feudal rule in Lebanon antedated the Ottoman conquest, but it reached its peak as a political and social system during the Ottoman Empire, first under the Ma'an Emirs, who controlled the mountain ranges from the advent of the Turks until the exile of Fakhr ad-Din Ma'an II in 1635, and later under the Chehab Emirs, who ruled from the fall of the Ma'ans until the removal of

Bechir Chehab III in 1841. The Ma'ans and the Chehabs, particularly Fakhr ad-Din Ma'an II and Bechir Chehab II, both powerful and shrewd men who were in power for half a century each, extended their influence and often effective control beyond the mountains into the inland plain of the Biqa' and the coastal plain and cities of Beirut, Tripoli, and Sidon. There were numerous population shifts within this area, especially in the mountains, during the Ottoman period. They were caused both by the influx of fresh waves of religious and national groups from the outside, which pushed older groups into other sections, and by the movement of the peasantry into areas which they considered offered greater farming opportunities.

Historical sources provide incomplete information on population movements within the emirate of Mount Lebanon (both under the Ma'ans and under the Chehabs) and on the size of each national or religious group. But it is generally agreed that the two groups that played the most important role in achieving and maintaining the unity and autonomy of the Mountain, as the whole collection of peaks under princely rule was called, were the Maronites and the Druze.[3] An alliance between the two communities concluded in the first quarter of the seventeenth century led to the incorporation of northern Lebanon into the emirate of Fakhr ad-Din Ma'an II of southern Lebanon and the establishment of the emirate of Mount Lebanon in 1627. Northern Lebanon, however, remained the stronghold of the Maronites, where the majority of the peasants and nobility belonged to the Maronite church. Druze nobility and peasantry were concentrated in southern Lebanon. Less important in size and influence were four other communities: the Metawilis or Shi'i Muslims; the Greek Orthodox and Greek Catholic (both Christian), who were settled in their own homogeneous centers and in mixed areas in both the Mountain and the Biqa' plain; and the Sunni Muslims, who, on the whole, lived in the coastal plains and coastal cities.[4] They were all, however, significant in the social structure of the Mountain and its environs, and each was later to play a role in the communal disturbances that erupted in the mid-nineteenth century.

In the 1840's an "official count" put the population of the emirate of Mount Lebanon at 87,727 Maronites, 12,023 Druze, and 6,744 Sunnis and Shi'is. Thus the Maronites, the largest Christian community, constituted 85 per cent of the population.[5] Though it is doubtful that this census was completely accurate, it does indicate in a general way that the Maronite Christians were in the majority. What is significant is that by the 1830's, when a number of developments contributed to the weakening of the Druze-Maronite alliance and the emergence of mutual suspicions, large numbers of Maronite peasants were living among the Druze in southern Lebanon and farming the lands of Druze feudal lords. In fact, so many of the Maronites from the north had moved south over the years that they now formed a larger population there than the Druze, the earlier settlers of southern Lebanon.

The seeds of the disturbances between the two communities during the 1830's had been planted by Bechir Chehab II, Emir of Mount Lebanon from 1789 to 1840. To consolidate his hold over the Mountain, the Emir, a Sunni by birth but a Christian convert, infringed upon the hereditary privileges of Druze feudal families and in some cases, such as the Junblatts, the 'Imads, and the Abu-Nakads, dispossessed them outright.[6] He followed a policy of favoritism toward the Christian majority and at times instigated them against the Druze. In 1822 he took temporary refuge from the wrath of the Sublime Porte at the court of Mohammed Ali and he and the overlord of Egypt plotted against their common suzerain, the Sultan of Turkey. Bechir hoped to secure his position in Lebanon and returned home to pursue with greater vigor his policy of creating communal strife. With the connivance of Bechir, Mohammed Ali planned to occupy Syria and Lebanon as a necessary first step for the realization of his dream of empire that would take him to the very gates of Constantinople.

Syria and Lebanon were occupied by the armies of Ibrahim Pasha, Mohammed Ali's son, in 1831–1832. In Lebanon the Christians welcomed the occupation, but the Druze opposed it and their leaders fled to a northern Syrian town to plot the ouster of the Egyptians. But the Egyptians maintained their strategic sway over Syria and Lebanon for nine years, during which time they helped Bechir II strengthen his hold over his domain. In 1840 the pressure of Turkey and the European powers (with the exception of France) and a revolt by the people of Syria and Lebanon forced the Egyptians to retreat. Bechir II was deposed and banished by the Sultan.

The occupation had a disastrous effect on Druze-Maronite relations. True, the Maronites had joined the Druze in revolt when Egyptian rule had become oppressive to them also, but the entente was short-lived. For each community looked back on the occupation in a different light. The Druze recalled that the Maronites had guided and helped Ibrahim's soldiers in entering Lebanon, and were later recruited and armed, along with other Christians, to put down Druze uprisings against the Egyptians. They recalled, too, how under Bechir II the Maronites had gradually gained political and numerical preponderance over them in their own traditional stronghold in the south. Now that Bechir was gone, however, and their own leaders were back from their forced exile, the Druze felt it was time to avenge their past humiliations and at the same time defend their right to continued existence in Lebanon.

The Maronites had other ideas. Having responded to Turkish and British encouragements to drive out the Egyptian armies, they now expected the Sublime Porte to sanction the position of ascendancy they had gained over the Druze.[7]

There were other contributory causes of the widening rift between the Druze and Maronites. For one thing, between the

1830's and the 1850's the Sublime Porte as well as France, Britain, and Russia were constantly meddling in Lebanese affairs. At the same time, the Druze and Maronite communities were reacting differently to social and political changes wrought by the Egyptian occupation.

The Sultan, who had been forced in 1833 to agree to Mohammed Ali's control of Syria and Lebanon, remained unreconciled to that situation, and, fearing that it might set a precedent for a further decimation of his empire, sent out his agents to stir up the discontented elements against Ibrahim Pasha's rule. These were the Druze and Sunni Muslims, who saw themselves gradually losing their influence to the Christian communities.

On their part, France, Britain, and Russia sought to establish durable ties, each with a different religious community within Lebanon and Syria. Each power hoped that its special ties with a community would help bring it a larger share of the Levant when the tottering Ottoman Empire finally collapsed. France, the protector of the Maronite community since the twelfth-century Crusades, temporarily lost face with its protégé when in 1840 it hesitated to withdraw support of the Egyptian occupation, which by then, despite their favored position, had become unbearable to the Maronites also. Yet France soon regained its old-time influence by championing the interests of the Maronites and other Uniate Christians.

Russia had gradually extended its protection over the Christian Orthodox communities as an excuse for interfering in Levantine affairs. Britain, however, remained without a protégé. But by the late 1830's it had sent out its agents to instigate Christians and Druze against the Egyptian occupation, and by 1840 it had decided to adopt the Druze as its protégés and to champion their interests against those of other communities.

Supported from the outside against each other by rival powers, the Lebanese sects themselves were undergoing different social experiences. The Christian peasantry as a whole, and the Maronite peasants in particular, appreciated the social and judiciary reforms that had been introduced under the aegis of Ibrahim Pasha, as well as the rational and fair system of taxation that had been imposed on rich and poor alike. They now felt that this democratic trend should be continued in the interest of their own social and economic betterment. Democratic thoughts soon sprouted a democratic movement among the Christian peasantry. It was directed against the nobility, whose heavy hand in the past had deprived the peasants of the greater share of their crops and earnings.

By contrast, the democratic spirit was noticeably lacking among the Druze rank and file. More warrior than peasant in outlook, they were neatly organized within the hierarchical structure of the Druze feudal system and were very loyal to their feudal lords.

The Lebanese feudal families had for some time been losing in influence and power, owing, on the one hand, to Bechir II's continuous efforts to consolidate his authority over the Mountain at their expense, and on the other to the democratizing reforms introduced during the Egyptian occupation and to Ibrahim Pasha's later attempts to limit the nobility's political and social predominance. Encouraged by the results, the Maronite clergy now sought to replace their nobility as leaders of their own community. Rising mainly from peasant backgrounds and harboring a strong resentment against the patronizing nobility, the Maronite priests pursued their ambition by feeding the spirit of revolt among their peasant congregations.

The social developments of the forties and fifties did not pass unobserved by the Sultan and his ministers. In fact, they planned to take advantage of them to accomplish their overriding objective of bringing Lebanon within the complete and direct control of the Sublime Porte. As an autonomous principality, Lebanon had encouraged revolutionary and separatist tendencies within the Sultan's European possessions, where he had been forced to make a retreat. It must not remain a symbol for the further decimation of the empire.

Well aware of his own military weakness and of the European powers' covetousness of his empire, the Sultan decided upon a shrewd course of action: he would encourage sectarian rivalries and set the Lebanese against each other until they themselves implored him to relieve them of their bankrupt autonomy. There were certain very useful methods he could employ. In 1839, making a bid for popular support within the empire and for the support of European opinion against the progressive Mohammed Ali, the Sublime Porte had proclaimed the *Hatti-Cherif* of Gulhane (named after the house of roses in the old seraglio), the first of the *tanzimat* or administrative reforms to be undertaken within the empire. The purpose of the proclamation was to procure for the provinces institutions which would effect the following reforms:

> 1. guarantees assuring the subjects of the Sultan a perfect security with regard to their life, honor and fortune;
> 2. a proper way of assessing and raising taxes;
> 3. an equally proper way of levying soldiers and regulating the duration of their service.[8]

No constitutional government was intended by these reforms, but simply a guarantee against official arbitrariness and bad administration. Yet the decree represented a major break with certain Islamic traditions of the empire. It announced extension of the reforms to all Ottoman subjects regardless of religion or sect, and thus introduced the principle of civil equality for the Christians and Jews of the empire. Traditionally, these people were not subject to the Shari'a, the Islamic law governing Muslims, but were organized according to religion and sect into semi-autonomous communities, each under its own ecclesiastical leader. These communities were tolerated and protected by the state as "people of the book"—i.e. the Old and New Testament recognized by Islam as books of divine revelation. But at the same time they were regarded by the Muslim faithful as separate and inferior for having rejected the revelations of Islam. Still, civil equality for them was officially proclaimed in the hope of winning the loyalty of dissident Christian groups and of dissipating separatist tendencies among the Christians of the Balkan region.[9]

In Lebanon, where the tradition of decentralization and feudal government had existed for so long, initiation of the reforms would be the means through which the Sublime Porte would carry out its policy of centralization. Using the reforms as a screen, it would aim at the subtle destruction of the feudal system, the mainstay of Lebanese autonomy, thus causing this autonomy to collapse and bringing Lebanon under its own direct control.

The first step toward centralization was taken in 1840, when the Ottomans returned to Lebanon. At the insistence of the French, protectors of the Maronites, who were well disposed toward the Chehab family, the Sublime Porte appointed Emir Bechir Kassim Chehab as Governor General of Lebanon. The firman of investiture, however, made it clear that the Emir must strictly obey the Sultan. The appointment offended the Druze, who had already suffered much under Chehab rule, but it suited the purposes of the Ottomans. And through Bechir Kassim they began institutionalizing the sectarian differences that had emerged to date. The Governor General was called upon to organize a *diwan* (provincial council) to hear disputes and carry on discussions in accordance with the laws. The council was to include

> twelve men, two from each of the major religious sects (Maronite, Druze, Orthodox, Greek Catholic, Sunnite Muslim, and Shi'ite Muslim), to assist him in the administration of justice. The Druze refused to cooperate in this arrangement by declining to choose their representatives, because they saw in the *diwan* an

encroachment on the traditional authority of the fiefholders. Bashir Qasim's reaction was a violent threat to dispossess the Druze shaikhs and divide their holdings among his own followers. This he actually did in the case of the 'Imad family, from whom he withdrew authority over the village of Shmistar and gave it to a branch of the Abi-l-Lami' family.[10]

Although Bechir Kassim was generally considered an unjust and incapable administrator who managed to displease at once the feudal lords, the clergy, Maronite peasantry, and Druze, a historian of the period, Michel Chebli, presents the following sympathetic picture of the Governor General:

> It is perhaps true to say that Bachir III "possessed neither the energy nor the prestige of his predecessor." But what could this emir really do against the outburst of passions excited by foreign politics? He was nicknamed "Abu-Tehine"[11] for having distributed flour in times of want. And when he became aware of the injustice of a measure, he hastened to correct it; such was the case when, through the simple intervention of the Maronite Patriarch, he restored to some Druze sheikhs, their villages in the Biqa'a that had been confiscated by their cousins.
>
> It was he, who, during his short government, established the electoral regime of Lebanon by creating the administrative Council. This Council, which had administrative and judiciary attributions had to be "elected and chosen" by the population and "had to settle matters according to the laws. . . ." It was composed of ten members of whom three were Maronite, three Druze, one Sunni, one [Greek] Orthodox, one Greek Catholic and one Shi'i.[12]

Not only was the sectarian composition of the Council proof of Bechir III's attitude of tolerance and appeasement, Chebli maintains, but it also attested to the spirit of conciliation that the Maronites exhibited. For though they constituted 85 per cent of the population, they were hardly represented on the Council in proportion to their numerical strength.[13]

There is still a third intimate though different description of the power structure within the *diwan* or Council. Agreeing with

Chebli on the numerical composition of the Council, M. Jouplain nevertheless points out the autocratic powers enjoyed by the Christian Emir:

> In effect, the equity in the distribution of mandates within the Council was but a fiction: the Emir Bechir-Kassim, as president by right, or his proxy whom he could appoint freely, could tip the scales to whatever side they wanted; but the Emir Kassim was a Christian and an enemy of the Druze. The Council, which was supposed to be a court of arbitration between the "nations", was thus threatening to become an instrument for Christian domination over the Druze, especially since the Emir Bechir-Kassim appointed as its effective head and as his proxy, the Christian Sheikh, Bechara el-Khouri, known for his hatred of the Druze.[14]

Whatever the personal merits or shortcomings of Bechir III, the Ottomans' administrative measures and instigation of classes and sects against each other soon paid off. Unable to remove Emir Bechir Kassim by peaceful and legal means, the Druze in 1841 turned to insurrection, which soon led to a sectarian civil war and the massacre of Christians in mixed areas. With the massacre well under way and no effective aid coming from the Ottomans, the Maronites requested the European powers to intervene on their behalf. France, Britain, Russia, Prussia, and Austria-Hungary responded most willingly and instructed their ambassadors to Constantinople to meet with the Sublime Porte to plan the administrative reorganization of the emirate of Mount Lebanon. The meeting was in fact precipitated by the Porte's bold step toward direct control of Lebanon and the final destruction of its autonomy. Removing Bechir Kassim from office at the end of 1841, the Porte sent in Ottoman troops, presumably to put an end to the troubles, and appointed a Turk, General Omar Pasha, as the new Governor General. He was also instructed to encourage the Christians to petition for direct Turkish control on a permanent basis. But opposition from the five European powers frustrated the plan, and in January, 1843,

Omar Pasha's regime was replaced by a new system of government they had worked out at the bargaining table with Turkey. The emirate was divided into two governorates, setting the scene for further sectarian strife and for further European intervention. The measures which led to these developments are set down below.

THE PARTITION OF LEBANON INTO A CHRISTIAN
AND A DRUZE GOVERNORATE

Although confessionalism in Lebanese politics is generally traced back to the establishment of the *Mutasarrifyya* (governorate) in 1861, the groundwork for this institution was actually laid down in the preceding nineteen years. During that time the once unified Mountain existed as two separate governorates, the Ottomans continued to organize and reorganize its political institutions along sectarian lines, and the European powers never ceased to interfere in its internal affairs to promote their own interests.

The partition plan of 1843 effected the following changes. The coastal plains and the Biqa' valley were put under direct Turkish control. The mountainous areas were reorganized into a northern governorate under a Maronite *qa'im maqam*, or governor, and a southern governorate under a Druze *qa'im maqam*. Both governors were put under the general supervision of the Pasha of Sidon, who was the Ottoman governor of both Beirut and Sidon and the direct representative of the Sultan. Furthermore, the office of *qa'im maqam* was made appointive and the controversial Chehabs were excluded as candidates for the governorship.

The reorganization of 1843 produced several negative results. The mountainous areas lost their economic prosperity by losing the fertile plains. Turkish appointment and supervision of the governors dealt a crippling blow to the institution of hereditary feudal rule; this, though it may be considered a positive step in itself, nonetheless weakened Lebanese autonomy, which rested on the power of the feudal lords. The arbitrary partition of the mountains into two about equal parts placed some of the Maronite communities within the Druze province; this became a constant source of trouble. The Christian province of the north was further weakened by the exclusion of the important district of Jbeil, nerve center of Maronite activity and seat of the Maronite Patriarch. Jbeil was attached to the Pachalik of Tripoli and thus came under direct Turkish rule.

The organization of the two governorates was not identical. In the Druze province of the south, where the nobility was predominantly Druze and the peasantry predominantly Maronite, steps were taken allegedly to safeguard the interests of both. In each of the mixed villages the Christian inhabitants could choose a Christian *wakil* or agent to look after their interests. He would be responsible not to the Druze governor, but to the Turkish governor in Sidon. The Druze population in the mixed districts also had their *wakils,* and both Druze and Christian *wakils* exercised judicial authority over their coreligionists and collected taxes from them on behalf of the *mukate'jis* or district feudal lords. Both functions had of course traditionally belonged to the *mukate'jis,* who now found their power sharply curtailed by the intrusion of elected *wakils.*

In the purely Maronite and purely Druze districts, however, the authority of the feudal lords was not curtailed. And the discrepancy was in time to fan the flames of dissatisfaction among the Christian peasantry in the wholly Christian districts and to lead to a peasant uprising.

Yet disturbances in both governorates continued unabated, and a serious outbreak of fighting between Maronites and Druze in 1845 elicited a formal protest from the Concert of Europe. The Sublime Porte responded by immediately sending Foreign Minister Shakib Effendi to Lebanon on an official mission of investigation. And at the end of the year a plan for reform which he had worked out was put into effect.

In accordance with the Règlement Shakib Effendi, as the plan was called, each governorate was endowed with a *majlis* or council composed of twelve members. It included the *qa'im maqam,* who presided over the meetings, a judge and a councillor from each of the Maronite, Greek Orthodox, Greek Catholic, Druze, and Sunni sects, and a Shi'i councillor. The Sunni judge also represented the Shi'is. The *qa'im maqam* was empowered to choose a deputy who would preside over the meetings in his absence. The first members of each council were nominated for life by Shakib Effendi, but their successors were to be chosen by common agreement among the bishops, the *okkals* (religious leaders of the three Muslim sects), and the remaining members of the council. Before any new member could be instated, however, he would have to be approved by the Pasha of Sidon. "The task of apportioning taxes, which was the more important function of the *majlis,* was to be undertaken collectively by the assessor members [the councillors] in the presence of the judges. In all other matters referred by the *qa'im maqam* the *majlis* would serve as a consultative council. The members were to be full-time officials receiving fixed salaries."[15]

The Règlement of 1845 achieved several objectives of the Ottoman authorities under the guise of a seemingly fair and considerate plan:

1. It undermined the influence of the feudal lords by making membership in each council elective rather than hereditary, and by requiring judges on the council to be professional men so that they could preside over both criminal and civil cases. Traditionally the feudal lords had acted as both administrators and judges in their respective districts. Now civil and criminal justice were lifted entirely from their jurisdiction. Furthermore, the principle of equality before the law swept away the special privileges that they had previously enjoyed, and imposed on

them the same personal and property taxes that the peasants had to pay.

2. It placed final authority and control of each *majlis* in the hands of the Turkish governor of Sidon. There were several avenues open for his interference. First, the councils were placed under the close supervision of the *qa'im maqams,* who in turn were closely watched and controlled by the Pasha of Sidon. Next, decisions by each council had to be unanimous, but because of sectarian rivalries the council was often deadlocked. So the Pasha intervened to settle matters his way. Finally, since new members of each council had to be approved by the Pasha, he was able to force the selection of men he could control, and later play them off against the *qa'im maqam.* This was not too difficult because the *qa'im maqams* were appointed by the Ottomans from among the nobility while the members of the councils represented the peasantry, especially those recommended by the Maronite bishops, who aspired to the leadership of their community.

On the village level, the Règlement Shakib Effendi continued the system of municipal representation, through elected *wakils,* in the mixed areas, but left the areas with homogeneous populations, as before, under the direct control of the hereditary feudal lords. Certain feudal privileges, such as the recruitment of labor gangs and the levying of special taxes, were also left intact. Such obviously deliberate discrepancies between the local governments of the different areas were bound to exacerbate, as intended, the class struggle.

FOREIGN INTERESTS AND THE PRINCIPLE
OF FOREIGN INTERVENTION

The preceding pages indicated that the Concert of Europe powers, and especially France, Britain, and Russia, acted as a self-appointed watch-dog committee over the affairs of Lebanon in pursuance of their own interests. A closer look at these interests is now in order.

Of the major European powers, France enjoyed the oldest, and apparently the most durable, relations with the Levant. French connections with Lebanon, as we have already seen, dated to the twelfth-century Crusades, when the Maronites became the friends and allies of the Frankish invaders. In 1250 King Louis of France sent a letter to the Maronite Patriarch and bishops expressing his gratitude for the friendship of the Maronites and extending to them French protection in the same measure as it was enjoyed by Frenchmen themselves. By cultivating the friendship of the Ottoman Sultans, the French monarchs acquired a series of capitulations from the sixteenth century on which gave France the right first to protect its own citizens within the Ottoman Empire, and later to extend this protection to all ecclesiastics of the Latin rite. Gradually, with the arrival in the Levant of Catholic religious orders, who were set on winning the dissident Eastern churches back to Rome, France came to claim the right of protection over all Catholics and Christians in the Levant. Such a right, however, was never formally granted in a capitulation. In the Lebanon, the only Christians who responded to France's bid to protect them were those of the Catholic rites, and mainly the Maronites, whose higher clergy paid visits to France to seek further support from the "compassionate mother," and whose upper-class families sent many of their sons to work for the French consular service in the Levant.

France strove to maintain its influence in the Levant through both its commerce and its culture. As long as it enjoyed friendly relations with the Ottomans, its trade with the area increased. French culture, on the other hand, was disseminated indirectly by the French religious orders, who performed religious, educational, and humanitarian work, and many of which were established in Lebanon. On two occasions France suffered a setback in its influence in the Levant: in 1799, when Napoleon invaded

Egypt, a province of the Ottoman Empire, and then undertook his campaign against Syria; and during the 1830's, when France supported the Egyptian occupation of Syria and Lebanon. On the latter occasion France temporarily earned the displeasure of the Maronites when it failed to support their revolt in 1840 against the armies of Ibrahim Pasha. In the critical years that followed it was anxious to prove once again that it was the good friend of the Maronites and to regain its influence with them.

The position of Czarist Russia was quite different. With most of its ports facing the frigid north, it had for a long time cast an acquisitive eye on Constantinople and the Turkish Straits as an outlet to the warm waters of the Mediterranean, and consequently sought excuses for interference in the internal affairs of the Ottoman Empire. The treaty of Kutchuk Kainardji of 1774, which ended the Russo-Turkish war of 1768, gave the Czar's government a vague right to protect the Greek Orthodox subjects of the Sultan. From then on it made it its business to "assure" the proper treatment of the Greek Orthodox, first in the Sultan's European holdings and later also in the eastern provinces.

Not much can be said for Austria-Hungary. As a Catholic power, it had sought at one time to rival France in protecting the Catholic sects of the Near East, but was unable to compete and had lost out to the latter by the middle of the nineteenth century. Prussia, another member of the Concert of Europe, was still a growing power in the nineteenth century, and more concerned with consolidating its strength on the continent than in carving a sphere of influence outside it. Neither Austria-Hungary nor Prussia, however, could afford to be left out of any joint European action in Ottoman affairs at a time when the "Sick Man of Europe" appeared so very sick.

Britain was France's main rival for influence in the Levant. But in order to preserve the balance of power in Europe, it found it imperative to preserve the territorial integrity of the decaying Ottoman Empire. For should the empire be liquidated, and an unfriendly power install itself in the Arab lands, it would pose a direct threat to British rule in India. It was the fear of such a possibility that prompted Britain to cultivate the friendship of the Druze of Lebanon and to champion their cause. As a protector of the Druze, Britain could at once checkmate French influence and offer its own legitimate excuse for intervention whenever there was trouble in the Levant.

Thus it was that from the 1840's until the end of the nineteenth century the ambitions and mutual fears of France, Britain, Austria-Hungary, Russia, and Prussia forced them to act more or less in unison when crises erupted in Turkey's eastern provinces. They spoke to the Sublime Porte with the voice of the Concert of Europe, but each watched the others closely lest one should break ranks and snatch a large or strategic piece of Ottoman territory.

The first important group action with regard to Lebanon took place in 1842. After Britain and France had done some hard bargaining with the Ottoman government in the interest of their respective protégé communities, the Concert adopted in May of that year the partition scheme that was to be put into effect the following year. In 1845, when the Turkish Pasha of Sidon arrested the Druze and Maronite *qa'im maqams* in an apparent move toward direct Ottoman rule, the Concert again acted in unison. The five powers sent identical notes to the Sultan protesting the arrests as well as the disarming of the Christian population of the mountains. They further demanded that the Porte carry out its earlier promises to see to it that the Druze paid an indemnity to the Maronites for the losses they had sustained during the Druze uprising of 1841. If Britain's action on this last point seemed contrary to its role as protector of the Druze, it was because it felt that intervention would be more difficult should the Ottomans succeed in turning Lebanon into an outright Turkish governorate. More important, however, was that the identical memoranda to the Sultan clearly proclaimed the five powers' right to protect the Christians of the Ottoman Empire through collective intervention and international control.

In the 1850's there were two developments outside the eastern provinces which concerned Lebanon and the rest of the Levant. These came right on the heels of the Crimean War of 1854–1856, in which Russia once again failed to take Constantinople, owing to the determined opposition of the other Big Four. As a result, Russia was deprived of its right of protection over the Orthodox Christian churches in the Ottoman Empire. But Turkey also found itself obliged to promulgate a new reform law, the *Hatti Hamayoun,* confirming and extending the civil rights and the spiritual and temporal privileges that had been promised in the reform bill of 1839 but in fact not fully granted. The law further proclaimed a new and radical change: the Ottoman Empire would abandon its traditional Islamic form of government, which sanctioned the inferiority of non-Muslims, and would become a secular state with secular and rational laws. To the Sultan, the law was a defensive measure against constant outside interference in his empire. But the European powers grasped it as a further justification for their collective intervention. Having been officially notified of the decree while sitting at the Paris Peace Conference of 1856, they announced their right to see that the promised reforms were carried out. The massacres of 1860 in Lebanon afforded them their next pretext for major intervention.

THE CLASS STRUGGLE TURNS INTO
A RELIGIOUS MASSACRE

The democratic movement that was sparked among the Christian peasantry by the more just and rational laws that they had enjoyed in the 1830's under the Egyptian occupation gathered momentum in the two decades that followed. Peasant restlessness was accentuated by other causes, of course. First, there was a general feeling among the Christian peasantry that having participated in the common effort to throw out the Egyptian invaders, they were now entitled to better treatment as a class. At the same time, their ambitious clergy kept prodding and instigating them against the nobility, while the Sublime Porte also followed a policy of pitting the two classes against each other. Matters came to a head when in 1858 the Christian peasants of Kesrouan in northern Lebanon rebelled against their Christian overlords, setting up a peasant government within the district the following year.

The immediate causes of the uprising and the developments contributing to its success bear a closer look. The Kesrouan peasants were irritated by the fact that whereas in the mixed villages of other districts the peasants enjoyed the protection of elected representatives against the abuses of the feudal lords, they themselves were denied such representatives. They now demanded the right to elect their own representatives, or village *wakils*, and the appointment of *ma'murs* or functionaries to represent the interests of their feudal lords. They were further incensed by the fact that the land in Kesrouan almost wholly belonged to the local feudal aristocracy, the Khazin family, who held an iron grip over the peasantry, and exacted from them unpaid services and a large share of their crops and income. The peasants now also wanted to throw off their obligations to the Khazins and to own the land they cultivated.

Support for their movement came from younger sons of the Khazin family and of other nobility, who resented the existing system of primogeniture, and from the Maronite clergy, who resented the Khazins' patronizing attitude and challenged their leadership of the population. Support also came from the new *qa'im maqam* of the Christian governorate, Emir Bechir Ahmad Abi-l-Lama', who had been appointed to the office after the death of Emir Haidar Isma'il Abi-l-Lama' in 1854. But the new governor did not feel secure in his office because the Khazin lords wanted to replace him by Bechir Assaf, nephew of the de-

ceased Haidar. As the British backed the Khazins' choice and
the French and Turks lent their support to Bechir Ahmad, the
latter tried to influence the outcome in his favor by encouraging
the Kesrouan peasants against their Khazin overlords. Finally,
when the revolt did break out in 1858, the Turkish authorities in
Beirut made no attempt to suppress it.

At first it was the whole institution of feudalism that was being
threatened. Because they recognized this, the Druze nobles of
the south offered to come to the aid of the beleaguered Christian
nobility of the north. But they soon withdrew their hasty offer
upon being warned by the Turkish governor of Beirut, Kourshid
Pasha, that the revolution was spreading southward through the
Matn and would soon hit their own district of the Chouf, and
that they would be wiser to stay home and guard their own
ramparts.

Kourshid Pasha was right. Prodded by their own clergy, and
encouraged by the success of the peasants in the north, the
Maronite peasantry in the southern district of the Chouf rose
against their Druze overlords in 1860, protested the multiple
dues they had to pay them, and made a bid for the latter's feudal
holdings. This class struggle soon turned into a religious war
when the rank and file of the Druze, seeing the uprising as a direct threat to the continued existence of their own people, came
to the assistance of their feudal chiefs. The Druze were well organized. The Maronites, although more numerous, lacked both
organization and adequate arms. And so a general massacre of
Maronite and other Christian villages ensued, while the local
Turkish authorities made no immediate attempt to put an end
to the bloodshed.

The three-month war which turned into a massacre was
mainly a Druze-Maronite affair, but other sects were also involved. Christians fleeing into the province of Saida, a Sunni
stronghold, perished at the hands of the Sunni. The Druze of
the Hauran region in Syria, coming to the assistance of the

Druze in Lebanon, fell upon Christian towns and villages, killing without discrimination Greek Orthodox, Greek Catholics, Syriacs, and Armenians as well as Maronites. The town of Zahle in the Biqa', with its Greek Catholic population, was besieged and attacked by both Druze and Sunnis. On the other hand, Shi'i Muslims offered protection to Maronite refugees and kept the Druze from exterminating the Christians of the Jabal ar-Rihan area in the south. In other areas Sunni Muslims also sided with the Maronites, whereas certain Greek Orthodox groups sided against them.[16]

But whatever the lines of division, the massacre provided the Sublime Porte with "conclusive" proof that the Lebanese were incapable of governing themselves. What would be its next move?

CHAPTER 2

The Establishment of the Mutasarrifyya of Mount Lebanon, 1861: A Firmer Foundation for Confessional Politics

The massacres of 1860 provided Turkey and the Concert of Europe—Britain, France, Russia, Prussia, and Austria-Hungary —with ample evidence of Lebanese "political immaturity"—although Turkey, Britain, and France, at least, had contributed through their policies over the previous twenty years to the growing tensions of Lebanon. Britain and France settled down to assessing the damage done to their respective protégé communities in preparation for further intervention. Turkey tried to present the European powers with a *fait accompli.*

When the fighting had been finally stopped, 11,000 to 18,000 Lebanese had perished. The death toll shocked both Druze and Maronite leaders, and at the prodding of the Sublime Porte, they were ready to make a quick and total submission to Turkish authority. Under Turkish auspices, they immediately signed a peace treaty in which they declared that their autonomy had engendered anarchy, and asked that Turkish authority be effectively and continually exercised in the affairs of Lebanon and in the administration of its justice.

But the European powers would not respect this treaty, concluded without their advice. They invoked the Treaty of Paris, which, they said, empowered them to see that the reforms promised in the *Hatti Hamayoun* decree of 1856 were carried out (see page 28). These reforms, they now announced, had not been carried out. Mutual fears, however, again dictated the need for collective action. Because France insisted on sending troops to "help" the Ottomans with the pacification of Lebanon, Britain and the other powers reserved the right to patrol the coastline to make the French undertaking a success. Then all together they compelled Turkey to join them in an international commission to work out a system for the administrative reorganization of Lebanon that would guarantee its continued autonomy. When the commission had finally finished its work, the Sublime Porte and the representatives of the five powers at Constantinople signed a protocol, on June 9, 1861, authorizing the administrative reorganization of Lebanon. As amended in September, 1864, this protocol became the charter of an autonomous Lebanese province which enjoyed autonomy until the outbreak of World War I.[1]

Under the new regime, the two governorates were reunited into a single governorate or *Mutasarrifyya* headed by a Christian non-Lebanese Governor General, who was appointed by the Porte upon the approval of the European powers. The Governor General was responsible not to the Turkish Pasha of Sidon, as in the past, but directly to the Porte. The new Lebanon was further put under the collective guardianship of the European powers and of the Sultan.

Physically, the *Mutasarrifyya* was much smaller than the principalities of either the Ma'an or the Chehab Emirs of the past. In the east, with the exception of the cantons of the Hermel and the town of Zahle and its environs, the eastern watershed of the Orontes and Litani rivers was excluded from the autonomous province and placed within the *vilayet* of Damascus as the *sandjaks* of Baalbeck, the Biqa', Rachaya, and Hasbaya. Lebanon was given an eastern frontier that followed generally the very crest of the chain of the Lebanon Mountains. Thus in the east the *Mutasarrifyya* was deprived of an area peopled by large

Christian communities and including indispensable fertile regions such as the Biqa' and Marjayoun valleys. In the west, the port city of Beirut, surrounded by a radius of a few miles, was excluded and placed under Ottoman authority, as were Sidon in the south and all of southern Lebanon. In the north, the port city of Tripoli as well as the districts of Tripoli and Akkar, both inhabited by large Christian communities, were similarly put under direct Turkish rule. With so much territory on all sides excluded, what was left in the *Mutasarrifyya* were mainly the range of western mountains known collectively as Mount Lebanon. These were inhabited by a population almost entirely Druze and Christian. And the Christians were mostly Maronites.

The governorate was subdivided at first into six administrative departments of varying sizes so that each could include a preponderant religious community.[2] Each was administered by a *qa'im maqam* chosen from among the largest religious group. Thus the *qa'im maqams* of the departments of Kesrouan, Jezzine, and the Metn were Maronites, that of Koura a Greek Orthodox, that of the Chouf a Druze, and that of the department of the city of Zahle a Greek Catholic. Under the 1864 protocol amendments, Kesrouan was subdivided into two districts, Kesrouan proper and the district of Batroun, each to be administered by its own Maronite *qa'im maqam*. The adjustment was made in order to give the Maronites, by far the largest community, a more equitable representation in the *Mutasarrifyya*'s central *majlis* or council. The latter was composed of twelve members, who, after 1864, included four Maronites, three Druze, two Greek Orthodox, one Sunni Muslim, one Shi'i Muslim, and one Greek Catholic.

The Governor General was invested with extensive powers, among which were the right to control the police force, nominate all functionaries and judges, and organize the collection of taxes. As chief executive, he convoked and presided over the central *majlis* and directed its debates.[3] He was required to abide by its

decisions on matters pertaining to the budget and the allocation
of taxes. On all other questions, he could convoke it as a consultative assembly if and when he pleased, but was not obliged
to accept its advice. When he himself could not preside over its
meetings, he was represented by a vice-president whom he chose
himself from among the Maronites outside the Council.

The seat of the government was Deir el-Kamar, a Maronite
town in the predominantly Druze district of the Chouf in the
south. As a Christian town, Deir el-Kamar came under the direct
jurisdiction of the Governor General.

The principal administrative aides of the Governor General
were the *qa'im maqams* of the six districts and of the town of
Zahle. Each *qa'im maqam* was assisted by a regional administrative council, composed of three to six members representing
the different elements of the population in the district. Each
qa'im maqam convoked and presided over his council once a
year for the purpose of receiving its advice on matters of regional importance, especially with regard to the collection of
taxes. The regional council was also charged with settling administrative differences and hearing the complaints of the resi-
dents of the district.

The districts—or departments—were in turn subdivided into
nahies or cantons, and each was administered by a *moudir* (director) named by the Governor General upon the recommendation of the district *qa'im maqam.* Each village in a canton was
administered by a *sheikh,* named by the Governor General upon
the recommendation of the villagers.

Autonomous Lebanon was also burdened with a judiciary
system of a confessional character in which the Governor General exercised the power of appointment and dismissal. A supe-
rior judiciary *majlis,* sitting as a high court of appeals, was established at the seat of government, Deir el-Kamar. The high court
was actually subdivided into two sections, one having final
jurisdiction over criminal cases, the other over civil cases, and

each presided over by a functionary nominated *ad hoc* by the Governor General. Each section consisted of six judges chosen by the Governor General from the Maronite, Greek Orthodox, Greek Catholic, Druze, Sunni, and Shi'i communities respectively. Occasionally, a Protestant or a Jewish judge would be added to the court when it heard a case involving a member of either faith. Simple cases were tried by courts of first instance and by the village sheikhs. According to Ottoman custom there was no jury at all in the court system, in which also the Muslim Hanafi law of the Ottoman Empire was applied. Finally, all judges were salaried, and were subject to dismissal and a penalty if an inquiry proved that they had acted either dishonestly or improperly. To prevent constant intrusion by Ottoman troops, a special police force was organized under the command of the Governor General.

Placed as it was under international protection, and endowed with institutions calculated to be democratic as well as representative of the whole population, the *Mutasarrifyya* enjoyed peace and tranquillity during the fifty-three years of its existence. Its overwhelming Christian majority became even greater when in 1863 and 1864 thousands of discontented Druze followed their leaders, who headed a tight social and military structure, into the Druze stronghold of the Hauran in Syria. The emigration had been encouraged by the first Governor General, Daoud Pasha, who, on behalf of the administration, bought up the properties of Druze landowners in the south and distributed them among those who had been clamoring for them for so long—the Christian tenant peasantry. And because of their preponderant numbers, not only in the south but everywhere, the *Mutasarrifyya* came to be regarded as a Christian refuge surrounded by a hinterland of Islam. The average citizen in this haven had a greater sense of security than he had enjoyed in the thirty years before the advent of the regime.

But how did the new institutions affect the practical politics of the regime?

In the interest of justice and equity, confessional representation was introduced at all levels of government—village, cantonal, district, and central. But the effect was also to sharpen existing differences among the various sects and to make religion, rather than common social or economic interests, the main channel of communication and understanding between the citizen and his official representatives. The system also prevented the development among the citizenry of a Lebanese national consciousness, for one owed loyalty not to the nation, but to one's religious community and to its spokesmen within the government. Based as it was on sectarian representation, the system further was grossly unfair to the sect for whose protection it was originally introduced—the Maronites. Despite their four seats out of the twelve in the central *majlis* and their four out of seven district *qa'im maqams,* as the majority community they still remained underrepresented.

Complicating the problems of confessional representation were the three interest groups that the *Mutasarrifyya* inherited from the earlier regime: the nobility, the clergy, and the newly awakened peasantry. Though feudal privileges were now abolished the nobility still owned most of the land. Old-time rivalries between aristocratic families continued, though less acrimoniously. But they now sought as a group to pursue their interests within the central government by obtaining for their members the high administrative posts and the seats in the Central Council earmarked for their respective religious communities. It was the Council which devised the rate of taxation, and by controlling it the nobility could prevent their properties from being heavily taxed. For personal reasons, also, they tried to exercise control over the judiciary.

As a new political interest group, the peasantry challenged the nobility at every turn. They also sought to fill the executive, legislative-advisory, and judiciary offices with their own representatives, and they continued to agitate for the parceling of agricultural land and for its outright ownership by the cultivators.

As the third group competing for power, the clergy enjoyed the special advantage of moral leadership with which they were endowed by the church as well as certain immunities from the law. Having undermined the position of the nobility in previous years, the way now seemed open to them to attain what they had striven for—the political leadership of Mount Lebanon. Their immunity from civil jurisdiction gave them an advantage over the Governor General, in whose extensive powers they saw a threat to the achievement of their own political ascendancy. Conversely, their own judicial autonomy helped the considerable extension of ecclesiastical mortmain, which became one of the major causes of heavy peasant emigration abroad. Growing constantly in numbers but finding less and less land to farm, hundreds of Christian peasants were forced to leave the country throughout the *Mutasarrifyya* period.

Occupying the highest office in the administration, the Governor General was able to use his vast legal powers to augment his authority still further. The rivalry among the six sects and three interest groups played right into his hands. In the central *majlis* especially, neither the seven Christian deputies nor the five Druze and Muslim deputies could often agree among themselves, let alone produce a majority vote. Thus with so much disagreement in the Council, the Governor General, who was also its president, could and did step in to direct its meetings, control its debates, and even bring a majority vote on the budgetary and tax measures he favored, although these were the only matters in which the Council was intended to exercise control over him. Through his power of appointment and dismissal, and his right to change the size and composition of the courts, the Governor General was also able to exercise a great influence over the judiciary. Finally, he used the nobility to check the strident politics of the clergy. In fact, each succeeding Governor General did his part in returning the nobility to a position of power and preeminence by both appointing them and encouraging their selection for public office.[4] Thus in the districts as well as in the central government many high offices came to be filled by members of the old-time aristocratic feudal families. Their return to power renewed a tradition that was to affect the course of Lebanese politics for many years to come.

Similarly, the extensive official and unofficial powers of the governorship, whether they were exercised harshly and abusively by some occupants of that office or benevolently and beneficially by others, nevertheless set a precedent for a much later generation. They accounted partly for that curious phenomenon in modern, democratic Lebanon: the strong-man tradition in the office of chief of state.

CHAPTER 3

The Establishment of Greater Lebanon
under French Mandate: A New Dimension
to Confessional Politics

The outbreak of World War I in 1914 brought stricter controls over the administrations of Turkey's eastern provinces. Lebanese autonomy was at first violated, then officially abolished in October, 1915, when the *Mutasarrifyya* regime was replaced by direct Ottoman rule. At the close of the war in 1918, Lebanon was temporarily administered by the French military authorities, and in 1922 it was confirmed by the League of Nations as a French mandate. The Lebanon of the mandate period was a much larger country than that of the *Mutasarrifyya* period. This fact alone brought many political headaches to the new nation and constantly threatened its geographical unity, for there were important segments of the population who wished to be united with Syria rather than attached to the separate state of Lebanon. But in 1943 Lebanon was able to declare itself an independent state within its existing boundaries.

The declaration of independence in 1943 was made possible by the united support of all sections of the population, their determination to achieve independence in the fullest meaning of the word (since only self-government was technically possible in 1943), and a general understanding on the nature and future course of the Lebanese state. It was in fact this understanding, which was embodied in the National Pact of 1943 (*al-mithaq al-watani*), which set the course for the common struggle. The Pact provided for a balanced partnership within the governing institutions of the state between the Christian and the Muslim population, and defined Lebanon's foreign policy to the satisfaction of all. It represented a giant step from a state of disunity to a state of unity on the political future of Lebanon. But the change was not accomplished overnight.

CONFLICT OVER THE NEW STATUS OF LEBANON:
BACKGROUND AND DEVELOPMENT

When the French arrived in the Levant in 1918 with the intention of assuming control of both Syria and Lebanon and of establishing a sphere of influence there, they were faced not with a docile population, but with a politically awakened people who very much wanted to determine their own future. The political awakening had blossomed first in Lebanon, and then spread to the rest of the Levant. In the last two or three decades of the nineteenth century Lebanon was seized with a new sense of revulsion against Ottoman suzerainty. Within Christian circles anti-Turkish sentiment ran high, mainly because of the accumulation of several things—the traditional connections of the Christians, and particularly the Maronites, with the West; the spread of Western education, culture, and political philosophy, particularly the ideals of the French Revolution; the more recent introduction of the Arabic printing press and the consequent revival of the Arabic language and Arabic literature. Secret societies were organized to work for the separation of Lebanon from the Turkish empire.

At about the same time, educated Muslim Arabs in neighboring Syria began to grow restive under the misrule of Sultan Abdul Hamid II, although the majority of Sunni Arabs, peasants as well as city dwellers, remained resigned to it because it was essentially a Muslim Sunni rule. The intellectual elite, however, began to agitate for representative institutions and for greater Arab participation in the administration of the Arab provinces. To achieve their ends they started collaborating with the Christian anti-Turkish leaders of Lebanon, who, in turn felt that a common Christian-Muslim effort would hasten their separation from the Ottoman empire. This Muslim-Christian collaboration was not, as was later assumed in the 1930's and 1940's, the beginning of modern Arab nationalism and the birth of the struggle for independence and complete separation from the Ottoman empire. At that time the Lebanese wished to throw off the suzerainty of the Sultan, whereas the Muslim Arab leaders of Syria wanted only to improve the political status of the Arabs within the empire. It was only after the first decade of the twentieth century, when these leaders saw in the revolution of the Young Turks not the hoped-for reforms but an autocratic pan-Turanian movement, that they began to think of independence.[1]

The First World War hastened the activities of Muslim Arab leaders on behalf of the hoped-for independence. They plotted against Ottoman rule through secret societies, such as *al-Fatat* (Youth Society). And in the summer of 1915 they secretly sent to the Sherif Hussein of Mecca in the Hejaz, where Turkish control was at its weakest, the Damascus Protocol, a paper visualizing Anglo-Arab cooperation to secure the liberation and independence of the Arab homeland. The messenger was Hussein's son, Prince Faisal, who brought back word from his father that Arab independence would be guaranteed by Britain in exchange for the participation of the Arabs in the British war effort, which was now being plotted by his father and the British.

Meanwhile, though nothing could be done openly, strong antipathies toward the Turks were building up among the people of both Syria and Lebanon because of the harsh and cruel rule of Ahmad Jamal Pasha, Turkish governor of both provinces and commander of the Ottoman forces in the area. He inadvertently gave the independence movement in both provinces its first martyrs, and a fresh impetus, when he summarily arrested, tried, and publicly hanged in Beirut and Damascus a number of Lebanese and Syrian dignitaries. The martyrs of Beirut included both Muslims and Christians.

In June, 1916, the long-planned Arab revolt broke out with an attack on the Turkish garrisons in the Hejaz. It continued as part of a joint Anglo-Arab campaign northward and eastward against the Turkish army until the Turks were completely defeated in 1918. The Arabs now claimed the independence that had been promised in the written understanding between the Sherif of Mecca and Sir Henry McMahon, British High Commissioner in Cairo. But they were sorely disappointed. First, it turned out that the negotiations between the Sherif and Sir Henry, known as the Hussein-McMahon correspondence, had been rather inconclusive with regard to certain areas of the former eastern provinces. One of the questions over which agreement could not be reached at the time was that of the littoral and coastal ranges of geographical Syria, the areas lying west of the districts of Damascus, Homs, Hamah, and Aleppo and including the territory of the former *Mutasarrifyya* of Mount Lebanon. The Sherif Hussein claimed all of geographical Syria as belonging to a future independent Arab state, and could not be induced to give up any part of it. Sir Henry did not wish to make precise commitments because of the interests of Britain in the area, as well as those of its ally, France. And so they decided to postpone the negotiation of these matters until after the war. Shortly before the end of the war, however, the Sykes-Picot agreement, which had been concluded secretly between Britain and France, came to light. It divided former geographical Syria into spheres of influence between the two. When the war was over, Britain assumed control of Iraq, Transjordan, and Palestine; France staked its claim to Syria and Lebanon. The newly formed League of Nations soon acquiesced in this arrangement when in July, 1922, it officially approved the draft mandates that the

mandatory powers, France and Britain, had prepared for the
areas they were controlling. The mandatory system of control,
devised only after World War I, interposed a period of so-called
political maturing for liberated peoples between the time of
their liberation and final independence. It visualized the encouragement and development of political responsibility in each
liberated area under the guardianship of a major democratic
power.

Before France could establish itself as the mandatory power
for Lebanon and Syria the situation in both areas remained
fluid. France itself was claiming rights and interests not only in
Lebanon, where it had built up a clientele among the Maronites,
but also in the whole of Syria and in the Mosul district of northern Iraq, which was inhabited by the Chaldean community, a
Catholic minority. In Syria, Arab nationalist leaders were clamoring for the immediate independence of Syria and Lebanon and
for the unification of the two. In Lebanon, however, Maronite
circles and clergymen were raising strong objections to the
Syrian claims for unity and were in turn demanding the establishment of an independent Lebanon. If outside assistance was
necessary to achieve the full and independent statehood of their
country, the Maronites preferred to receive it from France.

While the debate was going on, a temporary military administration organized in Damascus under the auspices of the British forces there was turned into a *de facto* Arab government by
Syrian and Iraqi participants. Headed by Prince Faisal of the
Hejaz, the new government assumed that its authority extended
over the whole of geographical Syria (all of the Arab area liberated from the Turks). Accordingly, in October, 1918, it sent
a representative with a token force to Beirut to establish Arab
authority there and in the coastal area. But the attempt was
thwarted by General Allenby, Commander-in-Chief of the Allied
forces. Instead, a French military administration was set up in

the coastal area and in Mount Lebanon, and was soon bolstered by the arrival of French troops.

In Mount Lebanon itself, the leadership was divided and sometimes vacillating on the political course to be followed. Reactivated by the Syrian nationalist-unionists, the old-time Central Council of the *Mutasarrifyya* period held meetings in Ba'abda, its former winter headquarters, and generally acted as a branch of the Arab government in Damascus. But as the French position became better established and the French administration of Lebanon became more effective, the Council switched from a pro-unionist to a separatist and pro-French attitude. Encouraged by the French, it soon made known that it favored the establishment, under French protection, of an independent Greater Lebanon through the restoration of the areas separated from the *Mutasarrifyya* in 1861. A delegation from the Council composed of two Maronites, a Greek Orthodox, a Druze, and a Muslim was sent by the French to the Paris Peace Conference in 1919 to make this demand in the name of all the Lebanese.

The demand for a Greater Lebanon was reiterated before the Conference by two other French-sponsored Lebanese delegations, both Maronite. The first visited Paris in 1919 and was headed by the Francophile Patriarch Mgr. Elias Boutros Hwayyik; the second arrived in 1920 under the chairmanship of Bishop Abdallah Khouri of Beirut.

Faisal, who had now been proclaimed King of Syria, was willing to accept the establishment of a separate Lebanese identity under French guardianship, subject, however, to a later definition of the frontiers between Lebanon and Syria. But Syrian nationalist leaders remained adamant, and on June 20, 1919, convened a National Congress which claimed the independence and sovereignty of the whole of Syria "within its natural boundaries" (i.e., including Mount Lebanon). Angry retorts from the Maronites and other Catholic communities of Lebanon toned down these claims, and in March, 1920, the Congress proposed the formation of a National Government of "all Syria," but with special guarantees for Lebanon. Muslim members of the revived Lebanese Central Council attended the Congress' meeting in Damascus and approved its resolution, but upon their return to Lebanon they were arrested by the French and sentenced to long prison terms. Christian Lebanese responded with an outright rejection of the Syrian proposal. Representatives of all their sects immediately held a meeting at Ba'abda and, with full French approval, proclaimed Lebanese independence from Syria.

The crisis came to a head in the summer of 1920, after the Supreme Allied Council had approved on April 25 the establishment of a French mandate for both Syria and Lebanon. The news was received with great elation by most of Lebanon's Christians, but it elicited a negative response this time from Christian as well as Muslim members of the Central Council. Meeting secretly on July 10, the Council resolved by majority vote to proclaim Lebanon's sovereign independence, without French tutelage, and to cooperate with Syria. If the Council has been credited with finally waking up to French ambitions in Lebanon, it has also been accused of receiving bribes from a young Sunni unionist from Sidon who had acquired the money for this purpose from a rich Beiruti Muslim.[2] A charge of bribery was in fact levelled against the Council members by the French as soon as they had heard of the secret resolution. The Council was dissolved by the French High Commissioner, General Gouraud, and its members sent into exile.

To secure the French position, Gouraud decided to follow this up with a French military occupation of Syria. He delivered an ultimatum to Faisal, who was still making claims over the coastal areas, and virtually demanded acceptance of a French mandate over Syria. Realizing the inadequacy of his own army to defend Syria, Faisal accepted Gouraud's terms, but the reply reached the latter too late to prevent a clash between Syrian and French troops. The Syrians were defeated at Maisaloun Pass and the French entered Damascus on July 25. Faisal fled the country, and the French established their authority.

But the irredentist movement was not dead in Syria, which now, too, was becoming a French mandate, though an unwilling one. The movement received fresh impetus when on September 1, 1920, General Gouraud proclaimed the "independence" of Greater Lebanon. The state now included the areas for which Maronite spokesmen had been clamoring—the Biqa' valley in the east, Jabal Amil in the south, and the coastal areas including the towns of Tripoli, Beirut, Sidon, and Tyre. Lebanese Christians on the whole accepted the measure as a restoration of lost territory. But Syrian nationalist leaders regarded it as an unjust and unnatural dismemberment of the Syrian homeland. Equally dissatisfied were the Muslim inhabitants of the newly acquired areas, who constituted the majority of the population there. Their dissatisfaction with this state of affairs was to have a disruptive effect on Lebanese politics for the next fifteen years.

The new boundaries also brought some major changes in the demographic picture of the state. Under the *Mutasarrifyya* Lebanon had been predominantly Christian; now, a large Muslim population was added. In fact the Lebanese Christians now only slightly outnumbered the Muslims. Furthermore, the Druze lost their former position as the dominant Muslim sect to the Sunnis, who now emerged as the main challengers to the Maronites' numerical preponderance and political predominance.

There were other aspects of the demographic change to be considered. From an overwhelming majority, the Maronites were now reduced to 30 per cent of the population. The next largest community were the Sunnis, followed by the Greek Orthodox, the Shi'i, then the Druze. Beirut contributed a population half Christian, half Muslim (mostly Sunni). The Biqa' gave twice as many Muslims, of the Sunni, Shi'i, and Druze sects, as Christians, mainly Greek Catholic. Tripoli and its environs added a population that was overwhelmingly Muslim. And the newly added south yielded a mixed population: Sidon was Sunni, but the hilly, inland region was about three-fifths Shi'i and two-fifths Christian, mainly Greek Orthodox. Though the new state became economically more viable it lost the social homogeneity that was Lebanon's during the *Mutasarrifyya* period.

The demographic pattern further revealed various degrees of commitment or noncommitment to the viability of the new state. In the summer of 1919, when the conflicting demands of the Lebanese separatists and the Syrian unionists had been at their shrillest, the King-Crane commission arrived to determine the wishes of the people. It had been appointed to the task by President Woodrow Wilson. Its survey revealed the following trend: the Maronite and Greek Catholic communities were overwhelmingly in favor of a French mandate; the Greek Orthodox community generally favored the unification of Syria and Lebanon, but could not agree on the choice of a mandatory power; the Muslims were overwhelmingly for union with Syria but against any supervision by France.

Within that general pattern, however, there existed some differences. Predominantly Maronite, Mount Lebanon was both separatist and pro-French-mandate, though some unionist sentiment was also present. The Sunnis of Beirut, Tripoli, Sidon, and other coastal areas were the most enthusiastic unionists. The Shi'is, concentrated mostly in the Biqa' and in Jabal Amil in the south, also favored union with Syria, but were not as determined about it; there was certainly significant dissidence within their ranks. The Druze of the Biqa' and of the south were divided somewhat like the Shi'is, but their primary concern was the preservation of their tribal autonomy, no matter what happened.

THE MANDATORY POLICY VERSUS UNIONIST OBJECTIVES

It was certainly a divided Lebanon which France was pledged to bring to political maturity. But it took on the task willingly,

for, despite the American survey of public opinion, it was determined to establish a sphere of influence both here and in
Syria. Its first task, in accordance with the terms of the mandate
for Syria and Lebanon (which the League of Nations approved
in 1922), was to frame an organic law for both states within
three years. Such a law, or constitution, would have to take into
account the rights, interests, and wishes of all the population of
the area. Its second task was to facilitate the progressive development of Syria and Lebanon as independent states.

From the beginning of the mandatory regime, France followed
a specific policy in discharging its obligations to both areas. Consideration for the "rights, interests and wishes of all the population," as specified in the first article of the mandate agreement,
was interpreted as consideration for the rights, interests, and
wishes of each of the various sectarian and regional communities of Syria and Lebanon. France was thus emphasizing regional
and religious distinctness, and making it a guide to the framing
of the organic law of each state and to its administration. The
policy could hardly be expected to contribute to the development
of national unity, the necessary corollary for eventual independence. But France had its reasons. First, it could justify the
policy, in Lebanon at least, as a continuation of the tradition of
sectarian representation and equity in government. But it also
wished to assure the Maronites and other Christians of Lebanon
of its support against any Syrian attempt at pan-Arab unity, for
many Christians saw in Arab unity their eventual engulfment in
a theocratic Muslim state. In Syria, France wished to grant Christian minorities and heterodox Muslim minorities the full equality
with Sunni Muslims that they had not enjoyed under Ottoman
rule.

By catering to the minorities, France was serving its own aims.
The mandatory mission, to which it could visualize no end, was
also a tool for the consolidation of the French position in the
Middle East. And this could best be done by strengthening the
traditional ties with the Maronite community, by cultivating the

friendship of the Druze, Shiʻis, ʻAlawis, and the Christian communities, and by securing their position vis-à-vis the Sunni majority in Syria. For France saw in Sunni Islam both the source and the strength of the Arab nationalist movement, which could develop into a serious threat to its own ambitions if it were not curbed. And France hoped to curb it by emphasizing the differences between the Sunnis and the other sects.

In Lebanon, the formal reinstatement of confessionalism began in 1922. Anticipating the early approval of the mandate by the League of Nations Council, on March 8 the French High Commissioner issued a decree calling for the election of a Lebanese Representative Council. Since distribution of the Council seats was to be on a confessional basis, a census of the various religious communities was first taken. Elections were held in April, triggering a series of protests and acts of violence. The Muslims boycotted the elections in protest against inclusion of their home districts within the new state. The Director of Interior, Asʻad Bey Khurshid, was murdered by unionist Muslims for his Francophile and anti-union attitude. A visit to Damascus by Mr. Crane of the former King-Crane commission was made the occasion for violent and bloody demonstrations in both Syrian and Lebanese towns. Muslims of Beirut, Tripoli, Sidon, and Jabal Amil in the south held a series of meetings to consider the unification of Lebanon and Syria as a first step toward the creation of a larger Arab union. In Cairo, a "Syro-Palestine Congress" issued manifestos calling for the establishment of an independent union of all Syria (i.e., Lebanon included). Though groups of Maronites, other nonunionists, and the Lebanese Representative Council all quickly retorted that the Congress did not represent the views of the Lebanese, the fact remained that large sections of the Muslim population within Lebanon were unionist in sentiment.

The divisions within Lebanon were compounded by other events. In the summer of 1925 open revolt broke out in the au-

tonomous Jabal Druze (within Syria) against French reform
measures which had struck at the traditional institutions of the
Druze. The revolt soon spread to other parts of Syria, taking on
the aspect of an Arab nationalist liberation movement, and in
the spring of 1926 it reached those districts of Lebanon that had
been annexed in 1920 to form the larger state. Druze, Shi'i, and
Sunni rebels attacked neighboring Christian villages, turning
the revolt into somewhat of a confessional fight.

Before the rebellion was finally quelled in the early months of
1927, rebel leaders in Jabal Druze had issued a list of demands as
a precondition for negotiating a peace with the French. They
called for the unification of all Syria (which had been divided
into four autonomous territories), the return of the areas that had
been annexed by Greater Lebanon, the immediate conclusion of
a Franco-Syrian treaty giving Syria home rule, and the withdrawal of French troops. These were essentially the same demands as those the Arab nationalists in Damascus, under the
direction of the People's Party, had been continuously making
ever since the establishment of Greater Lebanon in 1920. The
Damascus nationalists even visualized the inclusion of Mount
Lebanon within the union, allowing it at most an autonomous
status. What was significant, though, was that the Arab nationalist spirit had spread, perhaps temporarily, to the traditionally
insular Druze of the Jabal. Would it infect their kin in Lebanon?

In Lebanon, however, events took a different turn. Tired of
the struggle, the Druze rebels made peace by declaring their
allegiance to the High Commissioner and the Lebanese government. The Shi'is also came to terms with the French and were
granted early in 1926 political rights as a distinct religious community. Henceforth they would be able to participate more fully
in Lebanese political life and would be less dependent on the
Sunnis for guidance. For the latter, however, there were no concessions. They remained dissatisfied.

Even before the rebel areas had been completely pacified,

France forged ahead with its plans for carrying out the terms of the mandate agreement. A new High Commissioner for Syria and Lebanon, Henri de Jouvenel, made plans for the drafting of constitutions for both states. In Lebanon, a Representative Council elected, by Muslims as well as Christians, in the summer of 1925 convened in December as a Constituent Assembly. Protests immediately poured in from all over the country. Unionist nationalists, mostly Muslims, were objecting to the legalization of Greater Lebanon through an organic law. Nevertheless, the Assembly went ahead with its work. The constitution was drawn up and the Lebanese Republic proclaimed on May 24, 1926.

Publication of the new Lebanese constitution brought a torrent of protests from unionist circles in both Syria and Lebanon, particularly because it declared as unalterable the existing territory of Lebanon. Fuel was added to the fire when the newly elected President, Charles Dabbas, publicly declared the immutable integrity of the Republic and the French High Commissioner rejected the unionists' demand that a plebiscite be held in the contested areas to determine where the boundaries of Lebanon should be drawn.

In Syria, preparations in the winter of 1925–1926 for the drafting of a Syrian constitution precipitated further agitation from all parts of the country for unification with Lebanon. Nationalist leaders in Damascus, Homs, Hamah, and Aleppo pressed for a plebiscite in the newly annexed districts of Lebanon, sure that it would return an overwhelming vote for union. There was so much public disturbance on this and other questions of unification that the Syrian Constituent Assembly could not meet before July of 1928. The constitution that was finally drafted reaffirmed in article 2 the political indivisibility of the Syrian homeland and practically declared Syrian independence from French control. It ignored the separate existence of Jabal Druze, the 'Alawi state, Lebanon, Palestine, and Transjordan. Article 2 was the work of the minority of nationalist deputies who had dominated the Assembly and a reflection of public sentiment. But it did not please the French, who demanded deletion of its two unacceptable provisions. When nationalists and moderates could not agree on the French request, the High Commissioner, Henri Ponsot, prorogued the work of the Assembly *sine die* in February, 1929, and dissolved it in May, 1930. He then issued a constitution for Syria that was free of the two clauses that had offended the French, but otherwise contained all the essentials of the previous one.

Temporarily outmaneuvered, nationalists in Syria continued to plan for unification and kept in close touch with unionists in Lebanon, especially with a group of leaders, mostly Muslims, known as the Negativists. Despite their repeated failures to achieve unification, the latter and the Syrians felt morally obligated to continue with the struggle. For legally, they all maintained, France had no right as the mandatory power to enlarge Lebanon by annexing to it Syrian territory, and politically, it had ignored the principle of self-determination by denying the inhabitants of the annexed areas a plebiscite.[3] Nationalists on both sides of the border further felt that the creation of Greater Lebanon was part of a plot to divide the Arab world. It was in accordance with these long-held views that in 1928, on the occasion of the convening of the Syrian Constituent Assembly, a group of Negativists and other Lebanese unionists had visited Damascus to demand reattachment to Syria of the annexed areas of Greater Lebanon, and to ask for the inclusion of an article to that effect in the Syrian constitution. Although repudiated at the time by the Lebanese government, they had returned home to carry on a campaign for reunification.

PARLIAMENT: VEHICLE FOR CONCILIATION

On the other side of the political fence, the mandatory power, as well as responsible spokesmen for the Maronite community

who wished to consolidate the separate existence of Greater
Lebanon, decided from the beginning that denunciation of
unionist agitation would not alone solve the problem. Both the
unionist inhabitants and their leaders must be induced to accept
citizenship within the state. The confessional system of government was at hand. It must be used to achieve the desired objective. The constitution of 1926, as amended in 1927 and 1929,
provided the key to action. First, in line with previous measures
taken by the mandatory power, it called for proportional confessional representation within the Chamber of Deputies, and
through confessionalism for the equitable representation of the
regions as well. Further, to stimulate greater interest by all the
sects in the government, article 95 stipulated that they should
all be equitably represented in public employment and in the
Cabinet so long as this was not detrimental to the welfare of the
state.

But the Chamber remained the major vehicle for conciliation.
In order to make it an effective body, and at the same time lessen
the tensions of intercommunal rivalry, a decree was issued for
the purpose of bringing to this forum deputies of moderate views.
Thus, in accordance with the decree, each district elected a number of deputies belonging to the different communities living
within it, but each deputy was elected not only by his coreligionists but also by all the other voters of the districts, and he became
a representative of the whole nation. Application of the law in
the mixed districts, where the different religious communities
were numerically about equal, resulted in the election of moderate candidates, men who were acceptable to all the communities.
Candidates representing special interests were eliminated. In
predominantly Sunni districts, where the unionist sentiment was
strongest, there were always moderate candidates to be found
who would run against the militant unionists. And here, as elsewhere, the mandatory power was not loath to give the candidates it preferred assistance at the polls, if they needed it. Thus

the parliament was generally a place of intercommunal harmony and understanding. And to a certain extent it was able to promote national cohesion through legislation acceptable and beneficial to all the communities.

On the other hand, being a body of generally moderate views, the Chamber could not resolve basic differences between the sects, foremost among which was the Sunni-Maronite disagreement over the question of the territorial integrity of the state.

STATUS QUO DEBATED BY "SHADOW PARLIAMENT"

Strong, divergent, and sometimes contradictory communal interests, denied an airing within the Chamber, had to find some other means of public expression. They were represented by the institutions and recognized leaders of the respective religious communities, which, though not officially constituting part of the legislative or governing process, were able to set limits on what the legislature and the executive could do. In the Christian churches, hierarchically organized and enjoying a tradition of clerical leadership, the extraparliamentary communal spokesmen were the ecclesiastics themselves, particularly the patriarchs and the bishops. Within the Muslim communities, where no natural religious hierarchy existed, community spokesmen included both notables and religious magistrates such as *muftis* and *qadis*. In a sense, a hierarchical structure was imposed upon the Muslim sects through the official recognition at the beginning of the mandate of certain men of religion as the religious heads of their respective sects. They became respectively the Sunni *Mufti of* the Republic, the Shi'i *Mufti* of the Republic, and the *Sheikh al-'Aql* of the Druze, and, following the precedent set by the Christian ecclesiastics, they also came to be leading spokesmen for their communities.

Like a shadow parliament, the communal leadership carried on the debate and struggle over issues that were practically taboo within the Chamber. It was the Sunnis' favorite theme, union with Syria, that excited the passions of some and engaged the attention of all. What was the sectarian lineup on this important question, and how was the mandatory power guided by the developing debate?

The Maronites were clearly opposed to any union with Syria. Although a few of them made the pilgrimage to Damascus, the Mecca of Arab nationalism, on different occasions during the twenties and thirties, they were not representative. The community as a whole was represented by its Patriarch, Mgr. Elias Hwayyik, and other Maronite ecclesiastics, who were quick to counter any arguments for unification. The Greek Catholic community and its religious hierarchy were similarly opposed to any unification scheme, for they shared with the Maronites their traditional Western orientation. Both these communities favored continued French protection as a means of maintaining the Christians' political preponderance and of forestalling any attempts at unification. Since their attitudes coincided with the interests of France itself, both communities, and especially the Maronites, were treated with special favor by the mandatory.

The Greek Orthodox started out under the mandate in a different frame of mind. Under the *Mutasarrifyya,* they had been, on and off, the protégés of Czarist Russia, not of France. Furthermore, theirs was an Eastern church, and thus somewhat of a rival of the Vatican-affiliated Maronite church. Having lost their protector to the Russian Revolution, and fearing Maronite domination, they generally opted for union with Syria. The French soon realized that they were partly to blame; they had alienated the Greek Orthodox by being too openly solicitous of the Maronites. It was time to make amends. So in 1926, when the Lebanese constitution was promulgated, they promoted the election by the then two-chamber parliament[4] of a Greek Orthodox as the first President of the Republic. He was the eminent lawyer Charles Dabbas.

The election of Dabbas, a Greek Orthodox, instead of a Maronite to the highest office in the state served several objectives. First, of course, was the mandatory's desire to reconcile the Greek Orthodox community to the existence of the mandate and the separate status of Lebanon. Dabbas himself was a fortunate choice for another reason: having participated in the 1913 Arab Congress in Paris, which had demanded greater Arab autonomy within the Ottoman empire, he was acceptable to Lebanese Muslims also. Furthermore, he was a master of the French language, had studied in France, and was married to a Frenchwoman. The mandatory considered him to have strong attachments to France. Finally, the election of a man from only the fourth largest community gave the mandatory time to work out a policy in regard to the highest office in the state, a policy that would maintain communal equilibrium at the top of the political pyramid and avoid in particular a clash over the office between the largest community, the Maronites, and the next largest, the Sunnis.

Lebanon's Christian population also included several smaller communities, of which the Roman Catholics, the Syrian Orthodox, and the Protestants were officially recognized as early as 1922, when they were allowed collectively one deputy in the Representative Council.*

The attitude of these small communities on the question of Lebanese viability has never been definitely determined, although it may be assumed that the Catholics among them shared the views of the Maronites, while the Orthodox shared the views of the Greek Orthodox. At any rate, these communities were too small to play a significant role in the debate among the larger communities over the issue of independence versus union with Syria.

More important than the above groups were the Armenian Or-

---

* These small communities have continued to have their own representative in the legislature; in addition, the Protestants at times have had a representative of their own.

thodox and Armenian Catholics, a national minority who had arrived in Lebanon in the early twenties as refugees from Turkish Armenia and Cilicia, where large numbers of their compatriots had been massacred by the Turks. The Armenians were about 31,000 (25,000 Orthodox and 6,000 Catholic) in the twenties and early thirties. In 1938 they were joined by other Armenians fleeing the Syrian city of Alexandretta, which was ceded that year by the mandatory power to the Turkish Republic, and by the mid-forties they numbered around 70,000 (60,000 Orthodox and 10,000 Catholic).

Although the Armenians were not involved in the debate over the question of Lebanese viability, their presence in Lebanon was at first resented by the Muslims because it contributed to the enlargement of the Christian community. Furthermore, by the mid-thirties, the mandatory power considered the Armenian Orthodox community large enough to have separate representation in the Chamber of Deputies, and in 1937 two of its members were elected to that body.*

From the Sunni leadership outside the Chamber, there was no letup in the campaign for unification of the predominantly Muslim areas with Syria. There were also bitter attacks on the mandatory power itself: it simply had to go. Still, the mandatory had managed to attract some Sunnis to public service. Their reasons for participation in the government varied. Some found public office attractive, others saw it as a means of serving their own community. Still others saw in it an opportunity to protest the status quo. Sunni deputies, for example, helped draft the national constitution, but at the same time declared themselves against the consecration of the frontiers of Greater Lebanon, against the principle of territorial integrity, and against the choice of Beirut as the national capital.

* The Armenian Catholics were first allowed to have a representative of their community in the Chamber of Deputies after independence—in 1951.

In time, it became clear to some politicians as well as to the French in Lebanon that, as in the case of the Greek Orthodox, a bid must be made to win over gradually the loyalty of the Sunni community to the Lebanese state. Tripoli presented the first opportunity. A hotbed of Sunni unionist sentiment, the city boasted of two outstanding citizens, Abdel-Hamid Karame, the *Mufti* of Tripoli and an indefatigable spokesman for union with Syria, and Sheikh Mohammad al-Jisr, a respected man of religion and politics. In the hope of counteracting Karame's agitation and of winning the Tripolitanians' cooperation, President Dabbas and the mandatory maneuvered the Chamber in 1929 into electing Sheikh Mohammad as its president. As former Director of Interior and former senator, the Sheikh had already shown a willingness to cooperate with the administration.

Within the Druze community, some leading noblemen and their followers were moved by the Arab nationalist-unionist spirit. But the community as a whole put one thing above everything else: the protection and preservation of its traditional institutions and feudal organization from outside interference. If the mandatory was ready to guarantee their inviolability, then they, the Druze, would cooperate with it as they had cooperated with their former protector, Britain. Their participation in the 1925–1926 rebellion was primarily an expression of solidarity with their kinfolk in Jabal Druze, who had originally risen up to resist hasty French attempts to introduce social reforms in the Jabal at the expense of feudal organization. With the back of the rebellion broken, the Lebanese Druze declared their allegiance to their legal government and settled down to a fruitful participation in its institutions and to cooperation with the French. Lively competition between their two leading and rival families,

the Arslans and the Junblatts, netted them a greater share of
political power than would have otherwise been theirs.

There remained one other major community whose attitude on
the question of union with Syria was important—the Shi'is. They
constituted the majority population in the Biqa' valley and were
also predominant in Jabal Amil in the extreme south. At the beginning of the mandate, the Shi'is indicated a preference for unification. But they were not irrevocably committed to union, and
many among them did not wish it at all. Ottoman rule had left
them with some unhappy memories. They had been persecuted
by the Sunnis, who considered them a heterodox Muslim sect,
and placed by the Ottomans under the direct jurisdiction of
Sunni courts in personal status matters. In short, unlike other
communities, they had been denied the special status of a separate *millet*. Poor and with a high rate of illiteracy, the Shi'is were
a rural people dominated by a landed aristocracy, whose role in
public life at the beginning of the mandate was overshadowed
by the more vociferous Sunni elite. Thus because of their un-
fortunate experience and their sad state of affairs, the Shi'is
might well be induced to accept a happier and more rewarding
life as citizens of Greater Lebanon. Following their sporadic
agitation for unification with Syria in the early twenties and
their participation in the rebellion of 1925–1926 in the same
cause, the mandatory stepped in with a plan calculated to wean
them away from the attractions of Arab nationalism. Early in
1926 a statute was passed granting the Shi'i (Ja'fari) rite official
recognition for the first time. This meant a right of community
jurisdiction in personal status matters, which heretofore had
been within the jurisdiction of the Sunni courts. The measure
could not fail to win Shi'i approval, for it gave them the opportunity to work for the much needed social and material progress
of their community.

From then on, Shi'i leaders were encouraged by the French

High Commissioner as well as by shrewd Maronite politicians to play a wider role in government, and to share in the responsibilities of the state as a means of bringing greater benefits to their community. The mandatory was careful, however, to back only those feudal leaders who were willing to cooperate with it. Still, support from both the French and the Maronites eventually helped the Shi'i leaders to become independent of Sunni influence and to come into their own politically. Evaluating the far-sighted policy toward the Shi'is, a Lebanese journalist who had seen it in operation writes:

> There is no doubt that Shi'i strength was responsible more than anything else for establishing Lebanese entity on a firm basis after the evacuation of the French. Fearing for this entity, the French had imposed it through sheer will on the two Muslim communities [the Shi'is and the Sunnis], who constitute nearly half of the population of the country, and who did not accept the creation of Lebanon and had never once conceded that it was the embodiment of their dream and their final homeland.
>
> And here we must give credit to Mr. Emile Edde for having been the first to follow a pro-Shi'i Lebanese policy through which he gathered around him in parliament all the Shi'i leaders of the South and of Ba'alback, with the exception of Sabri Hamade, member of the Constitutionalist Party. And the French helped him [Edde] in winning over the Shi'is because they believed it was not really possible to win over the Sunnis to a cause that was purely Lebanese [and gain their allegiance to a Lebanon] separated from the interior [i.e., the predominantly Sunni Syrian hinterland].[5]

As the above quotation implies, official recognition of their rite was not sufficient in itself to win the Shi'is over completely to the cause of a Greater Lebanon existing independently of Syria. For this was an ambivalent community which could again be moved by the call for Arab unity (as it was in 1936) despite its resentment of past Sunni persecutions. The appeal of Muslim-Arab unity might be strong enough to submerge sectarian dif-

ferences.[6] Though agrarian, it was also a tribal community with
strong ties between its leaders and followers. With the power he
exercised over his followers, any tribal lord could easily make
trouble for the state if he chose to. Thus it was wise to keep the
Shi'i leaders friendly and contented, which would help keep
their followers satisfied too.

The task of wooing the Shi'i leadership over to the state was
undertaken primarily by the Maronite community, which also
undertook to win over the Sunni leaders. The effort fitted well
into the Maronites' plans for the administration of the state, on
which they did not see eye to eye with the mandatory. Though
favoring the mandate for the mantle of protection it provided
against the demands of Arab nationalism, Maronite ecclesiastics
and politicians were generally opposed to the French policy of
reserving initiative, advice, and approval for the French advisers
and the High Commissioner. They were just as anxious as the
other communities for a relaxation of French control, especially
since this would allow them, the majority community, a greater
share in decision-making.

Because of their dual interests, the Maronites followed a dual
policy toward the mandatory. On the one hand, they issued, with
French approval, statements on the indivisibility and the territorial integrity of Lebanon when a threat to the state was posed
from the Muslim side; on the other hand, they censured the
mandatory when it exerted too much control over the Chamber
of Deputies and the Cabinet, or when it suspended the constitution and ruled by decree. Censure of the French had of course a
further value: it demonstrated to the other communities that the
Maronites, too, rejected French domination and aspired to independence and self-government. Into this area of mutual interests
stepped two young and energetic Maronite politicians to take
the lead. They were Bishara el-Khouri and Emile Edde, both
lawyers by profession, and both groomed in politics by the
French. But each was a determined and shrewd politician in his

own right. And each was the rival of the other. How they played the game of politics and how they attracted the Muslim leadership to their rival political blocs are questions which belong in a wider discussion on political groups in Lebanon's confessional system of government. They are reserved for the next chapter.

CHAPTER 4

Political Groups in Lebanon's Confessional System

During its twenty-odd years as a mandate of France, Lebanon harbored within its borders three distinct types of nationalism which conflicted in their aims for its own political future. One type of nationalism stood for the continuation of the separate existence of Lebanon within its existing borders; a second hoped to see the state merged with a growing Arab political union that could embrace perhaps the whole area of the Arab Middle East. A third type of nationalism insisted that Lebanon could only become part of a specific geographic area known as the "Syrian homeland."

How did these disparate nationalisms find expression within mandated Lebanon? Did they find support within Lebanon's confessional system of government? Did they see their objectives modified by other forces or exploited for other purposes?

NONIDEOLOGICAL GROUPS AND ALLIANCES

Up until 1934 Lebanon remained without serious political groups. Since religious affiliation was the basis for participation in the governing process, the sects performed the functions of political groups in a modern state. Outwardly, each politician was known to represent the views of his religious community, especially on the vital question of Lebanon's viability. But in Lebanon, as elsewhere, each politician was of course also motivated by personal interests. These at times led him to make temporary alliances with politicians whose views on political issues were dissimilar if not contradictory to his, even with regard to the public posture he was taking on the primary question of Lebanese viability. Alliances among politicians were formed before elections and were generally continued within the Chamber of Deputies. They were the natural outcome of a combination of three factors present on the Lebanese political scene: the remains of a feudalistic organization, multiple representation constituencies with their attendant voting slates or "lists," and the apportionment of parliamentary seats on a sectarian basis.

Despite the blows dealt political feudalism in Lebanon both under the Ottoman reorganization measures of the 1840's and under the *Mutasarrifyya* regime of 1861–1914, and despite the breakup of large landed estates and their distribution among their former tenants, there still existed in certain areas a tradition of feudal patronage over the peasantry. This was as true of the newer areas c˙ Greater Lebanon, such as the Biqa' and Jabal Amil in the south, as it was of the basic core of the state, the ranges of Mount Lebanon. The apportionment of parliamentary seats on a confessional basis under the regime of the mandate and the introduction of multiple representation constituencies gave the old-time feudal families fresh opportunities for reestablishing their political dominance,[1] within the limits, of course, imposed by the mandatory. At the same time, the new electoral-parliamentary system encouraged the emergence in the coastal towns of Beirut, Sidon, and Tripoli of local *za'ims*, or strong men, who sought election to parliament as champions of the city masses. Like their counterparts from other areas, the *za'ims* also came from leading families and had their basic corps of workers and supporters.

An illustration will help explain how the heads of the feudal-aristocratic families succeeded in establishing their political power. Supposing, for example, that in a constituency two leading Maronite families were contending for supremacy. Supposing, too, that the population within the constituency was largely Maronite but had significant Sunni and Greek Orthodox minorities, so that in all it was entitled to elect three Maronite, one Sunni, and one Greek Orthodox deputy to the Chamber. Organization for the contest would proceed as follows: each of the two leading Maronite families would form a slate of candidates headed by its own most prominent and most powerful member or by a reliable family substitute. The slate would also include two other Maronites, a Sunni, and a Greek Orthodox. As minor, less prestigious, candidates, the latter would contribute to campaign funds, but would rely heavily on their association with the feudal name at the top of the slate to win the elections. If the leading candidate won, he would carry the whole slate with him. Determining the outcome of the elections would be such things as the relative prestige and popularity of the rival aristocratic families, the extent of the bribery used by either side, and sometimes even the mandatory's interference in the elections. The same procedures were followed in the coastal cities, where elections were contested by rival *za'ims* and by rival feudal sheikhs who had moved to the city, as heads of their respective "lists" or slates of candidates.

Once in the Chamber, each deputy could act and vote independently. But with an eye on future elections, and in the hope of getting on the winning team again, he could not but be guided by the views of his influential colleague who had headed the slate. Still, whatever his motivation, his action within the Chamber was greatly diminished by the fact that the area in which that body could legislate was limited, and that even within these limitations it had to heed the advice of the mandatory's representatives. Furthermore, the Chamber of Deputies, after it was enlarged by the constitutional amendment of 1927, consisted of only thirty elected members. Fifteen others, or one-third of the total, were appointed by the President (elected by the Chamber itself) upon the approval of the mandatory.

Though the Chamber was a body of severely limited powers, the pattern of alliances and the list system that were developed for the election of two-thirds of its members were important to the politicians themselves. During the late twenties and throughout the thirties, they refined the art of forming alliances and counter-alliances and of drawing up strong and balanced slates calculated to win them seats at the elections. When independence came in the 1940's, the pattern had become a tradition and was carried into the new era. The list system assumed greater significance because the removal of French controls meant that the political stakes were now higher and competition for parliamentary seats was now keener. And both developments inevitably led to an increase in the power of the feudal sheikhs and of the city *za'ims*, who had the prestige and influence to swing the votes for the candidates on their slates.

But in the meantime, during the mandatory period, the customs and traditions of politicking were being laid down mainly by two leading Maronite aristocrats, who constituted the hub of political activity. They were Emile Edde and Sheikh Bishara el-Khouri. Edde had been a member of the delegation from the revived Central Council that had been sent to the Paris Peace Conference in 1919 to demand independence for a Greater Lebanon under French protection. Later he became an adviser to the mandatory and was also a member of the Representative Council that preceded the constitutional regime. When the latter was inaugurated in 1926, he was named to the Senate, and when that body was dissolved by a constitutional amendment in 1927, he was transferred to the enlarged Chamber of Deputies. Fearing the absorption of part or all of Lebanon by Syria, Edde advocated an isolationist policy toward the Arab world, and one of cooperation with Europe, especially France. It was his view that the Lebanese were of Phoenician and therefore of non-Arab stock.

Despite his friendship for the French, Edde had in 1925 publicly censured their "dictatorial" measures when in January of that year they had appointed a Frenchman, Leon Cayla, as temporary Governor of Lebanon. The appointment was contrary to an earlier promise by the High Commissioner, General Sarrail, that the Representative Council would be allowed to elect a Lebanese Governor. Though he may have been prompted by personal ambitions for the governorship, Edde's pronouncements won him acclaim from Muslim circles. At the same time, he angered the French. This man could not be relied on completely if they were to succeed in carrying out their policy for Lebanon. It was necessary to encourage the ambitions of another Maronite to counterbalance the power of this leading politician. Thus Bishara el-Khouri, who had served for a few years as a judge, was invited in July, 1926, to join the first Cabinet as Minister of Interior. On October 14, 1927, he was appointed to the Senate to succeed a deceased member, and when that body was abolished three days later he, too, was transferred to the enlarged Chamber of Deputies. For the next few years el-Khouri and Edde remained colleagues, but rivals, within the same Chamber. There were higher offices to aspire to, and both men held the premiership briefly, but the presidency of the Republic remained the most attractive. Each man hoped to attain it.

Quietly, diligently, each of the two rivals began to build up his corps of supporters and political allies within the other religious communities. But of the two politicians el-Khouri seemed the shrewder. While the fiery Edde stood firmly for a policy of isolation from the Arab countries and for the inviolability of Lebanese territory, el-Khouri avoided the question and went about establishing good relations with Muslim notables. In 1934, when he announced the organization of a political group which he called *al-kutlah ad-dusturiyah* (Constitutional Bloc), he attracted to its ranks prominent Muslims from various parts of the country. El-Khouri formed the Bloc as an act of protest. In 1932 the mandatory had suspended the constitution and ruled through an authoritarian "temporary regime," which gave way two years later to a modified parliamentary regime. El-Khouri's Bloc pressed for the reactivation of full constitutional life.

Edde was not to be left behind. He immediately organized his own supporters into a political group which he called *al-kutlah al-wataniyah* (National Bloc), and proclaimed its principles to be "the defence of Lebanon in her present form and the maintenance of her independence against any forces that might attempt disintegration or separation."[2] But like its rival, the National Bloc sought to gather within its ranks prominent Muslim leaders, for, as one observer says, "every political party that was organized but did not include Muslim *za'ims* could not be considered a political representation of the country, but we used to consider it as a confessional representation only."[3] Still, el-Khouri remained more far-sighted: he began to work through his Bloc for a gradual rapprochement with those hard-core Arab nationalist spokesmen who were advocating union with Syria.

IDEOLOGICAL GROUPS

Neither the Constitutional Bloc nor the National Bloc was a real political party, for neither had a party doctrine, an organization for mass membership, or a definite legislative program to offer. Both were primarily convenient vehicles that rival politicians used to promote themselves into political office. During the twenties, Lebanon had no political parties as such. But within its borders, in its press, and between spokesmen for its various sects raged a heated debate as to whether Lebanon should continue its separate existence or merge with Syria and eventually into a larger Arab union. It was an argument between the Arab nationalist movement, seeking to satisfy its aspirations for Arab unity, and a crystalized Lebanese nationalism, determined to keep Greater Lebanon outside the confines of any Arab union that might develop. Arab nationalism had emerged at the turn of the century, and gathered momentum with the defeat of the Ottoman rulers in World War I. It was informed by the spirit of Islam; its leaders and followers were generally Muslims, for the Arab world was overwhelmingly a Muslim world.

Lebanese nationalism could trace its history to the *Mutasarrifyya* period, when Maronite circles began to plan and plot for complete independence from the Ottoman empire. The movement received a further impetus after the establishment of Greater Lebanon in 1920, when it became necessary to promote public allegiance to the Lebanese homeland within its new borders. Various spokesmen for Lebanese nationalism professed its origins to lie in Lebanon's Phoenician culture, which they considered as separate and distinct from Muslim Arab culture. Thus they advocated a "Lebanon first" policy in all inter-Arab and international dealings. The leadership and following of the Lebanese nationalist movement were Christian, primarily Maronite. It won no support among the Muslim masses, whose hopes were still pinned on an Arab homeland.

Onto this stage of conflicting demands for Lebanon's future a new movement emerged in the nineteen-thirties which offered a third solution. Its purpose was to avoid the traps of cultural distinctness based on religious association. The movement was in fact a reaction against both Arab nationalism and Lebanese nationalism. Its originator was Antoun Saadeh, a Lebanese Christian, who immediately institutionalized it by organizing secretly in 1932 the Syrian National Party. It was a party with a doctrine, a program, and it soon had a growing membership. Emphasizing the concept of historical continuity within a specific geographical area, it called for the reunification of this area of "Greater Syria" because of its "continued geographical unity." To Saadeh and his followers, the people of this "Greater Syria" homeland have had a long history as a complete nation within their natural geographic area of the Fertile Crescent and Cyprus, a history antedating the Arab invasion. Moreover, they have had only loose ties with the Arabs, the most important being their common Arab language.

Having emphasized the importance of geographical unity in their concept of nationalism, the Syrian Nationalists could reject religion as a reason for unification. Thus their party was a secular one, and it found a following among the youth who could accept neither of the religiously tinged Lebanese and Arab nationalist movements. The Syrian National Party (SNP) was investigated in 1935 and declared illegal. Still, its membership increased rapidly and branches were established in Syria, Palestine, and Egypt. It attracted both Muslims and Christians.

In its organization, the SNP was modeled after Fascist groups that flourished in Europe during the thirties. Saadeh was named *za'im*, leader, for life, and he stood at the top of the hierarchy, holding both legislative and executive powers. There was no room for individualism in the party, and the rank and file had to conform to rigid principles handed down from the top. But the combination of its strict discipline, leader worship, and armed preparedness made it a party to reckon with.

The first item on the agenda of the SNP was the unification of Syria and Lebanon as the preliminary step to achieving union between the various parts of "Greater Syria." Concentrating on this objective, Saadeh and a group of supporters petitioned the High Commissioner in March, 1936, for a Syro-Lebanese union. Not only was their petition turned down, but they were sent to jail for several weeks.

Still, the rapid progress and persistence of the SNP were now a cause for alarm among both Lebanese nationalist and Arab nationalist circles, and they set about organizing their own youth movements. In 1936 the *Kataeb* (Phalanges Libanaises) were established, and in 1937 the *Najjadah* were formed, both ostensibly as athletic organizations. Despite their claim to secularism, the former found adherents predominantly among the Maronite youth, the latter predominantly among the Sunni youth. Founded by Pierre Gemayel, a Jesuit-trained Maronite, the *Kataeb* viewed the existence of Greater Lebanon as separate and distinct, both geographically and historically, from its Arab neighbors, and advocated its preservation in this form. They tried to give the concept of Lebanese separateness a firm foundation by nurturing in the young a strong sense of Lebanese nationalism and a sense of duty toward the fatherland. They were quick to condemn any project for union, federation, or confederation since it would compromise the independence of the state.

The *Najjadah*, or Muslim Scouts, moved in the opposite direction. They glorified pan-Arabism and considered Lebanon as part of the Arab world. Organized and operated by Sunni Muslims, the *Najjadah* advocated the unification of the Arab countries, with local autonomy for Lebanon. But their insistence that the "civilizing heritage of Islam" was the life force of Arab nationalism repelled even those Christians who were not committed to Lebanese separatism.

Both the *Kataeb* and the *Najjadah* were paramilitary organizations, but the former were more tightly knit and resembled the SNP in their hierarchical structure and centralization of power. The *Kataeb* leader, Pierre Gemayel, had supreme authority, and like Saadeh of the SNP inspired hero-worship, though to a lesser extent. Furthermore, the *Kataeb* offered a broader program for youth service and athletic training, and thus attracted a much larger membership than the *Najjadah*. Both however were forced to go underground about a year after they had been established because the mandatory officially "dissolved" them for having engaged in other than purely athletic activities.

There were still two other programs to be offered in the thirties for the political future of Lebanon, and both were imports. The first came from the League of National Action, a Syrian group originally organized to work for the complete independence and unity of the Arab lands. In 1936 it established a branch in Lebanon for that purpose, but by 1939 it had modified its program and recognized Lebanon "as an Arab country with its own political entity, and not a part of another country."[4] The promise for a separate political entity was calculated to make an Arab Lebanon acceptable on a nonsectarian basis to Christians fearful of being submerged within a greater Muslim-Arab union.

The other program was hardly solicitous of Christian feelings. It was offered by the Muslim Brethren movement. Organized in Egypt in 1928, and spreading to Syria and Lebanon in 1936–1937 under assumed names for fear of persecution by the mandatory, the movement called for a return to puritan Islam in social life and for the unification of all Muslim nations, both Arab and non-Arab. Although it had a large following elsewhere, the movement remained limited in Lebanon and was little known because of its secretive ways and appearance in public simply as a Muslim social fraternity.

A BALANCE OF INTERESTS

Outside the Chamber of Deputies, the ideological parties and groups just described competed for the attention and support of Lebanese society. Inside the Chamber, none had a direct representative to plead its case or to seek legislation in its support. Such a thing, of course, would have been impossible, for with the exception of the *Kataeb*, who remained apprehensive about the future, the groups would have had to raise the question of Lebanese entity and sovereignty, or foreign orientation; and this the mandatory would not have tolerated. Besides, the electoral system that the mandatory had devised made the Chamber a moderate body, and not a place for political extremism. Thus the Chamber during the thirties remained dominated by the

National Bloc of Emile Edde and the Constitutional Bloc of Bishara el-Khouri.

Being nonideological, but merely vehicles for the promotion of men to power, the Blocs could not keep their members separated. Members of one Bloc sometimes ran for election on a slate organized by the other Bloc, or accepted portfolios in a Cabinet formed under its direction. For instance, during the presidency of Edde, the first of the two rivals to reach that high office, such "pillars" of the Constitutional Bloc as Michel Zakkour, Khaled Chehab, and Camille Chamoun deserted the Opposition to accept portfolios in various Cabinets. Chehab at one time even accepted the premiership.[5]

Still, the two Blocs performed a useful service other than accommodating the personal ambitions of their predominantly Maronite membership. They were instruments of protest: whenever the mandatory, for instance, suspended the constitution and ruled by decree, the Blocs were geared into high activity to demand the return of constitutional life. They were also organs of conciliation: both made allies among non-Maronite candidates and deputies from the various regions of the state, thus attenuating the confessional rivalries of parliamentary life.

By the middle thirties, thanks to the solicitations of the rival Blocs and to timely measures by the mandatory power, the major religious communities, except for the Sunnis, appeared to have settled to a fruitful participation in the political life of the state. Like the other communities, the Sunnis too had their representatives in the judiciary, legislative, and administrative branches of the government, but this gave more satisfaction to the officeholders than to the sect as a whole. It yearned for reattachment to predominantly Sunni Syria and for a return of the prestige it had enjoyed under the Ottomans. Furthermore, an incident in 1932 had left the Sunnis suspicious of official intentions. At that time the mandatory suspended the constitution, dissolved the Chamber and the Cabinet, and instituted an authoritarian regime, all because Sheikh Mohammad al-Jisr, Sunni deputy from Tripoli and president of the Chamber, insisted on announcing his candidacy in the forthcoming presidential elections and stood a good chance of winning. Sunni *amour propre* was slighted.

Although the candidacy of a non-Maronite for the highest office in the state was not prohibited in the constitution or in any secondary law, it became obvious that after the compromise presidency of Greek Orthodox Charles Dabbas (see pages 56-57), the mandatory power wished to reserve this office for the Maronites, the largest community, in accordance with its plan for maintaining a communal balance of power within the organs of the state in proportion to the numerical strength of the communities. Sheikh Mohammad's chances of election at that time derived from the fact that the Chamber, whose duty it was to elect the President, was very much divided as to which of the probable Maronite candidates to elect. Should Edde announce his candidacy, he could not of course count on the votes of the supporters of el-Khouri, who was himself determined to become a candidate. There were also other Maronites with presidential ambitions, and when election day came one of the hopefuls was sure to emerge as the French-approved candidate. Factional rivalry and an unwillingness to elect the "official" candidate, for fear that he would become a tool in the hands of the mandatory, decided many a Christian deputy to support the candidacy of Sheikh Mohammad. The dissolution of the Chamber, however, robbed them of this chance.

With the return of full constitutional life to Lebanon in 1937 and the election of Emile Edde to the presidency, it was time to tender the Sunni community a major gesture of conciliation. Thus the President called upon Khair ad-Din al-Ahdab, a Sunni deputy from Beirut and publisher of a unionist newspaper, to form a Cabinet. This was the first time that a Muslim was accorded this honor under the constitution, and from that time on it became the custom to reserve the premiership, the second highest office in the state, for the Sunnis, the second largest community in the nation. It was the mandatory power itself, however, that had pointed the way to this Maronite-Sunni partnership at the highest level of the executive when in 1934, while the constitution was still suspended, it appointed Maronite Habib Pasha al-Sa'd as provisional President and Sunni Abdallah Bey Beyhum as Secretary of State.

Did the appointment of a Sunni Arab nationalist as Premier by an isolationist Maronite President mean that a Christian-Muslim entente within the state had now been achieved and that the Sunni community were now reconciled to their future as Lebanese citizens? This certainly was the hope of those who favored a separate existence for Lebanon, but it was not a development that could clearly be identified and labeled. For the task of achieving Sunni integration within the state was dependent largely upon providing adequate satisfaction to the community's deep-seated reverence for Islam and Arabism. It was thus too early to answer the question.

There was, however, a gradual change of attitude on the part of some Sunni spokesmen who had thus far relentlessly asked for the reattachment to Syria of the predominantly Muslim areas. Events of 1935 and 1936 contributed to their change of heart. First, there was a rapprochement between the Maronite Patriarch, Mgr. Antoine Arida, and the unionist politicians in Damascus. In 1935 the Patriarch issued a scathing criticism of French political and economic policy in Lebanon and especially of the mandatory's grant in March of a new tobacco monopoly in both Lebanon and Syria after it had allowed for five years the competitive growth and manufacture of tobacco. Both Mgr. Arida and the Syrian nationalists claimed that the monopoly was against the interests of the local tobacco growers and workers, and their campaign against it led to common efforts and friendly contacts between them. The Patriarch did not allow this new spirit of understanding to falter. Thus, following the outbreak of disturbances in Syria in 1935–1936 for the restitution of constitutional life and the conclusion of a treaty with the mandatory, he sent messages of sympathy to those Damascus politicians who had been detained by the French.

The Syrian disturbances forced the mandatory to give in to the demands for a treaty of independence, and a Syrian delegation was sent to Paris in April, 1936, to negotiate it. In the meantime, the riots in Syria and reports of the impending treaty negotiations were having their repercussions within both Muslim and Christian circles in Lebanon. On January 10 a group of Muslim notables convened a conference at Beirut to demand reattachment to Syria of Beirut, Sidon, Tripoli, and the territories of Akkar, Jabal Amil, and the Biqa'. Popular support for this demand was shown in succeeding weeks "in the form of deputations from the Biqa', from the slopes of Hermon, from the Shi'is of southern Lebanon, from Tyre and Saida [Sidon], where strikes and rioting took place, and notably from Tripoli, where repeated demonstrations occurred."[6] Though popular Muslim acclaim was all too evident, strangely enough, the nationalist leadership in Damascus was generally not responsive to the unionist demands of the conference. A few individual voices were raised in Damascus for the annexation of Tripoli, whose sentiments for union were the strongest, and whose port facilities would also make it a definite gain for Syria. But the claim was roundly denounced by the Maronites and especially by Mgr. Arida.

The Christians rallied their forces to denounce the conference demands. Mgr. Arida issued statements to the press condemning unionist action and presented a "Green Book" to the mandatory in which he called for Lebanese economic and political independence. Similar views were expressed by prelates and laymen from the Maronite and other Christian communities. A Lebanese Unity Party was organized by Patriarch Arida's nephew, Tewfiq 'Awwad, to press the cause of Lebanese integrity. It attracted a number of Muslim notables to its ranks. In turn, unionist Sunnis in Beirut organized a Muslim Consultative Council under the auspices of the Sunni *Mufti* of the Republic to protect Muslim interests—i.e., unification with Syria. The French position on these conflicting demands was revealed when the High Commissioner gave assurances that Lebanese integrity would be preserved.

The demands of the Beirut conference were also cold-shouldered by a number of Sunni notables as well as by the Sunni and Shi'i deputies in the Chamber. Thus there was an obvious split between some of the leadership and the rank and file of these communities. Furthermore, during the conference itself, a minority group led by some Negativists (see page 53), one-time staunch supporters of union with Syria, opposed the return of the annexed areas of the state to Syria, and demanded endorsement of Lebanon within its existing boundaries. Why had the Negativists now changed their minds? Why had the nationalist-unionist leaders in Damascus changed their minds? Why did both sides now accept the principle of Lebanese political and territorial integrity?

Tactical reasons appear to have been responsible for the change of attitude on the status of Lebanon. Gradually with the years, Arab nationalist leaders on both sides of the Syro-Lebanese border had come to realize that their unrelenting stand on the question of the annexed territories was not bringing them any nearer to independence. It was obvious now that they had been using the wrong tactics in harping on the illegality and injustice of the act of annexation. They had helped neither the cause of Lebanese nor of Syrian independence. Furthermore, their attitude had only accentuated Christian fears in Lebanon, thus perpetuating the presence of the French. Logically, too, they reasoned, should the annexed territories be regained by Syria, Lebanon would become an isolationist Christian enclave, harboring an enmity toward the surrounding Arab areas and allying itself with any major power having designs on the Arab world. It would be better then to accept the status quo, work for the separate independence of both countries, and seek Arab unity later.

Lebanese Christians, too, were now thinking more seriously of gaining their independence. They found French autocratic methods exasperating and the limitation of constitutional life humiliating. Mgr. Arida had never ceased to lash out at the mandatory for its high-handedness, and was becoming impatient with its delay in granting independence. Yet he wanted an independence that would include the annexed areas, and it was with this in mind that he had made friendly overtures to Damascus and was now supporting the Syrian independence movement. Meanwhile, Christian spokesmen, with Bishara el-Khouri in the lead, sought an understanding with the Negativists on a joint Christian-Muslim effort to terminate the French mandate. When the Franco-Syrian negotiations for a treaty were announced early in 1936, the Christians, and especially the Maronites, became particularly anxious to have a Franco-Lebanese treaty of independence concluded at the same time. They had two things on their minds: they wanted a guarantee for the territorial integrity of Lebanon, and they wanted the same international status for their country as Syria would be getting so that they would not be put at a disadvantage vis-à-vis the French or the Syrians.

The Franco-Syrian and Franco-Lebanese treaties for the termination of the mandate were initialed respectively in September and November, 1936, and conformed to the general Syro-Lebanese understanding on an equal independence. Although the former treaty "contained no formal recognition by the Syrian Government of the separate existence of Lebanon . . . such recognition was implied by a protocol which declared the readiness of the Syrian Government to enter into negotiations with Lebanon for the regulation of all outstanding questions."[7] The

Franco-Lebanese treaty guaranteed the status quo. Both treaties were ratified in the same year by the Syrian and Lebanese parliaments respectively. But the act of ratification in Lebanon evoked a series of disturbances among the Muslims as well as communal clashes.

Syria and Lebanon were now ready to assume the full reins of self-government. France, however, was not yet ready to hand them over. Negotiated by the leftist Front Populaire regime of Léon Blum, the treaties remained unratified by the French Assembly, for it appeared to the conservative politicians in that body that France could not relinquish its position of strength in the eastern Mediterranean. The deteriorating international situation in the latter thirties favored their view.

France's failure to ratify the Lebanese treaty did not perturb Muslim public opinion in general. Neither did it perturb certain Maronite circles, who felt that the treaty did not give their community any special guarantees. But for the Muslim and Christian leaders who had worked hard on behalf of the treaty the struggle for independence was still an urgent matter. They continued to work together in the years that followed in an effort to find common ground for achieving it. What was really needed was a working partnership between the two sides that would help attain and maintain Lebanese independence.

Bishara el-Khouri of the Constitutional Bloc decided to take the lead in hammering out the partnership. The task was particularly suited to his talents. Furthermore, he was quick to realize that although Lebanon had a Christian majority, its Muslim population was not far behind, and that Lebanese viability would have to depend to a great extent on Muslim satisfaction and sense of belonging within the state. There would also be a personal dividend for him for his troubles: he would gain Muslim support against the ambitions of his political rival, Emile Edde. Thus while President Edde was still advocating a continued French connection as a means of guaranteeing independence after it was achieved, el-Khouri began speaking of the necessity of a friendly, brotherly cooperation between Lebanon and the Arab countries to attain full independence for all from foreign control.

World War II brought Syria and Lebanon closer to independence. When Paris fell to German troops in the summer of 1940, nationalist leaders in both countries knew that France, too weak to defend itself, could not hope legally or morally to defend its continued presence or its privileges in the Levant. Within the small isolationist camp of Lebanon, composed mainly of Uniate Catholics, there were now fewer people who still shared Emile Edde's view that France could and should continue as the protector of Lebanese independence against possible Arab domination. Nevertheless, to the advocates of unconditional independence, the position of the Christian hard-core isolationists appeared dangerous, for it meant that in exchange for giving protection, France would necessarily acquire concessions and privileges in Lebanon that would compromise its sovereignty. Something had to be done to set the mind of those Christians at rest, and at the same time deny the French a foothold in the Levant and avoid the evils of foreign protection. The formula that emerged in answer to those needs, as well as to the needs of the Muslim communities, was a Muslim-Christian understanding for the maintenance of an independent, sovereign, and viable Lebanon. It went into effect in September, 1943, when, in accordance with promises for Lebanese independence, a newly elected Chamber of Deputies* itself elected Bishara el-Khouri (against his rival Edde) as first President of the sovereign Republic.

Independence and sovereignty, however, were more formal than actual. It now became evident that General Charles de Gaulle intended to place limitations on the independence that

* The constitution had again been suspended between 1939 and 1943.

he had promised the Lebanese in 1941 in the name of the Free French forces. He wished to reactivate the defunct Franco-Lebanese treaty of 1936, and through it to secure for France political, military, economic, and cultural privileges in Lebanon. But conditions had changed since 1936 and the Lebanese were now unwilling to submit to such limitations. Under the leadership of the new Cabinet and the new Chamber, they rallied to the cause of unconditional independence, joining ranks in a truly national effort against the odds that lay ahead. All this was made possible by the newly concluded Muslim-Christian understanding, which had now come to be called *al-mithaq al-watani* or the National Pact of 1943.

The Pact was not a formal document, but merely a verbal agreement between the Maronite President, Bishara el-Khouri, and the man he had appointed as Prime Minister. He was the well-known Riad es-Solh, a Lebanese Sunni who had for many years agitated for the return of the annexed provinces to Syria, but had now come to accept and pledge himself to the cause of Lebanese independence and territorial integrity. With the consent of the Christian and Muslim leadership, the President and Prime Minister committed the two communities to the following principles:

> First, the Christians gave up the idea of an isolated Lebanon and accepted an independent and sovereign Lebanon within the Arab world. The Muslims in return, gave up the idea of giving back to Syria the territories which had been annexed to Lebanon; and also the aim of uniting Lebanon with the Arab world. . . .
>
> Secondly, the Christians gave up the idea of foreign protection, either by way of occupation, military outposts or the concluding of treaties with the Western Powers. . . . In return, the Muslims agreed to stop working to make the Lebanon submit to Syrian or Arab influence.
>
> Thirdly, the number of seats in Parliament was to be distributed in such a way as to ensure a majority to the Christians.

Also, the President of the Republic was always to be a Christian while the Premier in the Government was always a Muslim. . . .[8]

The principles set forth in the first and second paragraphs above reassured Christians and Muslims on the regional and international policy of Lebanon. Those in the third paragraph provided the basis for a Christian-Muslim equilibrium within the structure of the state. Since the Christians were a slight majority, they were given a slightly larger representation within the Chamber of Deputies, in accordance with a set ratio of six Christian to five Muslim deputies. Agreement on this ratio had been reached only after a crisis threatened to disrupt Muslim-Christian cooperation. The crisis was precipitated by Dr. Ayub Tabet, who had been appointed in March, 1943, by the French Delegate General[9] as temporary Head of State with the task of conducting the elections. He began by issuing a decree enfranchising all Lebanese émigrés who had not adopted foreign citizenship. Muslims of all sects were outraged and threatened to boycott the elections, for the émigrés were predominantly Christian and would have assured an overwhelming Christian representation within the Chamber. Only the removal of Dr. Tabet could conciliate the Muslims, and when this was done and he was replaced by Petro Trad, they accepted a proposal from the British Minister for the redistribution of parliamentary seats into 25 for themselves against 30 for the Christians. It was a ratio of five to six and it remained the formula for future elections.

The balance of power thus established in the Chamber of Deputies was continued by virtue of the National Pact into the executive branch of the government. The Pact of course merely followed a trend that had been set during the mandate period: the presidency was reserved for the Maronites, the largest community, and the premiership for the Sunnis, the second largest community. Previously those two communities had stood at opposite poles with regard to the future of Lebanon; the Maronites had generally favored isolation from the Arab world; the Sunnis had pressed for integration within the Arab world. Now the Maronites were satisfied that Lebanese independence would be preserved through the Christian majority within the Chamber and their own control of the highest office in the land. The Sunnis were equally gratified that a fair Muslim representation within the Chamber and their own occupancy of the premiership would guarantee the rights of Muslims within the state and prevent their alienation from the Arab world.

To give the other major sects the same peace of mind, Prime Minister es-Solh also included in his Cabinet a Greek Orthodox, a Shi'i, a Greek Catholic, a Druze, and a Maronite. The communal balance he devised set a precedent for the composition of future Cabinets. This, of course, did not mean that Premiers would always maintain this exact balance. It did mean that they would balance sectarian interests within their ministries in accordance with their size.

The third largest sect within the state was not to be left without its own compensation. And so, in keeping with the spirit of conciliation of 1943, the Shi'is were accorded the right to the presidency of the Chamber.[10] Henceforth deputies would elect their own president from among their Shi'i colleagues.

Meanwhile, the unconditional independence in whose cause the National Pact was concluded was far from achieved. With public support behind him, Prime Minister es-Solh made his first move to shake off the fetters of the nation and to indicate its course in the future. Speaking before the Chamber on October 7, 1943, he declared that his Government would work for the following objectives:

1. Modification of the Lebanese constitution so that it would conform to a true state of independence, i.e., vesting sovereign powers within the nation and eliminating all references to the mandatory and to its right of limiting sovereignty.

2. Conducting the business of government in a manner that would benefit all the Lebanese and bring them into a closer national union.

3. Establishing a relationship between Lebanon and "the sister Arab states" on a strong basis "which will guarantee the respect of the Western states for the independence of Lebanon, her full sovereignty and the integrity of her present borders. For Lebanon is a nation with an Arab face, that selects what is good and useful in Western civilization."[11]

Es-Solh justified this policy of closer cooperation with the Arab states as well as his official recognition of the "Arab face of Lebanon" on the ground that Lebanon's "geographical position, the language of her people, her culture, her history and the circumstances of her economy put her relations with the sister Arab states at the foremost of her concerns."[12]

4. Maintaining Lebanon as "an independent, sovereign and free nation" because "we do not want her to be a foothold for imperialism; they [the Arab nations] do not want her to be a path leading imperialism to them."[13]

Thus, with their interests neatly balanced and guaranteed within the institutions of the state, Lebanon's sectarian communities could now work in unison for the liberation of their homeland. For the time being the arrangement proved effective. As the following pages show, it contributed immensely to the attainment of unconditional independence. But how long was this delicate confessional machinery going to last? In the absence of a binding secular nationalism, how would the state weather any disruptive influences that might sweep in from the outside? This was the problem of the future.

CHAPTER 5

Regional Developments and Lebanese Politics: From Harmony to Disharmony

Fifteen years elapsed between Lebanon's first official act of independence, when in November, 1943, the Chamber of Deputies abrogated all reference in the constitution to the mandatory regime, and the crisis of 1958, when the country was divided between two warring camps of Christians and Muslims. The two dates are significant in the political life of independent Lebanon. In 1943 there was maximum cooperation between the sects for the achievement of one major objective: complete independence and sovereignty. By 1958 the pendulum had swung to the other end: armed strife between the Muslims and Christians caused concern for the very future of Lebanese independence and sovereignty. What happened in the intervening years to change a situation of harmonious communal coexistence into one of conflict between the sects was due to an interplay of outside pressures and influences, regional developments, Big-Power politics, and the internal disruption of the confessional balance of power.

The years between 1943 and 1958 cover two contrasting periods in Lebanon's political development; the first period coincides with the presidency of Bishara el-Khouri, ending in 1952; the second period coincides with the presidency of Camille Chamoun, who succeeded el-Khouri in September, 1952, and remained in office until September, 1958.

FIRST DECADE OF INDEPENDENCE—PROPITIOUS FOR LEBANON

Between 1943 and 1946 Lebanon waged an all-out struggle to attain complete independence from French control. The el-Khouri regime wanted no foreign protection whatsoever, no foreign military bases within the country, and no special privileges for any power. France, on the other hand, wished to continue to enjoy the privileges it had in Lebanon under the mandatory regime and hoped to negotiate a treaty of alliance that would guarantee these privileges, even though it would abridge Lebanese sovereignty. France still exercised control over certain aspects of public life, and its Free French forces were stationed in Lebanon. It planned to use both as levers to attain its ends. Circumstances, however, favored the Lebanese objective rather than the French. On the domestic and regional level, Lebanon could count on the following assets:

1. The Lebanese people individually and as members of the different sects were wholeheartedly behind their government.

2. The government of Syria, which was also fighting for unconditional independence from the French, acted in unison with the government of Lebanon for the attainment of their common objective. Furthermore, there was spontaneous public support in each country for the efforts of the other.

3. Lebanon also received the generous support of each of the other Arab states, and in turn fully supported the efforts of Egypt and Iraq to free themselves from unequal alliances with the British.

4. The League of Arab States, which came into existence in 1945, unanimously upheld the mutual cause of Lebanon and Syria, who had joined the organization as "sovereign nations."

Despite the favorable circumstances, the Lebanese government had to proceed cautiously. For the French were physically in the country and in a controlling position. They supervised the governmental services, commanded the *troupes spéciales* (the local militia), and administered the Common Interests, the public services and economic enterprises that Lebanon shared with Syria. Furthermore, French troops were stationed in the country, and could not be made to leave before the end of the war.

The Lebanese government decided to do first things first, and to make Lebanon legally sovereign. On November 8, 1943, the Chamber of Deputies by unanimous vote[1] repealed all references to the mandate, to France as the mandatory power, and to the League of Nations. On November 9 the government published the amended constitution, which brought upon its head the wrath of the French Delegate General, Jean Helleu. As spokesman for General de Gaulle's Committee of Liberation, he had previously insisted that the Lebanese constitution could not be changed by the independent action of the Lebanese themselves, and had demanded the reactivation of the 1936 treaty as a basis for the negotiation of any transfer of powers. On November 11 he summarily arrested the President of the Republic, the Prime Minister and his Cabinet, and a number of deputies. He then issued decrees calling for the dissolution of the Chamber, the suspension of the constitution, and the appointment of Emile Edde as Chief of State and head of the government. But two of the ministers, Habib Abu Chahla and Majid Arslan, escaped arrest, and together with the president of the Chamber, Sabri Hamade, they moved to a village near Beirut and carried on as the legal Government of Lebanon. Members of the Chamber who were still at large continued to meet in various places.

For twelve days Lebanon was in a state of crisis. The Christian *Kataeb* and the Muslim *Najjadah* parties clashed with the French troops. The people stood solidly behind their government, and no politician would consent to join the Cabinet that Edde was trying to form. In Syria, public demonstrations were held in support of the Lebanese, while the governments of Syria,

Iraq, and Egypt and the Muslims of Palestine publicly denounced the French measures.

Arab solidarity and the pressures exerted by the British, who were in a controlling position in the Middle East, finally forced the French to give in. On November 22 they reinstated the President of the Republic as well as the ministers and deputies they had arrested. Helleu was replaced by another Delegate General and the decrees he had issued were rescinded—with the exception of the clause which had nullified the constitutional changes of November 8. In practice, however, the constitution stood as amended.

In the wake of the crisis Syria took the opportunity to amend its own constitution and assumed full legal sovereignty. Then without much ado both Syria and Lebanon gradually took over from the French in 1944 control of their public services and of their Common Interests.

Working hand in hand, Syria and Lebanon next attempted to take over from the French command of their respective *troupes spéciales,* for these were to serve as the nuclei of their future armies. But here they met with resistance. In May of 1945 General de Gaulle's government, now sitting in Paris, proposed the conclusion of treaties with both states as a condition for the transfer of these troops. The terms would guarantee for France a position of cultural and political preeminence in both countries as well as the continuance of its military bases there. The Syrian and Lebanese governments refused to negotiate on this basis. A deadlock developed and demonstrations and strikes broke out in both countries. On May 29-30 the French tried to force compliance by shelling and bombing Damascus from the air. But instead pressure was applied to them from various points. There was a general strike in Lebanon, a protest from a "National Congress" meeting at the seat of the Maronite patriarchate in Bkerke, further protests from the Lebanese government, from its delegation to the United Nations Charter conference in San

Francisco, and from the newly organized League of Arab States in Cairo. On June 21 the Lebanese and Syrian governments "announced their joint resolve to refuse a 'special position' to any European Power, to dismiss French officials, abolish the Mixed Courts, take over the *troupes spéciales,* and continue pressure for the total withdrawal of French troops."[2] Under such attacks the French position collapsed, and France was forced to accede to the nationalization of the *troupes spéciales* before the year was out.

The last thing that remained now was to obtain the evacuation of French troops from Lebanon. The government announced its intention to do so in January, 1946, and together with the government of Syria, which also was suffering the presence of French troops, lodged a complaint in February with the U.N. Security Council. As a tactical maneuver, both governments also complained about the continued presence of British wartime troops within their territories. Privately, however, they were assured of Britain's intention to move out its troops, and only hoped that they would stay long enough to act as a lever to push out the French troops also. Although the Security Council did not take positive action on the matter, the airing of the joint complaint forced the hand of France. Negotiations were held between the parties concerned and led to the evacuation of French and British troops from Syria by April, 1946, and from Lebanon by December of the same year. Lebanon was now a completely sovereign and independent nation. It had succeeded in avoiding the conclusion of a subordinating treaty of alliance with France.

During the same years of the national struggle, Lebanon had also succeeded in consolidating its sovereign status vis-à-vis the Arab world. It received special guarantees for its independence and sovereignty within its existing borders in the Alexandria Protocol of October, 1944, the document envisaging the forthcoming organization of the League of Arab States (Arab League). It obtained implicit recognition of its new status in the

Arab League Pact of 1945, which committed each member to respect the systems of government of the other members and emphasized the right of each to decide whether or not it wished to establish a closer relationship with any other member.

Thus internally and externally, Lebanon now fulfilled the terms of the National Pact. A sectarian balance existed within its governing institutions. No restrictive ties subjugated it to any big power or any Arab state. Its Christian and Muslim communities were both satisfied. Furthermore, since it was a charter member of the United Nations, there could be no question now from any quarter as to the meaning of its sovereignty. It looked to its membership in the world organization as the ultimate guarantee for its continued independence.

Thus assured, independent Lebanon, under its first President, Bishara el-Khouri, followed a policy of maintaining friendly relations with all nations, with the exception of the common Arab enemy Israel. It contracted no military or political treaty with any power that might have abridged its sovereignty. Within the United Nations it defended eloquently the cause of its sister Arab nations for complete emancipation from the last vestiges of foreign control. Within the Arab League it participated willingly in mutually beneficial economic and social programs, and effectively mediated quarrels and misunderstandings between rival Arab states. In its relations both with its sister Arab nations and with foreign powers Lebanon during these years followed a policy of neutrality. It protected itself from charges of favoritism by taking no sides in the disputes of the Arab nations—no less could be expected of it as a mediator. It protected its sovereignty by making no concessions to any big power. Its policy of neutrality was in fact in keeping with the spirit of the National Pact.

There is no doubt that conditions in the Middle East up until 1952 contributed significantly to the success of Lebanon's regional and international policy. For one thing, most of its sister

Arab nations were still preoccupied with obtaining full independence from the West. Despite their quarrels, they needed
and received the diplomatic support of each other at the United
Nations and in the world capitals. Then from 1948 and on, they
were drawn together on one overriding common cause of concern: the establishment of the state of Israel in their midst. One
and all regarded the alien state as a beachhead of Western imperialism, making its return to the Middle East in a new guise.
They saw in Israel's actions along its common borders with
theirs and in its Zionist ideology a militant aggressiveness whose
purpose was to enlarge Israel at their own expense. Zionism was
the new kind of imperialism in the Middle East and it must be
kept at bay. Because of their military weakness, they resorted to
the next best weapon of defense: nonconclusion of a peace treaty
with Israel and a boycott of Israeli goods.

For the first few years of the postwar era, the Middle East was
still regarded as a Western sphere of influence. The Soviet Union
had not yet bid for a major role in the eastern Mediterranean.
The cold war winds, blowing so gustily across Europe, only indirectly touched the shores of the Arab world. Thus Lebanon
and the other Arab states were not called upon to make a choice
between the Western alliance and the Communist world. Only
in 1951 were they approached, Egypt in particular, to join a
Western military alliance against the Soviet Union, but they declined. Lebanon declared that membership in such an alliance
would be incompatible with the principles of its National Pact.
Furthermore, though it was culturally and spiritually a Western-
oriented nation, it considered the Soviet Union a friendly power
which must not be unnecessarily antagonized. In fact, the Arab
League nations one and all saw no danger to themselves in Communism. It was Zionism that offered the major threat to their
security. And so, in 1951, in answer to the West's bid for an alliance, they drew up their own Collective Security and Economic Treaty under the aegis of the League. It was essentially a

defense alliance against Israel, but it remained a weak instrument of defense.

But Lebanon was not completely without danger to its national sovereignty and territorial integrity during the el-Khouri regime. The dream of Arab unity that had been cruelly betrayed after World War I received fresh hope with the termination of World War II. During the forties, two plans for unification were proposed and debated by the Arabs. The "Greater Syria" plan (not to be confused with the Syrian National Party's Greater Syria project) was put forward by King Abdallah of Transjordan, and visualized the unification of his kingdom with Arab Palestine, Syria, Lebanon, and possibly Iraq under his leadership. The "Fertile Crescent" plan, proposed by Premier Nuri es-Said of Iraq, called for the same arrangement, but under Iraqi leadership. Realization of either plan depended on the initial unification of the sponsor country and Syria, but Syria was lukewarm to Nuri's and Abdallah's advances because it did not wish to substitute its republican regime for the monarchical one that union would have brought. Furthermore, both men were suspect because of their personal ambitions and because of their continued connections with the British, which made them also unpopular with the masses. Thus for the time being, thanks to Syria's indecisiveness, Lebanon escaped serious pressures for unification.

There was, however, one sudden threat to Lebanese sovereignty, but the Lebanese government disposed of it promptly. Early in July of 1949 the Syrian National Party of Antoun Saadeh launched an attack on Lebanese gendarmerie posts in accordance with a plan to get control of the Lebanese government as a first step toward establishment of a Syro-Lebanese union and the eventual unification of the "Syrian homeland." The attack was repelled and Saadeh fled to Syria. But he was soon handed over to the Lebanese government, which gave him a summary trial and executed him on July 8. Other than his own party, which harbored a strong resentment against the government, the public had displayed no sympathy for Saadeh's unsuccessful "revolution."

LEBANON UNDER THE CHAMOUN REGIME:
NEW CHALLENGES TO NEUTRALITY

Shortly before Camille Chamoun assumed the duties of the Lebanese presidency in September, 1952, an event took place in the Middle East which was soon to change the balance of power within the area. In July of that year a group of Egyptian army officers overturned the monarchy in a bloodless coup, and set up their own revolutionary regime. The man who soon emerged as their leader was Gamal Abdel Nasser. At first, he set himself two major objectives: to make Egypt's nominal sovereignty complete by disposing of its unequal treaty alliance with Britain; and to reform Egyptian society for the benefit of the overwhelming majority, the hitherto downtrodden peasantry. By 1955 he had added a third objective to his list: to thrust out all British influence within the Arab Middle East, and to unify the area under his own leadership. He had become convinced that as long as the British maintained their influence in the Arab world, the West could divide the Arab states against each other and encourage the aggressive and expansionist policies of Israel.

In July, 1954, Abdel Nasser fulfilled his first objective. He signed a treaty with Britain which called for the evacuation of the British military base in the Suez Canal Zone. This put an end to the last of the privileges the British had enjoyed in Egypt. The Egyptians felt masters of their own house. But the British were unhappy. No longer was the eastern exit of the Mediterranean Sea under their watchful eye. They felt apprehensive about their trade with the Far East, which necessarily passed through the Suez Canal. They worried about their shipments of oil from the Arabian peninsula because oil was the backbone of their economy. Then there was the ideological struggle in which the Western world was engaged with the Communist world. The struggle was still in the cold war stage, but there was no telling when it could turn into a hot one. Military bases were important for the protection of the West. The United States, which had helped mediate the Anglo-Egyptian differences over the Suez Canal treaty, felt the same way.

Anticipating the loss of the Suez Canal base, Britain and the United States thus made a new attempt in 1953-1954 to bring the Arab Middle East into a defense alliance with the West. They needed a new military foothold in the area to link with their defense system around the periphery of the Communist world. They tried to get all the Arab states to join their proposed alliance, and particularly Egypt and Iraq. At first hesitant toward the proposal, Abdel Nasser soon rejected it for two reasons: he saw in Nuri as-Said's great haste to get into the alliance ahead of him a desire to establish Iraqi hegemony over the Arab world and to exclude Egypt from any meaningful role in Arab affairs; he also saw the proposal as a trick designed to bring British troops back to Egyptian soil under cover of an international agreement.

Nuri, on the other hand, favored the proposed alliance not only because he felt that Iraq's proximity to the Soviet Union warranted special protection, but also because he did indeed hope to use the alliance as a cloak for unifying the Fertile Crescent countries under Iraqi leadership. Thus he advocated Arab participation in the alliance. But Abdel Nasser was against it. To resolve the deadlock, the foreign ministers of the Arab League members held a meeting in Cairo in December, 1954. They declared that the foreign policy of their respective states should rest on the Arab League Pact, the Arab Collective Security Pact, and the Charter of the United Nations. But Iraq had some reservations and on February 24, 1955, it signed a defensive alliance with Turkey in accordance with the Anglo-American proposal. The alliance, which came to be known as the Baghdad Pact, soon acquired the membership of Iran, Pakistan, and Britain. Iraq and its new allies now tried to get the other Arab states to join the Baghdad Pact. Egypt, on the other hand, tried to keep them from joining.

Two other developments sharpened the conflict between Cairo and Baghdad over the course that the other Arab countries were to take. In the spring of 1955 Abdel Nasser embarked on his policy of positive neutralism, or nonalignment with either the Communist or the Western armed camp. By the fall of that year the policy was paying dividends in the form of an arms deal with the Soviet bloc. This meant, of course, that the West no longer held a veto over the supply of arms to the Middle East. It also meant that the Soviet Union had now entered on the scene of Middle East politics. It became increasingly urgent to Iraq and the West to get Syria, Jordan, and Lebanon to join the Baghdad Pact. They stepped up their campaign. Egypt responded by pressing on all three a policy of positive neutralism.

Although Lebanon finally rejected the Baghdad Pact, it did not do so wholeheartedly. There was a period of indecision which reflected official and public division on the issue of the Pact. The National Pact of 1943 called on Lebanon to cooperate with its Arab neighbors, but Iraq and Egypt were now deeply divided against each other. Which way should the Lebanese government turn? It was evident to the Chamoun regime that Egypt, with the support of Saudi Arabia, traditional enemy of the Hashemite dynasty of Iraq, was trying to isolate the latter from the Arab world or force it to renounce the Baghdad Pact. The Chamoun regime did not wish to see Iraq isolated, for its isolation would upset the balance of power and subject Lebanon to the dictates of Cairo. Furthermore, Iraq was free to seek greater security by adhering to the Baghdad Pact, for there was nothing in the Arab League Pact that prohibited it from doing so.

On the home front, the *Kataeb* Party of Pierre Gemayel, with its large Maronite membership, favored cooperation with the West, but directly and not through an alliance with Turkey. The Syrian National Party was eager to have both Syria and Lebanon join the Baghdad Pact. Its attitude was understandable: closer cooperation among the countries of the Fertile Crescent could lead to the unification of the "Syrian homeland." On the other hand, strong objections were raised among the Muslim leadership to any Lebanese membership in the Pact.

An exchange of visits in 1955 between President Chamoun and his Prime Minister, on the one hand, and the Turkish President and his Premier, on the other, indicated at least official interest in the possibility of Lebanese membership in the Baghdad Pact. Still, the Government held back, and in March, 1956, it presented a policy statement to the Chamber of Deputies in which it emphasized its "determination to refrain from joining the Baghdad Pact and any other foreign pacts. Lebanon was determined to realise the purposes of the Arab League Charter and the revival of the Collective Security and Economic Cooperation Treaty."[3] But the Chamber endorsed this policy by only a slight majority.

Technically, Lebanon's rejection of the Baghdad Pact now placed it officially in a position of neutrality between Cairo and Baghdad. But practically, there were many who felt that from then on President Chamoun supported the Hashemites in Baghdad and Amman in their quarrels with Abdel Nasser of Egypt,[4] thus deviating from the neutrality that had served Lebanon so well in its relations with its Arab neighbors.

CABINET CRISIS OVER RELATIONS
WITH BRITAIN AND FRANCE

In the years that followed the uproar over the Baghdad Pact, two events served to exacerbate relations between Cairo and

Beirut and, consequently, to stoke the fires of the Lebanese revolution of 1958. The first was the crisis over Lebanon's nonseverance of diplomatic relations with Britain and France following the Anglo-French-Israeli attack on Egypt in October-November, 1956. The second event was Lebanon's acceptance of the American Middle East policy known as the Eisenhower Doctrine.

There are two conflicting versions of the details of the first event and both bear a full report.

On November 13 and 14, 1956, President Chamoun was host in Beirut to a conference of Arab kings and chiefs of state to discuss what concerted action the Arabs could take to censure and stop the tripartite aggression on Egypt. One version of the story claims that the President had extended the invitations to the conference through Prime Minister Abdallah al-Yafi, and through him had relayed the promise that Lebanon would sever diplomatic relations with Britain and France as an expression of solidarity with Egypt. It was specifically on such a promise, the story goes, that the other Arab governments accepted Chamoun's invitation to the conference. When the delegations met, however, Chamoun considered their joint censure of the aggressor states as fulfilling Lebanese obligations, and refused to sever diplomatic relations with Britain and France. When his Prime Minister and Minister of State Saeb Salam asked him at least to withdraw his ambassadors from London and Paris, he turned them down. Both men then resigned in protest. It is further claimed that Chamoun had acted contrary to Lebanon's obligations under the Collective Security Pact of the Arab League (of 1951), and had thus broken Arab solidarity in the face of the aggressors.

In an interview with the writer on October 20, 1960, Chamoun denied that he had promised to sever diplomatic relations with Britain and France. "Speaking of the cutting off of diplomatic relations between Lebanon and France and Lebanon and Britain," he said, "there was never any kind of promise nor will [intent] from my government to cut off these relations. Even more, three days before the cease-fire I received a visit from an emissary who after having flown for nine hours from Cairo via the Sudan, Saudi Arabia, and Damascus reached Beirut at nine o'clock in the evening. Accompanied by a member of Parliament, Mr. Emile Bustani, he called on the presidency, bringing the salaams of Nasser and asking me to intervene with the British and the French for a quick cease-fire. The name of the messenger was Mustapha Amin. I did what I could do and was able less than forty-eight hours later to give him good news about the cease-fire. Well, this is the proof that it has never been either in Nasser's mind or my mind that diplomatic relations would be cut off. Otherwise, how could you cut off diplomatic relations and still intervene with these two nations?"[5]

On November 1, 1960, the former President's statement was repeated to the Arab News Agency and published in the Beirut daily *L'Orient*. But before the ANA report was published, private sources in Beirut had corroborated part of Chamoun's story and added their own explanations. Before President Chamoun received the verbal message from Cairo, they said, he had at least been considering withdrawing his ambassadors from Paris and London. Both Saeb Salam and Abdallah al-Yafi knew of the message, but ignored it when they quarreled with the President, attributing their dispute and their resignation from the Cabinet to his refusal to sever diplomatic relations with Britain and France. The true cause of the dispute, these sources continued, was the fact that the Government was functioning poorly because of friction among its members over economic questions. Chamoun, however, had no defense against the accusations of his ministers because the request from Abdel Nasser had been verbal. As for Salam and al-Yafi, since they criticized Chamoun for not severing diplomatic relations with Britain and France, they now had to proceed along the road of Arab nationalism in the interest of their political careers.

In Damascus, Chamoun's statement to the ANA was denied, and this writer was referred to the Cairo daily *Akhbar al-Yom* of November 5, 1960, for an official refutation by Mustapha Amin, the man Chamoun claimed to have been the messenger from Cairo. The issue contained an interview by Amin, coeditor of the daily, with U.S. presidential candidate John F. Kennedy in which the latter charged Republican bungling in the Middle East. There was, however, no denial of the Chamoun allegations.

Mr. Amin's silence was perhaps due to his inability to refute at least part of the former President's story. For Mr. Amin's visit to Chamoun had already been confirmed by his alleged companion, Deputy Emile Bustani, a friend of the Egyptian President and an advocate of more amicable relations with Cairo. In an attack on the Government's foreign policy in the Chamber of Deputies on August 29, 1957, Mr. Bustani took time out to defend the Government on at least one action. He stated that Lebanon had been the first to call for a severing of diplomatic relations (with Britain and France). But then, as the Arab conference was meeting in Beirut to discuss this matter, a messenger from President Abdel Nasser arrived to ask that Lebanon intervene (with the two aggressors). Consequently, Lebanon decided that it could not sever relations when it was being asked to act as a go-between. Bustani further claimed that the crisis that ensued over this matter had been provoked by the former Premier, Abdallah al-Yafi, to win public support for himself.[6]

If in fact President Chamoun had promised to sever diplomatic relations with Britain and France, he did not, on the other hand, all alone disrupt the solidarity of the Arab front by not fulfilling his promise. For apart from Egypt, only Syria and Saudi Arabia severed diplomatic relations with both countries, while Iraq and Jordan severed relations with France only. The degree of support that these states gave Egypt was of course in line with their own economic and political interests. But it did appear to those who could not see all the issues involved that Lebanon was doing even less for Egypt than the latter's rival, Iraq.

Within Lebanon, the incident provoked disagreement along religious lines on the ethics of the Government's behavior. Generally, Christian spokesmen felt it unreasonable to ask for a diplomatic rupture with Britain and France. To them such a step would have meant the economic ruination of Lebanon and the isolation of its Christian community. Sunni spokesmen, on the other hand, felt that the Government's attitude was a betrayal of the Arab cause.

The public did not have to wait long to guess in what direction President Chamoun was looking. The resignation of al-Yafi and Salam called for the immediate formation of a new Cabinet. Sami es-Solh, cousin of the deceased nationalist leader Riad,[7] became Premier and chose for his foreign minister Charles Malik, professor of philosophy and former ambassador to the United States and the United Nations. The choice of Dr. Malik for the foreign ministry was generally interpreted as a move toward closer collaboration with the West, especially with the United States. Educated at Harvard, he was an outspoken admirer of the spiritual tradition of Western democracy and a relentless critic of Communist ideology. In the months ahead he was to attract much attention as spokesman for President Chamoun's new foreign policy, for that policy was to become hopelessly involved in domestic and regional politics.

CHAPTER 6

The Eisenhower Doctrine versus Middle East Realities

The Arab world was still reeling with shock from the recent Anglo-French-Israeli attack on Egypt when President Dwight D. Eisenhower went before Congress on January 5, 1957, to request specific measures to protect the Middle East from the imminent and mortal danger of international Communism. Enumerating previous executive declarations on the Middle East, he added: "Nevertheless, weaknesses in the present situation and the increased danger from International Communism, convince me that basic United States policy should now find expression in joint action by the Congress and the Executive. Furthermore, our joint resolve should be so couched as to make it apparent that if need be our words will be backed by action."[1] He proposed a three-point legislative program authorizing the executive to:

1. Cooperate with and assist any nation or group of nations in the general area of the Middle East in the development of economic strength dedicated to the maintenance of national independence;

2. Undertake in the same region programs of military assistance and cooperation with any nation or group of nations which desire such aid;

3. Employ the armed forces of the United States to secure and protect the territorial integrity and political independence of nations in the area requesting such aid against overt armed

aggression from any nation controlled by international Communism.

The whole tone of the President's address was one of extreme urgency. Implying that the Middle East was in imminent danger of Communist armed aggression, he outlined the calamities that would befall the free world should this area of economic, geographic, strategic, and political importance be allowed to fall behind the Iron Curtain. It was therefore necessary to declare clearly and promptly to friend and foe alike that any such armed aggression against the area would be considered a serious threat to the vital interests of the United States, and that the United States stood ready to defend the area militarily. The President's warning was directed against the Soviet Union; it was a unilateral declaration of United States intent. The purposes of the powers he ·was seeking from Congress, however, did not directly concern the Soviet Union. They concerned a third party —the nations of the Middle East. Mr. Eisenhower wished to be authorized through a joint resolution to pursue a new policy toward these nations—a policy which depended on their cooperation for its success. To elicit this cooperation, he declared that he would send a special mission to the Middle East to explain the new program.

The President was in a hurry, and Congress hastened to study his proposals, the House in hearings before its Committee on Foreign Affairs and the Senate in hearings before a joint meeting of its Committee on Foreign Relations and Committee on Armed Services. Two months later, after extensive and sometimes conflicting and confusing testimony at both hearings, and long-drawn-out probings in the Senate, Congress presented him with House Joint Resolution 117. It was essentially what he had asked for and the President signed the bill into law on March 9.* The Administration could now proceed with the most urgent task of

---

* See Appendix, page 219.

preventing and deterring international Communism from closing in on the Middle East. This is how the Administration saw
the Middle East situation and this is how it reasoned. But unfortunately it had misread the facts of the situation, it had
ignored basic issues, it had calculated without considering the
feelings and desires of the people who were to receive the pre-
sumed benefit of this new policy. And so this new policy, based
on House Joint Resolution 117, which came to be known as the
Eisenhower Doctrine, was a failure. Instead of promoting
American interests in the Middle East it set them back; it forced
a polemical argument on the Arab world and aggravated the
Lebanese crisis of 1958; it afforded the Soviet Union greater opportunity to engage in anti-Western and anti-American propaganda in the Middle East.

MIDDLE EAST REALITIES: RECENT HISTORY

Of all the Arab countries that were expected to adhere to the
new American policy, Lebanon was the only one that accepted
the Eisenhower Doctrine. An isolated case, it could not isolate
itself from the storm of Arab protest that raged around the doctrine. Already at odds with Abdel Nasser's Egypt over its diplomatic relations with Britain and France, it found itself severely
shaken when the Egyptian President took up the cry against the
doctrine and found a responsive audience in approximately half
the population of Lebanon. Because Lebanon's problems with
the Eisenhower Doctrine were intermeshed with problems of
the rest of the Arab Middle East, a brief summation of the area's
political realities may help to reveal where the doctrine erred,
from the point of view of both content and tactical presentation.

The Arab world's most burning issue in 1957, as it had been
ever since the establishment of the state of Israel in 1948, was
the problem of Palestine. As President Eisenhower was calling
upon Congress for new powers to save the Middle East from

possible armed aggression by international Communism, Israeli forces were entrenched in Sinai, in Gaza, and in the Gulf of Aqaba, in irrefutable evidence of Israel's latest and most flagrant violation of Arab territory. Arab public opinion felt strongly that they were in imminent and continuous danger of expansionist Zionism, not from any nonevident troops of international Communism. The United States was barking up the wrong tree. Was it perhaps deliberately confusing the issues, they asked? Having been equally responsible with Britain for the creation of Israel, it could redeem itself only by attending to first things first: finding a solution to the Palestine problem acceptable to the Arabs. Its preoccupation with Communism was none of their concern.

At the same time, and with recent events to support them, the Arabs saw Western imperialism as the second major threat to their independence. Slowly and painfully, the Arab states had one by one rid themselves since World War II of the final vestiges of British and French control. There were still a few problems to be solved—Palestine primarily, Aden, and the Arabian sheikhdoms in treaty relations with Britain. And in North Africa, Algeria was still fighting its bloody war of independence. With these questions already making them wary of the West, the Arabs had been plunged into even greater fear and suspicion of Western intentions when Britain and France, in collusion with Israel, launched their attack on Egypt.

The United States immediately condemned the aggression and by taking the initiative at the United Nations and through direct pressure on the attackers played a major role in bringing it to an early halt. Egypt and the other Arab nations noted with gratitude the United States' salutary action. They saw too, that it was continuing to bring pressure on Britain and France, its two major NATO allies, for a withdrawal of their troops from Egyptian territory, and to press Israel to withdraw from the Sinai Peninsula, from the Egyptian islands of Tiran in the Gulf of Aqaba, and from the Gaza Strip. The United States was thus supporting the United Nations' efforts to bring the crisis to a just conclusion.

American prestige, recently at an ebb in the Arab world, was boosted high in the post-Suez days, but not for long. For there soon came the Eisenhower Doctrine, professing to save the Arabs from the clutches of international Communism. They looked around and saw no imminent threat from that quarter. But Communism apart, Russia, too, had just demonstrated its support of the Arabs by espousing the Egyptian cause in the United Nations and by threatening to hail missiles on London and Paris if the aggression on Egypt did not stop. And it was even now continuing to show its friendliness to the Arabs by championing the Egyptians in the Suez Canal settlement at the U.N. So why take a slap at a friendly nation? Why be dragged into the power struggle between the United States and the Soviet Union? The issue of the day in the Arab world was imperialism, not Communism. The Eisenhower Doctrine had no place in the hearts of the Arabs.

Yet apart from disenchantment with the West and fear of Zionism, the Arabs could not possibly look with favor on the Eisenhower Doctrine. Caught in the immense surge of nationalism that was sweeping across the new nations of Asia and Africa, they were too involved in working out their own destiny, in seeking a mode and standard of living adequate to their own needs. They could not afford to disrupt these efforts by aligning themselves with one big power against another, thus bringing the cold war to their own doorstep and possibly a hot one, too. There had already been so much pushing and shoving from both armed camps that in 1955 the new nations of Asia and Africa, led by Prime Minister Nehru of India, met at Bandung, Indonesia, and evolved a policy for their world, a third world, vis-à-vis the Soviet Union and the West. The new policy, positive neutralism, rejected alignment with either side, offered trade to all comers on a mutually acceptable basis, and sought to create an international atmosphere in which burgeoning national societies could grow and prosper free of the pressures of big-power politics. President Abdel Nasser of Egypt had come home from the Bandung conference eager to try out the new policy of positive neutralism, and had used it with dramatic success. He had forced his way out of dependence on the West through his daring arms deal with the Soviet Union and opened up new avenues of trade with the Communist nations. In Arab eyes in general, positive neutralism was now the new formula for success, the new tool for seeking on the international scene support for national objectives. And it was incompatible with the Eisenhower Doctrine, which took a rigid stance against the Communist world.

SECRETARY DULLES' DOCTRINE

This was the mood and temper of the Arab world when the United States debated and launched its new policy toward the Middle East early in 1957. Designed primarily for the Arab world, it was not acceptable to the majority of Arabs. It was therefore a self-defeating policy. But it was pursued with the hope of achieving impressive results. The fault lay with Administration thinking, which had misread, misinterpreted, and at times ignored the realities of the Middle East, and with Secretary of State John Foster Dulles, whose obsession with the Communist threat permitted no flexibility in his approach to this problem. It was inconceivable to Mr. Dulles that nations could prefer not to side with either Moscow or Washington. His reasoning seemed to imply that those who would not declare themselves for us were against us.

In the immediate postwar world, the two colossi of East and West stood facing each other across a ravaged Europe. Soviet armies posted across the eastern half of the continent as well as strong Communist parties within the western half posed an immediate threat to the economically weak but still free nations of the West. Boldly, imaginatively, the United States put them back on the road to full recovery with generous economic aid, strengthened their defenses with military aid and defense pacts. But to Mr. Dulles this was not sufficient; the encircling belt of containment against the Communist menace needed a link in the Middle East, and he set about devising it. The Greeks, Turks, and Iranians were already parties to defense pacts with the West. But the Arabs would enter into no such agreements. Unlike their neighbors to the north, they had had no brush with either Czarist or Soviet imperialism, but were full of fresh memories of British and French power and were also keenly aware of the alien state that the West had placed in their midst. When finally a defense treaty was devised in 1954 in the hope of attracting Arab membership, only the unpopular British-supported regime of Iraq elected to join. It signed the treaty, the Baghdad Pact, as much for reasons of rivalry with Egypt as for any real fears of Soviet aggression. Almost four years later, a new revolutionary regime in Iraq summarily denounced and abandoned the Baghdad Pact in expression of the true sentiments of the Iraqi people.

But before Iraq had shaken loose this weak link in the West's defenses, Secretary Dulles came face to face with new challenges in the Middle East—challenges posed by the aftermath of the tripartite attack on Egypt. Whether he saw the facts of the situation clearly or hazily, he chose to tailor them to fit his containment policy rather than modify this policy to take advantage of the facts. How did the Secretary see the Middle East in the months after the Suez war?

Mr. Dulles surveyed the situation and was greatly shocked by what the war and other developments had done to weaken the influence of Britain and France in the area and to send their prestige plummeting to zero. Russia, on the other hand, had gained tremendous prestige and popularity through its voluble support of Egypt against the aggressors and its previous arms sales to Egypt and Syria. And now there were Communist technicians and advisers working closely with the governments of both countries. Surely the position of the West was at stake. The United States must act, or Soviet "imperialism" would in a twinkling envelop the Middle East. Mr. Dulles warned of this danger in a New Year's message and forecast the President's proposals to Congress. "The United States," he said, "will have to accept an increasing responsibility to assist the free nations of the Middle East and elsewhere to maintain their freedom and their welfare. We must live by the Golden Rule. By serving others, we serve ourselves."[2]

This approach to foreign aid, though generous in intent, was unfortunately directed by the following guide lines:

1. Soviet policy in the Middle East was informed primarily by the objectives of international Communism.

2. Soviet popularity automatically promoted Communist influence in the area.

3. Communist influence in Syria and Egypt was dangerously high. Should the Communists gain complete control in both countries, they must not be allowed to overrun neighboring Arab countries. Syria and Egypt must therefore be isolated or forced to relinquish their Communist connections.

4. Nationalism and neutralism were dangerously susceptible to Communist pressure, and could easily be subverted by Communism. In fact, owing to the Anglo-French debacle in the Middle East there now existed a "power vacuum" in that area into which Communism could move if the United States did not act quickly to stop it.

Testifying before the Senate and House Committees which were studying the proposed resolution on the Middle East, Secretary Dulles and other Administration spokesmen sketched out the above points, sometimes by implication and sometimes by direct contention, as constituting the realities of the Middle East situation at that time. Yet at best they projected a picture of hasty assumptions and impressions motivated by the realization that the United States had been overtaken by events, that it lacked influence with the real sources of power in the area, and that it must now quickly get into a position where it could influence developments there. In other words, the United States had not pursued a clear and consistent policy, had consequently been rejected, and was now impelled to devise a new policy for the Middle East. And what was it based on?

Let us take the assumptions one by one. Was Soviet interest in the Middle East really motivated primarily by a desire to establish international Communism there? Secretary Dulles admitted in the hearings that Russia had exhibited an interest in the Middle East since Czarist times, yet he chose not to consider this as a legitimate national interest of a big nation in her neighbors to the south, like American interest in Latin America.

As Geoffrey Wheeler has written:

> For reasons of national security, national prestige and national economy, Russia has for the past 150 years wished to supplant the West as the political, economic and cultural mentor of the Middle East countries as well as of other Asian countries lying on her borders. The present Russian government is always prepared to use communism as a means toward achieving this end when and where it seems appropriate. At the same time, in order to preserve the monolithic position of the Communist Party inside the U.S.S.R., it must always seek an ideological justification for its foreign policies. These two factors have resulted in a disproportionate importance being attached to communism as the deciding factor in the formulation of Soviet policy, whether in Asia or elsewhere.[3]

Is it any wonder, then, that when President Abdel Nasser was refused American arms and in turn refused to join the Baghdad Pact, Russia vaulted this cordon sanitaire and offered arms to Egypt? Of course, we cannot discount the Soviet Union's Communist mission in its relations with other countries, but we must not equate Soviet popularity with acceptance of Communist ideology. The Arabs were jubilant to receive the support and assistance of an international power like the Soviet Union, but the Communist parties within the Arab world remained weak and frustrated, and were generally persecuted.

But what of the talk that Communist influence in Syria and Egypt was dangerously high? That those two countries were putting themselves and their neighbors in jeopardy? "The danger of Syria is primarily one of subversion and indirect aggression, not of overt attack,"[4] Secretary Dulles told an interrogator at the House Committee hearings.

"If this legislation were passed, do you anticipate that conditions would develop in such a way that our economic aid will be of help to such nations as Syria and Egypt in fighting international communism?" he was asked again.

"We would, I think, be prepared to aid both Egypt and Syria," replied the Secretary, "if that aid stimulated a fight against international communism, yes, but we do not want to give such aid if it merely supports governments which are subservient to or sympathetic to international communism."[5]

Thus, by conjecture, Secretary Dulles threw a mantle of suspicion over Egypt and Syria. And if action were to be taken against them, it would be taken under still more tenuous conditions, as the Secretary explained in this exchange with Senator Fulbright at the Senate hearings:

> Senator Fulbright: . . . Who determines whether or not a country is Communist-dominated, and what are the criteria of determining that under this resolution?
>
> Secretary Dulles: That determination would be made by the President. . . . That phrase "a government dominated by international communism" was picked because it is a phrase which has a legislative history. . . .
>
> Senator Fulbright: Does that history . . . set down a criteria by which you could judge whether a particular country is Com-

munist-dominated? I do not mean one like Russia. I mean bor-
derline cases, such as Syria. Does it give you a guide as to
whether or not Syria today is Communist-dominated?

Secretary Dulles: I do not think it lays down any precise formula, Senator, and I do not think any precise formula is possible. The determination of whether a country is dominated by
international communism is a close question in some cases, and
the answer to it is to be found, I think, not by any mathematical
rule of thumb. It is determined by a whole complex of actions or
lack of action which the government takes in its international
and domestic affairs.[6]

It was up to the President then, depending on Mr. Dulles'
"reading of the signs," to make a decision should friction arise
between one country and its neighbor as to which was dominated by international Communism and which was not. The proposed resolution ignored traditional rivalries and problems of
the area or saw them only in the light of the Communist-anti-
Communist struggle.

Like a part of a jigsaw puzzle, this false premise had to be
fitted into a total picture to give it meaning. One was at hand,
the Administration's fourth assumption that nationalism and
neutralism were dangerously susceptible to Communist pressure, that in the present state of "power vacuum" the United
States must come forward to keep the Middle East open to the
West, to save the Arabs from the claws of Communism.

The United States had long needed a clear and realistic policy
toward the Arab Middle East. But what it came out with in 1957
served neither its own interests nor those of the area it was trying to protect. First and foremost, it injected the cold war into
inter-Arab politics. With a moralistic approach to the whole area,
the State Department separated the "good Arabs" from the "bad
Arabs." It counted in the first group Nuri es-Said's Iraq,
Chamoun's Lebanon, Hussein's Jordan, and hopefully Saud's
Arabia. These rulers could definitely be considered as anti-Communist. It relegated to the second group Abdel Nasser's Egypt

and al-Quwatli's Syria, for both had resisted efforts to make them join the Baghdad Pact, had bought arms from the Communist bloc, were now receiving economic and technical aid from the same source, and were pursuing a policy of positive neutralism which seemed to Washington as favoring the Soviets. Still, an attempt should be made to entice them away from the Soviets and into the arms of the Eisenhower Doctrine. If they refused, then the United States was doubly justified in strengthening the defenses of their neighbors against possible armed aggression from their territory should either Syria or Egypt fall under the control of international Communism.

But the Arab world could not be divided by decree from Washington. In Iraq, Lebanon, Jordan, and Saudi Arabia, as in Egypt and Syria, the people saw themselves as nationalists, not as Communists or anti-Communists. Governments and people were united in their attitude toward Israel and the Palestine question. Governments were disunited in their approach to the solution of this problem. What was important to the area, of course, was the attitudes of the two major and rival powers of the Arab world, Egypt and Iraq, and also that of Syria, the heartland of Arab nationalism and cornerstone of the union that each of the two rivals aspired to lead. Under Nuri es-Said, traditional friend of the British, Iraq saw the way to a satisfactory solution of the Palestine problem through continued friendship with the West. It joined the Baghdad Pact not only because of its proximity to the Soviet Union, but also to keep the door open for a dialogue on Palestine with its partner in the alliance, Britain. And of course, in the game of regional politics, Nuri hoped that under the aegis of the Pact he could soon launch his plans for a union of the Fertile Crescent.

Disenchanted and suspicious of the West, and unwilling to trust the wily Nuri, Egypt and Syria in 1954-1955 followed the neutralist road of Bandung. It was the beginning of a concerted effort to build up their economies and their defenses, not only because that was the right thing to do for new and developing nations, but also because they needed the strength to prevent any aggression or expansion by Israel, with whom they shared common borders, and eventually to be in a position to settle the Palestine problem. The Bandung road led to Moscow, and both Cairo and Damascus began to trade and barter with the Communist nations because they were satisfied that there were no strings attached. Arab public opinion saw this as a great victory, for Egypt and Syria had shown that it was no longer necessary to depend on the good will of the West for the arms they needed to defend themselves against Israel. In Arab eyes this was the crux of the whole matter—defense against Israel.

The issue was aired in the Senate committee hearings on the proposed legislation:

> Senator Kennedy: As I understand it, the arms deal [with Egypt] came about because the United States, the British, and the French under the tripartite agreement were enforcing equality between the Israelis and all the Arab countries together, because they were together in the Arab League against Israel, which meant that Egypt, in relation to Israel, was at a sharp military disadvantage. Is that more or less correct?
>
> Admiral Radford: I would say that is probably a good estimate of the situation.
>
> Senator Kennedy: Therefore, when the Gaza raid [by Israeli troops against the Egyptians] occurred, then he—Nasser—turned to us for military assistance, and we felt because of the tripartite agreement we could not give it. We used economic reasons as the excuse. Nevertheless we didn't feel we wanted to break that balance and give him the arms.[7]

Even though the Eisenhower administration had inadvertently pushed Abdel Nasser toward the Russians, it did not like the results. The Soviet Union was now a Middle East power and, in the administration's view, Abdel Nasser was to blame. It felt also that because the man was getting to be very popular with the Arab masses, his present relationship with the Soviets posed a danger to Western interests in the Arab world. The Eisenhower Doctrine would rectify the situation by putting the Soviet Union on notice, and by weaning away or isolating him and other suspect Arabs.

Apart from being intrinsically the wrong kind of policy for the Arabs, the Eisenhower Doctrine committed several tactical errors. First, it was a unilateral declaration directed at the Soviet Union. It was a haughty and undiplomatic approach to the countries upon whose cooperation its success depended. The psychological advantage that the administration hoped to gain by the unilateral warning to the Soviet Union turned into a disadvantage even before the resolution had become law. The British criticized it as an attempt to supplant them in the Middle East, the Soviets attacked it mercilessly in broadcasts to the Middle East, most of the Arabs felt insulted because, though it concerned them, it was to be issued over their heads and because word had reached them that the purpose of the resolution was to fill the "power vacuum" left by the departing French and British. Later denials of the "power vacuum" theory by administration spokesmen made no impression on Arab nationalist leaders. Separately and collectively they denounced it, for what appeared at first to be merely an indiscretion of the administration soon turned out to be the pivotal idea of the whole resolution: there being now no Western presence in the Middle East, the United States was willing to employ its armed forces to prevent the Soviet Union from taking over. And the Arab states, the Arabs felt, would have to concede this interpretation in advance through formal commitments to the Eisenhower Doctrine. But the policy of positive neutralism was adopted by the Arabs precisely because it would avoid military entanglements, not lead into them.

"We refuse to be satellites of anybody," said Syrian President Shukri al-Quwatli on January 8, expressing a general feeling. "We accept to be satellites only of the Arab world. We live as

Arabs in culture, civilization and political thinking, seeking benefits where we get [them] and fighting danger. It should be the policy of the Muslim world. This is the spirit of the Koran which does not accept any easterly or westerly directions."[8]

On January 19, Abdel Nasser, Hussein, Saud, and al-Quwatli held a summit meeting in Cairo and issued a communiqué rejecting the "vacuum theory." They resolved "never to allow their countries to become a sphere of influence for any foreign power," and determined "that Arab nationalism was the sole basis on which Arab policy could be formulated."[9] Another communiqué by the four leaders was issued in Cairo on February 25 upon the return of King Saud from an official visit to the United States. Reiterating the principle of positive neutralism, it indicated no change of policy of their four governments. It was a defeat for the United States, for the administration had hoped that Saud, after his consultations in Washington, would attempt to elicit Arab support for the Eisenhower Doctrine.

The Arabs recognized two other fundamental drawbacks in the proposed resolution: it attempted to bypass the United Nations and it failed to condemn armed aggression from *all* sources. That of course was legitimate criticism from the point of view of the Arabs and in fact of all the small nations that had placed their hopes in the world organization. They felt that America, which had so dramatically worked through the U.N. only recently to put a stop to the armed aggression on Egypt, was now attempting to weaken the world body through a plan that called for American military intervention first and consultation with the U.N. later.

Preoccupied as it was with its fears of a possible Soviet takeover of the Middle East, the Eisenhower administration deliberately left out of the resolution any mention of the rankling problem of Palestine and of the nearly one million embittered Palestinian Arab refugees. It was avoiding the Arab-Israeli dispute, but could not avoid the anger of the Arab press and of Arab spokesmen. Why pick out Soviet aggression only? Why not make a blanket condemnation of all aggression—including the imperialist and Zionist brands? There were many leaders in the Arab world who felt that by avoiding the basic issue of the region, the United States was casting a protective mantle over an expansionist Israel, only recently an armed aggressor against the Arabs. If on any other basis the Arabs were inclined to reconsider their rejection of the Eisenhower Doctrine, this particular argument against it stiffened their resistance. To them the doctrine was Zionist-inspired.

ONLY LEBANON SUBSCRIBES

For two whole months before its adoption, the Eisenhower Doctrine was debated by the press and radio of the Arab world. By the time President Eisenhower's special representative, Mr. James P. Richards, arrived in the Middle East early in the spring to explain and solicit support for the new formal resolution the lines were already drawn. Public opinion was overwhelmingly against it. Like other Baghdad Pact members in the Middle East, Iraq had given it a nod of approval but the British-oriented Nuri made no attempt at closer identification. There was no worry, however, on that score in Washington because Iraq was considered a pro-Western nation that would be willing to cooperate in any move against international Communism should the need arise. Syria and Egypt stood squarely against the doctrine and had won over to their side Jordan and Saudi Arabia. Their common anti-doctrine stand had been formalized in the communiqués of January 19 and February 25, which committed them to a neutralist policy.

But the reasons behind this common front were not all mutual. Abdel Nasser and al-Quwatli had come to the conclusion that if any solution was to be found to the Palestine problem and if Israel was to be deterred from expanding into Arab territory, the Arab states must not align themselves with the Western camp, whose sympathy and support for Israel had worked against their interests. They must all follow an independent, neutralist policy seeking support for their cause where they could find it. A break in the ranks in favor of the Western camp would only give the West an advantage without contributing anything to the solution of their common problem: Israel. Although he had no direct relations with the Soviet Union and felt that Syria and Egypt were perhaps dealing too closely with that power, Saud had himself been following a policy of neutralism, or more correctly noninvolvement in world politics, and could not therefore endorse the Eisenhower Doctrine. National sentiment in Saudi Arabia, furthermore, was running with the tide of Arab nationalism, now fully attuned to the leadership of Abdel Nasser, so it was imperative for Saud to identify himself with the Cairo communiqués.

As for King Hussein, he personally favored the Eisenhower Doctrine, but he was in a very difficult position. Traditionally, the Hashemites in Amman, like the Hashemites in Baghdad, had cooperated with Britain, for she had started both dynasties after World War I. When independence came, they continued to cooperate with their former mentor under treaty obligations that constituted part of Britain's sphere of influence in the Middle East. In return, they received British backing against their traditional rivals in Riyadh and Cairo in the race for leadership of the Arab world. Hussein's grandfather, King Abdallah, had had ambitions of his own for hegemony over the Arab world. Hussein was willing to follow the lead of the richer and stronger family branch in Baghdad; he had enough troubles of his own, and felt in need of the backing of both London and Baghdad to maintain his kingdom. He saw Israel poised on the west, ready to move in and annex the western half of Jordan—what was formerly part of Arab Palestine—at the opportune moment. She had already declared her intentions in no uncertain terms on several occasions. But the British presence in Jordan was making her pause. Hussein also relied on a British subsidy for his army, the Arab Legion, which had been trained, armed, and officered by the British, and on other British assistance to shore up his nonviable economy.

But Hussein was not to be allowed to continue unhampered in these inclinations. Since the Bandung Conference, Damascus and Cairo, both campaigning seriously for an Arab policy of neutralism and nonalignment, forced him in 1955 to abandon plans for joining the British-dominated Baghdad Pact and in 1956 to abrogate his treaty with the British, forgo the subsidy, and sack his British chief of staff, Glubb Pasha. For Hussein was not a complete master of his own house. Two-thirds of his 1,600,000 subjects were Palestinians, some 600,000 of whom were refugees with bitter memories of lost homes in Israel. They listened eagerly and approvingly to the propaganda broadcasts of Cairo and Damascus, and those who were free took to the streets to influence their government's foreign policy. They were very effective. Early in 1957 Hussein found himself again limited by the neutralist sentiments of his Palestinian subjects as well as by the left-wing government of Suleiman al-Nabulsi, who categorically rejected the "vacuum theory" and the need for any foreign power to fill the empty shoes of the banished French and British. Hussein had no choice. He subscribed to the Cairo communiqués. For the moment, anyway, the answer to Mr. Richards had to be no.

There was only one Arab government left in the Middle East to welcome Mr. Richards' mission—that of Lebanon. Through his foreign minister, Charles Malik, President Chamoun had hailed the Eisenhower Doctrine long before it had become law and had thus sparked a lively public debate about its merits and the advisability of Lebanese adherence. Many voices were raised against it among the Opposition and Muslim leadership, though there were also voices raised in its defense. And from outside the country, the Syro-Egyptian campaign for nonalignment was gathering momentum. Still, making his calculations, President Chamoun decided to commit his country to the new policy, and on March 16, on the occasion of Mr. Richards' visit to Beirut, they issued a joint Lebanese-American communiqué based on the Eisenhower Doctrine. It called for the extension of American economic and military aid to Lebanon to fortify it against the advances of international Communism; it authorized Lebanon to request the assistance of American armed forces to repel a Communist aggression. However, the assistance would not be automatic. For in accordance with section 2 of the doctrine, it would be up to the President of the United States to determine whether or not Lebanon was really being threatened by armed aggression from a country controlled by international Communism, and to decide on the use or withholding of American armed forces in accordance with this determination.

If the Washington and Beirut governments felt a sense of accomplishment in issuing the joint communiqué, both were later disabused. Washington was dangerously intruding on regional politics. Beirut was splitting the nation.

THE DOCTRINE IN DOMESTIC AND REGIONAL POLITICS

A look at the Middle East political map of March, 1957, would show the following configuration. Having declared its neutralism, Saudi Arabia stood to one side, cautious but watchful. Egypt and Syria stood together for positive neutralism and against a military alignment with either the Eastern or the Western bloc. They wanted other Arab nations to follow their lead and conducted a belligerent press and radio campaign for that purpose. Cairo's Voice of the Arabs especially, which was blasting the Baghdad Pact and Iraqi membership in it, now turned on the Eisenhower Doctrine. Through its participation in the

Baghdad Pact, Iraq stood firmly in the Western military camp, or so its leaders thought. But people and government were not at one in this attitude, and there was a strong undercurrent of discontent. In Jordan the situation was unpredictable. Hussein stood for cooperation with the already committed Baghdad government and with the West. But for the moment the pressure of public opinion made him declare for positive neutralism. Still, he might seesaw back into the Western camp should his uneasy throne be threatened once again, when he would need protection. Israel stood belligerently facing them all. With British and French assistance she had just struck and was likely to strike again. Her many friends and influential protectors in the West, the Arabs thought, would find some justification for her new aggression. Whether they were in the Western camp or neutralist and whatever their personal differences, the Arab nations of the Middle East without exception saw her as the common enemy who had usurped Arab rights and was continuing to threaten Arab territory.

With this threat uppermost in the Arab mind, and especially in the minds of the Egyptians, the victims of the tripartite aggression, the Lebanese Government hastily stepped forward and signed up for the Eisenhower Doctrine. Why did Lebanon endorse the doctrine at this critical moment? Beirut had its reasons. Washington knew and shared some of them. Cairo reserved the right to make its own interpretation of the arrangement.

Let us first look at the reasoning in Washington, or more precisely that of Secretary of State Dulles. It was no secret that he disliked and mistrusted Abdel Nasser (the Egyptian leader felt the same way toward him). He, Dulles, was fighting Communism on all fronts and yet Abdel Nasser would not cooperate: he resisted joining the Baghdad Pact in 1955, then immediately began attacking it; later, when he could not get arms from Britain and the United States, he obtained them from the Soviet Union and mortgaged his cotton crop to the Russians for many years to come; he continued receiving economic and military assistance from the Communists and trading with them; he had provoked the recent war on Egypt by nationalizing the Suez Canal Company and brought the Soviets in the Middle East stronger than ever. Dulles held Abdel Nasser responsible for the popularity of the Russians in the Middle East and for the fact they were now a Middle East power. He was also furious with him for the effectiveness of his propaganda broadcasts among the Arab masses everywhere. With such great influence, and his own agents at work, Abdel Nasser was harassing Arab governments friendly to the West and was making it difficult to dam the Soviet-Communist tide in the Middle East. Dulles decided to checkmate him. Friendly rulers would be built up and supported as a counterbalance to Abdel Nasser. For the moment there was one Arab ruler available: Chamoun of Lebanon.

On January 8, the second day of his testimony before the House Committee on Foreign Affairs, Mr. Dulles gave a clue to what he was thinking:

> Mr. Burleson: Mr. Secretary, perhaps it would be more considerate just to ask the purpose of the Richards mission to the Middle East which is anticipated, but to put it more bluntly, let me ask: Since we assume that Turkey, Iran, Iraq, Pakistan and others of the Baghdad Pact, and Israel, would agree pretty much with what we are doing, is the purpose of the Richards mission to influence Syria, Jordan, and Egypt and maybe other countries in the area, to request our economic aid?
>
> Secretary Dulles: The purpose of the mission would be, I think, to visit the capitals of most of the countries of that area to see what can be done to bring about stability and to avoid economic distress of which Communism would certainly take advantage.
>
> That would probably involve Lebanon. Lebanon is a country which particularly needs our help and support at this present time. It is one of the most western-oriented of the countries of the area. It is very concerned about what is going on in its neighborhood.

I think very much can be done and needs to be done to
bolster up a government like Lebanon. Perhaps the example set
there would have an influence in the rest of the area.[10]

President Chamoun also saw the need to bolster up the government of Lebanon. But against what and whom? The enterprising
and free-trading Lebanese had built a strong economy. There
were still pockets of poverty no doubt, and the country needed
rural and urban development, but these problems could be
tackled through the ordinary channels of economic aid. There
was really no threat from international Communism. Though at
times banned, the Communist party in Lebanon had been operating undisturbed for a long time, but had attracted no significant
interest. The Lebanese were too smart to join. And Communism
was not on President Chamoun's mind. When before Mr. Richards' arrival in Beirut he was asked how serious he felt the threat
of domestic Communism was, Chamoun replied, "No doubt communism has made some progress here. But with appropriate
measures its advance can be halted."[11] These complacent words
do not indicate any great distress over Communism.

But Mr. Chamoun was having political troubles at home of a
non-Communist nature, and he was also experiencing continued
difficulties in his relations with Cairo. Ever since Abdel Nasser
appeared as the standard-bearer of Arab nationalism in 1955, the
Muslims of Lebanon, and particularly the Sunnis, made the mis-
take of supporting him and showing him a greater loyalty than
they showed to their own national leaders. This set off a reaction
among the Christians. Fearing that Lebanese independence
might be lost in the tide of Arab nationalism, they began supporting Chamoun in self-defense. At about the same time the President and his government became embroiled in the Iraqi-Egyp-
tian dispute over the Baghdad Pact. In 1955 there was an exchange of visits between Chamoun and President Bayar of Turkey, Iraq's pact partner. Pressure at home kept Lebanon from
joining, but the move was nonetheless interpreted by pro-Egyp-

tian nationalists as a deviation from the strict neutrality Lebanon was committed to in inter-Arab affairs. In the months that followed, Chamoun was also suspected of using his personal diplomacy to support the Hashemites in Amman and Baghdad in their quarrels with Gamal Abdel Nasser.

By the winter of 1956–1957 Lebanon was seething with unrest. The state of emergency that had been declared during the tripartite aggression on Egypt was continued. The Government was having difficulties with internal security. Opposition leaders felt they were being alienated from the sources of power and from their right to share in decision-making. They wanted Lebanon to follow a more pro-Egyptian policy, they wanted a voice in the government. Abdallah al-Yafi and Saeb Salaam, who had just lost their cabinet posts over Lebanon's nonseverance of diplomatic relations with Britain and France, felt especially bitter.

It was a difficult situation at best, and the Government needed to proceed with extreme caution and wisdom to reduce suspicions on either side, to return to the conditions of a mutual symbiosis between Christians and Muslims that is so essential to the integrity and independence of Lebanon. Later troubles might have been avoided if the Government had made an effort at a rapprochement with disgruntled Opposition leaders, who represented a large segment of public opinion, and pursued a more moderate foreign policy. Instead, it endorsed the Eisenhower Doctrine, embroiling itself still further with a growing opposition at home and bitter debate with Cairo. And it could not afford the dispute with Cairo, which was turning half of Lebanon's population against it.

At about this time, too, President Chamoun, with the apparent blessing and encouragement of Washington, London, and Paris, decided to seek a second term in office. The plan seemed mutually beneficial. The West found a friend who could be used as a front to challenge and counter the growing influence of Abdel Nasser. Chamoun saw in the Eisenhower Doctrine a chance to ward off the storm against his regime and to continue in power for another six years. Only, since it was unconstitutional for the head of state to succeed himself, the constitution would have to be amended.

Gamal Abdel Nasser looked upon Lebanon's acceptance of the Eisenhower Doctrine as both deviationist and unfriendly. He was convinced that the doctrine was nothing but an extension of the Baghdad Pact formula, concealed this time in a tempting economic aid package but nevertheless designed to herd the Arab nations into a military alliance with the West. He saw Lebanon's acceptance of the doctrine as weakening the bargaining position of the Arabs vis-à-vis the West on the vital issue of Palestine, and strengthening the hand of Iraq's Nuri in his pursuit of the Fertile Crescent plan. If Nuri managed to extend his hegemony over Syria, Jordan, and Lebanon behind the smoke screen of the Baghdad Pact, he would effectively isolate Egypt from the Arab world. This, thought Abdel Nasser, was also the objective of the Western powers. If Egypt were isolated from the Arab world instead of getting the chance to lead it, its revolutionary regime might not survive denial of the ebullient support of the Arab masses. The Egyptian President decided that Lebanon must be pried away from the Eisenhower Doctrine.

A VOTE OF CONFIDENCE
FOR THE LEBANESE GOVERNMENT

On April 4 and 5 the new es-Solh Government appeared before the Chamber of Deputies and sought a vote of confidence on its domestic and foreign policies, including the recently proclaimed Lebanese-American communiqué. Debate centered almost exclusively on the communiqué. The eight deputies who opposed it delivered a scathing and sometimes impassioned attack reflecting the arguments of the Opposition outside the Chamber and those of Cairo and Damascus. They scorned the communiqué for the following reasons. It was contrary, they said, to the National Pact of 1943, which imposed on Lebanon neutrality in inter-Arab relations; it deviated from the traditional Lebanese foreign policy of maintaining a common front with the Arab world, thus forcing Lebanon to forfeit its role of peacemaker among the Arabs; it made Lebanon party to an effort to isolate Egypt from the Arab world; it did not condemn aggression from all sources, and in its preoccupation with the nonexistent Communist threat it put aside the very real Zionist and imperialist threats; by ignoring the Israeli question it forced upon Lebanon acceptance of the status quo; it would bring the cold war to Lebanon by putting it in the Western armed camp against the Soviet camp, when there was no need to assume such a posture against the Soviet Union, with whom Lebanon had good relations; it was a military pact whose purpose, from the American side, was to erect a cordon sanitaire around the Soviet Union, a purpose which Lebanon should not become a party to; it was a military treaty in the tradition of the Baghdad Pact, in whose various committees the United States was now a participant, and its purpose, like that of the Pact, was to extend Western domination over the Arab world; it was a military pact also in the sense that in order to defend Lebanon American forces would first have to occupy Lebanese territory; finally, it made Lebanon a protégé of the United States, whereas Lebanon had traditionally drawn strength from its membership in the United Nations in maintaining its independence and integrity.

Pro-Government deputies and Foreign Minister Malik rejected these interpretations placed upon the communiqué. Lebanon, said Malik, was not deviating from the National Pact; it had always consulted with the Arab League on foreign policy matters but could not favor one Arab bloc against another and would not have its policy dictated by any nation. The communiqué did not give the United States any political or military concessions within Lebanon, he said, but was merely a justified declaration of the country's intention to defend itself in the event that Communism declared war against it. He conceded that the communiqué was concerned only with Communist aggression and made no mention of possible imperialist or Zionist aggression, but added that there was no reason to conclude that Lebanon was thereby relinquishing its position on these latter issues. It was doing nothing of the sort.

On the whole, the arguments of each side made sense within the context of its own evaluation of the Middle East situation. The overriding concern of the Opposition deputies was that Egypt would be isolated or forced to give up its policy of positive neutralism, and they would have found much substance for their fears had they been privileged to attend Congress' hearings on the Eisenhower Doctrine.

The Government treated the communiqué matter-of-factly, as not an unusual step in its foreign policy. There was, of course, the economic assistance clause, which immensely appealed to it and to its supporters in the Chamber. But more important, and whether all the ministers were aware of it or not, it gave Chamoun American backing should his difficulties with Cairo and the popularity of Abdel Nasser in Lebanon escalate into an attempted subversion of his regime. In this context, of course, one could understand the Government's arguments that it could not favor one Arab bloc (i.e. the Egyptian-Syrian) against another (i.e. Iraq), and could not have its policy dictated by any nation (i.e. Egypt). But putting the question in the perspective of the whole Middle East, was not the Government really favoring Iraq, in view of that nation's membership in the Baghdad Pact and of Nuri's affiliated plan for unity of the Fertile Crescent to the exclusion of Egypt? Furthermore, by endorsing the Eisenhower Doctrine, the Lebanese Government was not only aligning itself with the American government against international Communism but facilitating Secretary Dulles' objective to quarantine Syria and Egypt until they relinquished their own policies of positive neutralism and put themselves squarely in the Western camp. Again, although as Mr. Malik rightly judged the communiqué did not impose on Lebanon acceptance of the status quo with regard to the Israeli question, it did require Lebanon to assume a public posture against international Communism, and by implication against the Soviet Union, in order to qualify for military and economic assistance. This was a gratuitous gesture toward the Soviet Union not in keeping with Lebanon's traditional policy of maintaining friendly relations with all nations. If anything, it put Lebanon in a dangerous position by making it a party to the cold war. The communiqué, of course, was not a military pact in the traditional sense; it did not call for the exchange of military personnel or the granting of bases (the United States did not need bases when the Sixth Fleet was in constant patrol of the Mediterranean), but it did have military implications.

But if all these weaknesses of the joint Lebanese-American communiqué could be ignored, the crucial test of its advisability was still to come: would it unify the nation or divide it further? Would it preserve or jeopardize its integrity? Compromise and conciliation among Lebanon's various religious communities had won and maintained Lebanon's independence, and only compromise and conciliation could preserve its integrity. A significant community, the Sunni, felt very sympathetic to the revolutionary leader in Cairo and to his appeals to Arab nationalism and unity. The Eisenhower Doctrine, they were told, was designed to ostracize Abdel Nasser from the Arab family. But they wished to express solidarity with him, especially since Syria, with whom they had the closest ties, was also identifying with him. By subscribing to the Eisenhower Doctrine, it seemed, the Lebanese Government would be feeding this passion and creating more difficulties for itself. If economic and military aid were so vital, both could be had outside the scope of the doctrine, without any formal commitment to fight Communism (which could be done anyway) or acceptance of the premise that American forces might some day be fighting on Lebanese soil. The obvious implication of this premise was that Americans would be fighting Syrians should President Eisenhower determine that Syria was a country controlled by international Communism attacking Lebanon. And as for economic aid, Lebanon had been receiving it quietly under the Point Four program for some time. Furthermore, without accepting the doctrine, Lebanon could still continue in friendly relations with the United States.

During the parliamentary debates of April 4 and 5, Opposition deputies asked the Government to limit itself to seeking a vote of confidence on its domestic policy alone, and not in conjunction with its foreign policy. New elections were coming up in June, they said, and it would be preferable to wait until the new Chamber was in session to see what was the desire of the whole nation on foreign policy. Confident of its support in the existing Chamber, the Government, however, would not wait. On the second day the debates were closed and the vote requested. The results gave the Government a vote of confidence of 30 to 1.[12]

But before the voting started seven of the eight Opposition deputies stomped out of the Chamber in protest against the Government's foreign policy. They were Abdallah al-Yafi, Hamid Frangieh, Rachid Karame, Ahmad al-Asaad, Kamel al-Asaad, Sabri Hamade, and Dr. Nazih al-Bizri. Along with Deputy Abdallah al-Haj, the first six deputies soon resigned from the Chamber and began to campaign against the Eisenhower Doctrine in preparation for the forthcoming elections. They were confident that their resignation would soon be vindicated by the voice of the people. But the coming months were to show that for these traditional leaders there was more at stake than reversal of an unacceptable foreign policy. Most of them felt disenchanted with President Chamoun; most of them felt he was denying them their rightful exercise of political power. Yet they were to become even more concerned after the June elections.

CHAPTER 7

Lebanon's Foreign Policy in Local Politics: A Study in Political Opportunism

The sudden merger of Egypt and Syria into the United Arab Republic in February, 1958, had an electrifying effect on Arab masses throughout the Middle East. There were spontaneous demonstrations of joy everywhere, for this was the tangible beginning of the Arab dream of unity. In Lebanon, unionist sentiment among a large section of the Muslim population was much revived, and many delegations from among leaders and the general public visited Damascus in the following days to pay tribute to their towering symbol of Arab unity: Gamal Abdel Nasser. Three months later, when the revolution broke out, unionist sentiment was still at a peak, and there was much yearning for a merger with the U.A.R. But though it fed the fires of the revolution, unionist sentiment was not its true and original cause. Along with other feelings of dissatisfaction, unionism was being channeled and synchronized by a group of politicians for a rebellion against the Chamoun regime whose roots lay elsewhere, and whose purposes were other than union.

Why did these politicians resort to armed strife? The reasons were primarily personal, though they had both national and regional implications. In brief, over the past year President Chamoun had made enemies out of a number of important political leaders who either claimed to have been deprived by him of their rightful share of elective office, or otherwise felt that they had been denied their proper influence within the governing institutions of the country. Furthermore, since Chamoun held the supreme magistracy in the state, they feared that he would use his position to renew his mandate for another six years and prolong their alienation from the sources of power. They did not of course openly express their fears for their political future; instead, they hit back at the President by accusing his regime of corruption and discrimination at home and of deviation in foreign policy.

MOUNTING CONFLICT OVER ELECTORAL LAW
AND FOREIGN POLICY

Serious opposition to the Chamoun regime began to build up in the wake of the parliamentary elections of June, 1957, in which four important traditional representatives had lost their seats. They were Ahmad al-Asaad, Shi'i feudal leader from South Lebanon, Kamal Junblatt, Druze feudal leader from the Chouf district of Mount Lebanon, and Abdallah al-Yafi and Saeb Salam, both Sunni city *za'ims* from well-known Beirut families. But even before then, the Government and Opposition were moving to irreconcilable positions. Although the great debate centered on foreign policy, namely on Lebanon's acceptance of the Eisenhower Doctrine, there was also bitter controversy in the spring of 1957 over the enactment of legislation for the enlargement of the Chamber of Deputies in time for the June elections. The majority of deputies, loyal to the Chamoun regime, supported a plan for increasing the size of the Chamber from 44 members to 66. The Opposition, composed of individual deputies who were disenchanted with the regime (as distinguished from a united party Opposition), held out for an 88-member Chamber, and so did a few independent deputies. It was the contention of the Opposition that the Government wanted to limit the size of the Chamber to 66 members so that it could continue to control it and thus be able to perpetuate domestic discrimination and a deviationist foreign policy. They challenged the Government to rescind the state of emergency decrees that had been in effect since the Anglo-French-Israeli aggression on Egypt. By maintaining these no longer necessary decrees, they charged, the Government was limiting public debate on the proposed legislation for a larger Chamber, especially through its continued censorship of the press.

The Government was not without a defense. Prime Minister es-Solh affirmed that the Government favored neither the 88-member plan nor the 66-member plan for the Chamber, but that since the majority of deputies themselves preferred the latter it was bound by democratic principles to accept it. As for the state of emergency decrees, the Government pointed to the continued state of restlessness within the country, which made emergency controls necessary.[1]

The parliamentary debate on the alternative proposals for the enlargement of the Chamber began on March 28 and ended on April 3, when the 66-member plan was adopted. Subsequent sessions were devoted to the reapportionment of parliamentary seats in accordance with the plan and to a redrawing of constituency boundaries. The new electoral law was voted in its entirety on April 16. But the debates and voting on this law were not undertaken consecutively. They were interrupted by meetings devoted to the discussion of the Government's domestic and foreign policies. Thus on April 3, when the Chamber voted for the plan of 66 by a show of hands, the important Opposition deputies were in attendance. But they were not there when on April 9 it resumed discussion and voting on those clauses relating to the reapportionment of parliamentary seats and the redrawing of constituency boundaries. For on April 5 they had all resigned in protest against the vote of confidence that the Government received that day on its foreign policy. The men in question were Rachid Karame, Hamid Frangieh, Abdallah al-Yafi, Kamel al-Asaad, Ahmad al-Asaad, Sabri Hamade, and Abdallah al-Haj. By

their hasty withdrawal from the Chamber they denied themselves the right to be heard on the important question of the redrawing of constituencies. It was a question that was to bring
some of them bitterness on the heels of the elections.

Having failed to win any arguments by parliamentary debate
within the Chamber, the Opposition deputies, even before they
resigned, sought mass support to carry on their fight for a return
to what they considered to be Lebanon's traditional neutralist
policy and for "just" elections. They found support among important personalities and sectarian spokesmen outside the Chamber, and early in April they organized a "National Front" to represent all the elements that were dissatisfied with the regime.
Though predominantly Muslim, the Front also included some
Christian politicians. It began its work by presenting President
Chamoun with a memorandum demanding the following: (1)
abolition of the state of emergency; (2) increasing the number
of deputies to 88; (3) making each administrative district a self-
contained constituency; (4) calling upon a neutral, caretaker
Government to preside over the elections; (5) abstaining from
the conclusion of any foreign agreement pending the outcome of
the elections.

In a public manifesto issued at the same time, the Front
indicated that Opposition candidates for the forthcoming parliamentary elections intended to campaign on issues that presumably had already been settled to the satisfaction of both the Christian and the Muslim community. Among the objectives it listed
in the manifesto were these demands: adherence to the National
Pact of 1943, to the Arab League Pact, and to the principle of
neutrality between foreign nations. Were the old ideological differences to be raised again? Were the pre-independence fears
and suspicions between the two communities to be revived? Apparently so, for another step was soon taken in this direction. On
April 24 Sheikh Shafiq Yamut, head of the Muslim High Court
of Appeals, held an *iftar*[2] supper in his capacity as head of

rabitat al-'ulama' (Society of the Learned, i.e. sheikhs well versed
in Muslim law), and there delivered a speech emphasizing the
Muslim community's attachment to the National Pact, its support
of a policy of positive neutralism, its refusal to accept any foreign
military pacts, and its complete adherence to the "Arab policy of
liberation." Among Sheikh Yamut's 300 guests, in whose name he
issued these warnings to the Government, were Muslim Opposition politicians Rachid Karame of Tripoli in the north, Saeb
Salam and Abdallah al-Yafi of Beirut in the west, Sabri Hamade
of the Hermel in the east, and Ahmad al-Asaad of the south. All
were acknowledged leaders in their respective areas and all were
candidates for the forthcoming elections.

On May 7 the Government issued decrees terminating the
state of emergency to allow for free campaigning for the elections and specifying four Sundays in June for balloting in the five
mohafazats (administrative regions) of Lebanon.[3] A few days
later the Opposition, now operating under the name of the National Union Front, organized a mass rally in Beirut, with Opposition politicians Hamid Frangieh, Saeb Salam, Philippe
Takla, Ahmad al-Asaad, and Abdallah al-Yafi prominently in attendance. Resolutions were passed setting forth the following
objectives: adherence to the National Pact of 1943 after rescuing
it from the hands of those who had misused it (i.e., the Government), returning to a policy of real cooperation with the sister
Arab states, maintaining Lebanese neutrality in any political or
military conflict between foreign nations, denying foreign powers any military bases on Lebanese territory, rejecting the Baghdad Pact and all other foreign military pacts, and refusing any
kind of conditional aid that might place a limit on Lebanon's free
conduct of its foreign policy or might impinge on its independence and sovereignty.

This was a bid to the electorate to punish the Government's
candidates at the polls for its recent acceptance of the Eisenhower Doctrine, and for its deteriorating relations with Syria

and Egypt. The call was taken up by the Opposition press and candidates. The electoral campaign was launched.

On their part, the Government and the loyalist candidates countered by accusing the Opposition of advocating a policy of subservience to Cairo and proclaiming that a vote for the Opposition would be a vote against Lebanese sovereignty. The battle was thus joined on a doctrinal front. The settled question of Lebanon's regional and international orientation, with which the state's viability was so closely linked, was to be dragged out and openly debated again.

Sensing the danger implicit in such campaigning, the Beiruti dignitary and former foreign minister Henri Pharaon attempted to put an end to it. On May 10 he published an appeal for national unity in which he pointed out that the discords and divisions that had characterized the electoral campaign to date were not inevitable and did not really derive from any fundamental conflict over doctrine. The bonds of national unity, he asserted, could be reestablished on the basis of the following principles:

1. Safeguarding the independence and sovereignty of Lebanon.
2. Cooperation with the Arab countries within the framework of the [Arab] League Pact.
3. Cooperation with foreign countries within the framework of the United Nations Charter.
4. Acknowledgment of the fact that the Communist doctrine is incompatible with our religious beliefs and our political and social principles; and maintaining and even reinforcing our legitimate defense against Communism inside our frontiers—as also against all subversive propaganda capable of dividing the Lebanese and weakening Lebanon.
5. Accepting American aid if it is furnished without political or military conditions.[4]

Because these were basic principles over which there were, and should be, no disagreements among the Lebanese, Pharaon said, their adoption as campaign policies would lead to a peaceful and honest resolution of all controversy over the interpretation of texts and procedures. What Pharaon wanted was that the candidates campaign along the traditional lines of individual and group interests and put aside their polemical and doctrinal arguments, which camouflaged but did not eliminate these interests, and which only served to divide the nation against itself. But the appeal went unheeded. In March the Government had interpreted and justified its foreign policy, its acceptance of the Eisenhower Doctrine, and its relations with its Arab neighbors in terms of the principles enunciated by Pharaon. It had then received an overwhelming vote of confidence from the Chamber. Now loyalist candidates campaigned on this record. In the Opposition camp, however, it was maintained that the Government had not in fact adhered to the basic national tenets of safeguarding the independence and sovereignty of Lebanon and of cooperating with the sister Arab countries. The result was that charges and countercharges of disloyalty and deviationism and of subservience to outside interests were hurled back and forth between the two sides.

ATTITUDES OF THE VOTERS

The electoral campaign of May and June of 1957, as conducted by both the Government and the Opposition, was calculated to arouse fears in the hearts of the voters for the future of Lebanon. In this it differed markedly from previous campaigns. How did the voters react? To the volume of words that poured out from the campaigners they reacted generally in accordance with their own basic fears and inclinations. Thus the most admiring listeners to Opposition oratory seemed to be the Sunni voters of Beirut, Tripoli, and Sidon. And it was to them mainly that Sunni Opposition candidates addressed themselves on the need for a "liberated Arab policy." This, of course, had the opposite effect on Christian circles, where it was feared, with much encouragement from the regime, that "liberated" meant a policy dominated by the dictates of Cairo. Both the *Kataeb* and the Social Nationalist Party (formerly the Syrian National Party) now had candidates for the elections, and both identified themselves with the Government's platform on foreign policy. Though not quite happy with the Government's domestic policy, the Christian *Kataeb* were devoted to Lebanese independence and sovereignty, and it seemed to them that the Opposition was advocating a limitation of both through its identification with the Egyptian position. The Social Nationalists shared these views about the Opposition, but for another reason: the "Greater Syria" plan they visualized excluded union with Egypt. Thus it was expected that strict party discipline would make both the *Kataeb* and the Social Nationalists' rank and file vote for the candidates approved by the party leadership.

And yet it seemed that the ideological struggle could not dominate the actions of all voters. Indeed, press reports at the time of the elections indicated that voters were generally behaving in typical fashion, even though the votes of some appeared to have been cast for ideological reasons. As usual, the determining factor in the attitudes of voters seemed to be the immediate or long-range personal, family, or communal benefits that could be derived from voting for one candidate as against another. Where feudal and family ties were strong, and in Tripoli, Beirut, and Sidon, where local *za'ims* each had his own following, loyalty to the leader-candidate was the tradition. For only by voting him into office could his supporters count on special benefits and favors which he could dispense only as a member of the Chamber or the Government. In Beirut, for example, the two leading Opposition candidates, Saeb Salam and Abdallah al-Yafi, each had his own personal following among the Muslim voters. Prime Minister Sami es-Solh, who was also running in Beirut, also had his own following. Similarly, in Tripoli Rachid Karame could count on those who had supported him in previous elections and had supported his father, Abdel-Hamid Karame, before him as the champion of Tripolitanian demands. In the Hermel in the east, Shi'i feudal leader Sabri Hamade was assured the traditional backing of the Shi'i tribes of the area, while the Shi'i feudal leader Ahmad al-Asaad and his son Kamel both enjoyed similar tribal support in the south.

In Mount Lebanon, the traditional Druze feudal leader Majid Arslan, a minister in the es-Solh Government, had his own following, and so did Kamal Junblatt, another Druze feudal leader whose family had been the political rivals of the Arslans for decades.

In North Lebanon, the constituency of the Maronite town of Zgharta and its environs could be expected to vote in accordance with traditional loyalties. For decades the area had been the scene of sometimes bloody feuds between the two rival clans of the Frangieh-Mouawad and the Doueihy-Karam. Now the head of the Frangieh clan, Hamid Frangieh, and René Mouawad were running on the same ticket for the two Maronite seats for that constituency against the team of Father Samaan Doueihy and Yousef Karam. The former team was associated with the Opposition, which was advocating a foreign policy more favorable to Cairo. The latter team was endorsed by the Government, which was calling for a policy free from the pressures of Cairo. Yet to the voters of Zgharta this foreign policy debate was not the main issue. The main issue was the rivalry between President Chamoun and Hamid Frangieh over the former's office. Chamoun's term in the presidency was due to expire the following year, but there were already indications that he was anxious to succeed himself. Yet Frangieh had aspired to the presidency for a long time, and would stand a better chance of getting it if he were elected to the Chamber. It was up to the Zgharta voters to decide whether or not to give him that chance. The town was a stronghold of old-fashioned Maronite parochialism whose fighting sons had on occasion terrorized the Sunni Arab nationalist inhabitants of neighboring Tripoli. But it did not matter to Frangieh's clansmen that he was now identifying himself with the Opposition and had in fact joined the National Union Front and endorsed its resolutions. These were merely campaign tactics. They would vote for him.

In certain communities it was not the tradition of feudal and family loyalties that determined the voting attitude of the electorate, but rather the question of whether or not the candidate seeking a community's votes had already bestowed upon it tangible favors and services. Surveying the attitudes of the electorate in the *mohafazat* of Mount Lebanon, the Beirut Arabic daily *al-Hayat* reported what happened in a previous election:

> To give an example of this [method of winning votes through special favors to the electorate], a Deputy was able to win the votes of a large family, which included some 200 voters, by simply appointing a municipal policeman. Before then, this family had supported the rival of the said Deputy through three electoral periods.[5]

Al-Hayat concluded by pointing out that many voters in Mount Lebanon were influenced by appointments to municipalities and to investigation commissions in their districts and villages. This fact, it added, had prompted a number of deputies recently to make changes in town and village municipalities in the district of Ba'abda.

Still other voters were influenced most of all, it seemed, by cash renumeration for their votes. In some voters this attitude was born out of despair: selling their votes was the only benefit they felt they derived from the elections. To others, selling their votes was an extra dividend they derived from voting for a particular candidate that they hoped would do more for them after his election. Vote buying was a standard procedure in Lebanese elections, and was indulged in by various candidates regardless of affiliation. It was practiced openly but invariably became the object of charges and countercharges after the elections. Those

who profited most from this practice were the agents who
rounded up the paid voters for the candidates willing to pay. At
times, even, paid voters would be kept away from the polls until
late in the day, when rival candidates believed to be running
neck-and-neck would each raise his cash award in the hope of
attracting a sufficient number of extra votes to win.

To what extent vote buying influenced the outcome of the
1957 elections is hard to say because of the very nature of the
transaction. It was significant enough, however, to attract editorial comment. Toward the end of the elections, the independent Arabic Beirut daily *al-Jarida* spoke of the fantastic sums of
money both Government and Opposition candidates had already
spent on vote buying. In Zahle, it stated, the heads of the two
slates spent together over two million Lebanese liras for votes. In
Beirut, South Lebanon, and Mount Lebanon, it added, similar
sums of money were spent by rich candidates.[6]

THE REWARDS OF POLITICAL OFFICE

Why were candidates willing to spend so much money to get
elected to the Chamber of Deputies? To a large extent it was because of the political prestige, the *wajaha*, that membership in
the Chamber offered. To the lucky few, the more prominent of
the politicians, membership also meant a good chance of being
asked to join the Government, which offered even greater prestige than the Chamber. Then of course membership in the Chamber or Cabinet meant access to power. And it was the confessional system of government which made competition for the
prestige and power of office so keen. For by creating sectarian
harmony within the governing institutions through the proportional representation of the sects, confessionalism was at the
same time consecrating the feudal and regional rivalries inherited from the past. Thus ever since the office of Prime Minister was reserved in 1937 for a member of the Sunni community

from within the Chamber, each of the three Sunni strongholds of Beirut, Tripoli, and Sidon, and particularly the first two, had vied with the others to present the state with a Prime Minister from among its own leadership. Similarly, ever since the presidency was reserved for the Maronite community with the election of Emile Edde in 1936, Maronite strongholds, particularly in Mount Lebanon, had vied to fill that most prestigious office. To the Shi'is independence also meant that from then on the presidency of the Chamber was theirs. Thus it became a matter of prestige for each of the Shi'i communities of the Biqa' and South Lebanon to have its own leading deputy occupy that high office.

But it appeared that there was another compelling reason that drove some politicians to seek elective office. A seat within the Chamber or an appointment within the Cabinet opened the door to self-enrichment and made it easier to help one's friends and supporters. Seeking an explanation of why candidates spent so much money on the buying of votes, *al-Jarida* editorialized:

> People . . . understand very well that some of those who spend millions to become deputies have no doubt set their sights on regaining this large sum many times over through the means and ways provided by representation [in the Chamber] for using their influence and compensating for what they lost and regaining what they spent.
>
> And here lies the danger, all the danger, for it represents complete moral disintegration! Deputies who are expected to represent the nation are sold votes by some willing members of this nation just as slaves and concubines are sold in the slave market, and they [the deputies] in turn will sell this nation, in some tomorrow, for the same currency with which they have bought it![7]

THE LIST SYSTEM: FORMING THE WINNING TEAM

Because the office of deputy and of minister offered so many personal rewards, it was imperative for the parliamentary candidate to consider carefully the various possible alliances he could make and to decide which ones would give him the best chance of winning the elections. The pattern of alliance-making had been set under the French mandate and was carried over into the era of independence. Its characteristic feature was that personal rather than ideological interests determined what group of candidates shared the same slate to run for office. But in 1957 the crucial and divisive issue of Lebanon's international orientation was intruded on the campaign scene. Apparently it did not disrupt the traditional pattern of alliance-making. Personal interests won over doctrinal commitments. A review of the whole system would put the 1957 alliances in the proper perspective.

As already noted, in Lebanon's confessional democracy feudal and sectarian combinations have taken the place of ideological parties found in other systems of representative government. Feudal interests have been able to work through their respective sects to get to the sources of power. The Lebanese constitution and electoral laws, whose object is to achieve cooperation and moderation within the Chamber of Deputies, have facilitated their task. The laws require that deputies of whatever sect must be elected by a majority of all the electors in the constituency where they declare their candidacy, and that once elected they must act as the representatives of the whole nation. Furthermore, most constituencies must elect two or more deputies depending on the size of their respective populations and sects. From the beginning, both these requirements of the law have prompted candidates running in multiple seat constituencies to adopt the slate system, which gives each candidate a greater chance of winning than if he were running alone. This is true because of the relationship that exists between at least the leading candidates and their supporters. And who have been these leading candidates? Generally the scions of old-time feudal families or members of the upper-class city families, to whom confessional representation has offered the greatest opportunities.

Competing for political office over the years, leading politicians within the various constituencies have each developed his own group of loyal followers within his own sect. The relationship between the politician and his followers is usually a paternalistic one, based on personal interests and not on party doctrine. Thus followers vote for the politician during elections and he in turn watches out for their needs. If he is the dominant politician in the constituency who is assured of sufficient votes from his sectarian followers to get him elected, he is sought by other politicians, who wish to team up with him on the same ticket in order to win the votes of his supporters too. For followers generally vote for the whole slate on which their chosen candidate is running.[8] If a candidate is not sure of his own drawing power at the polls, he seeks to join a slate of candidates that he feels altogether makes a winning team.

Slates, or "lists" as they are called in Lebanon, are often made and remade. There is usually a lot of activity behind the scenes before a "list" finally emerges as complete. Since politicians do not run for office on a platform of party doctrine, they move freely among loyalist, Opposition, and independent or uncommitted groups until they find the slate they wish to join. This method of slate-forming has even imposed itself on the ideological parties, the *Kataeb, Najjadah,* and National Socialists, since they began running their own candidates for office. They have had no opportunity to present a straight party ticket.

In May of 1957, as loyalist and Opposition politicians were carrying on their loud and acrimonious public debate over which direction Lebanese foreign policy should be taking, they were quietly making and remaking their slates of candidates for the June elections. In Beirut, the first head of a list to announce his completed slate was Prime Minister Sami es-Solh. On May 21 the Sunni Premier told the press that his fellow candidates were Khalil al-Hibri (Sunni), Pierre Edde (Maronite), Ghassan Tueni (Greek Orthodox), and Khatchik Babikian (Armenian Orthodox), and added that they were running in the first constituency of Beirut.[9] Announcement of Edde's name on the list came as a surprise to everyone, for until then Alfred Naccache (Maronite) was known to have agreed to run with es-Solh. What had prompted the change, when both Edde and Naccache shared almost the same benign attitude toward the Chamoun regime and toward its foreign policy? The story finally came out: Edde of the National Bloc had insisted on declaring his candidacy for the one Maronite seat allowed to Beirut.[10] If he could not run on the Government ticket then he would run on the Opposition ticket headed by Abdallah al-Yafi, who had already indicated that he was ready to receive him. But if Edde were left to run on the Opposition ticket, this might alienate the National Bloc from the regime. To prevent such a possibility, es-Solh decided to dump Naccache and take Edde on his slate.

Soon after es-Solh's announcement, the Opposition invited Naccache to run on al-Yafi's slate, but he declined. Al-Yafi then took on as Maronite candidate, a former supporter of the National Bloc, Louis Ziadeh.

What was significant in this little incident of list-making was that a leading member of the Opposition, al-Yafi, had invited to his side first one and then another politician who was only moderately critical of the regime, but completely in agreement with it over its foreign policy objectives. On the other hand, one of these politicians, Edde, had himself considered joining the slate of the Opposition, though it was calling for a negation of this policy. Thus it appears that while the politicians were raising the pulse of the electorate with the most serious and disturbing arguments, they themselves were primarily concerned with getting elected—even with the help of candidates snatched from the opposing camp.

ELECTION RESULTS: THE BALANCE
OF POWER IS UPSET

The elections took place as scheduled on consecutive Sundays in June. The results were generally disappointing to the Opposition. In Beirut, the two Sunni Opposition leaders Abdallah al-Yafi and Saeb Salam, who ran in the first constituency on the same ticket against the slate of Sami es-Solh, lost to the latter and his fellow candidates. Only the Greek Orthodox candidate on the al-Yafi-Salam ticket, Nassim al-Majdalani, won out over his rival Ghassan Tueni. In the *mohafazat* of South Lebanon, Shi'i feudal leader Ahmad al-Asaad lost in the constituency of Tyre to the Government-endorsed candidate Kazem al-Khalil. Al-Asaad's son, Kamel, however, won the Shi'i seat for the constituency of Marjeyoun. In the *mohafazat* of Mount Lebanon, Druze feudal leader Kamal Junblatt, who had cooperated with the Opposition but not completely associated himself with it, was defeated along with his two fellow candidates by the Government-sponsored ticket of Greek Catholic Naim Moghabghab in the constituency of Baakline-Joun.

Leading Opposition candidates who won were Shi'i Sabri Hamade, Maronite Hamid Frangieh, and Sunni Rachid Karame. Running in his native Baalback-Hermel constituency of the Biqa' *mohafazat*, Hamade carried with him his three fellow candidates. Karame also carried with him his three fellow candidates in his native city of Tripoli in North Lebanon. Frangieh won with his teammate René Mouawad in their native Zgharta in North Lebanon.

There were, of course, other Opposition candidates who won. But this was not a straight Opposition-Government contest. List-forming had produced some unnatural alliances, while personal interests had pitted some candidates sharing the same views against each other. In the constituency of Sidon, for instance, where the population was predominantly Sunni and Arab nationalist in sentiment, Marouf Saad, Nazih Bizri, and Salah Bizri, all advocates of better relations with Syria and Egypt, contested the one Sunni seat for that city. Saad won primarily because the Bizris had to share the votes of their family clan and supporters. Had one of them withdrawn in favor of the other, the combined votes received by the two would have won the

Sidon seat for a Bizri. Furthermore, independents, some mildly critical of the Government's domestic and foreign policy, some approving it, had somewhat confused the lines of division between the Government and Opposition by allying themselves with both sides as well as forming slates of their own.

On the whole the elections were considered a victory for the Government since its own candidates generally won over those sponsored by the Opposition. And at the end, four important Opposition leaders, each with his own large following, stood outside the Chamber. Defeated were al-Yafi, Salam, Ahmad al-Asaad, and their new ally against the regime, Kamal Junblatt. These were men who had previously won their seats in the Chamber. Their defeat rankled with them. The Opposition press now charged that the Chamoun regime had planned the outcome of the elections in advance, first by pushing through the Chamber a law limiting the number of parliamentary seats to 66 instead of 88, the number preferred by the people, then by making the Chamber redraw the boundaries of constituencies in a way that would ensure the election of loyalist candidates and the defeat of the Opposition. In addition, the Opposition press continued, the regime had turned Christian voters against Opposition candidates by depicting them as "the candidates of Abdel Nasser" and "the candidates of certain Arab nations." Charges of bribery, pressure, terrorism, interference, and dishonest propaganda were made by losing candidates from both sides against their opponents. The Government and its winning candidates, however, maintained that the elections had been completely clean, calm, and orderly.

There were also mixed reactions to the elections. For instance, Philippe Takla, a member of the Constitutional Bloc who had won the Greek Catholic seat for the Baalback-Hermel constituency on Sabri Hamade's Opposition slate, had this to say: "The balloting in itself was proper. I want to say that technically, with regard to the way voting was conducted, I did not observe any fraud in favor of this or that candidate. But from the point of view of pressure on the electors, there was enough to write a book on the means that were used to defeat us. . . ."[11] But the man who was running against Takla, Finance Minister Nasri Maalouf, himself had a complaint against Takla and his teammates. Maalouf attributed his defeat to money spent by his adversaries, interference by "certain nonpolitical personalities," and the fusion of the former two constituencies of Hermel and Baalback into one.[12] But if, as charged, the two constituencies had been combined to give Government candidates an advantage, here, at least, the Opposition could find no serious cause for complaint: all four of its candidates won a clear victory. One good reason for their success was that Sabri Hamade's tribal followers from the Hermel had turned out in overwhelming numbers to vote for their leader and his entire slate.

PRESIDENT CHAMOUN'S POLITICAL RECORD

There was nothing new in the charges of interference that were exchanged between candidates for the parliamentary elections of 1957. All this had happened before. It was typical of the aftermath of every election. What was troubling the Opposition leaders now, however, was something more serious. President Chamoun's six-year term in office was due to expire the following year, and they felt that he had obtained a docile parliament which would do his bidding and pass a constitutional amendment to allow him to succeed himself for another term. The few dissident deputies who had managed to get elected, despite the regime's gerrymandering and other interferences, they reasoned, could not possibly put a stop to passage of the amendment. The implications of another six years of the presidency for Chamoun spelled political disaster to a number of politicians who were at odds with the President. Henceforth they would find their ambitions blocked.

Chamoun himself made no public statement that he wished to run for office again. But it was feared that when the time came for the necessary constitutional amendment he would have his friends in the Chamber initiate a draft movement. A precedent had already been set for such an eventuality: in May, 1948, a predominantly loyalist Chamber amended the constitution at the request of the Cabinet in order to allow President Bishara el-Khouri to succeed himself for another six year term. El-Khouri was sworn in for his second term in the fall of 1949, which meant of course that the same clique that had gathered around the President during his first term would continue to dominate the sources of power, and to use and misuse the machinery of the state for their own private benefit. The Opposition remained frustrated.

In view of the Opposition's growing suspicions about Chamoun and its mistrust of his regime, a look at his own record would be in order. Chamoun began his political training during the French mandate as a member of el-Khouri's Constitutional Bloc, where he was in charge of organizing the party's election campaigns.[13] It appears that his experience with managing campaigns and elections made him an enemy of political feudalism. Feudal leaders in various regions were taking advantage of the large-list system in large constituencies to pick and choose the candidates for the tickets they were sponsoring. These feudal interests working through the system of confessional representation caused the election of a largely loyalist Chamber in 1947. Chamoun and a few others were strongly critical of the methods used and the results obtained in the election, for a loyalist Chamber was a controlled legislature ready to do the President's bidding.

In 1948 President el-Khouri seemed to be interested in another term in office, but he could not legally succeed himself. It was thus necessary to amend the constitution to open the way for renewal. Chamoun, who was a minister in Riad es-Solh's Cabinet at the time, did not like the idea of a renewal because he felt that it might set a precedent of amending the constitution for personal reasons. Still, he did not wish to stand in el-Khouri's way, and on May 19 he resigned his post. In his letter of resignation, he indicated to the Premier the need for various reforms, including reform of the electoral law, which still provided for the large constituency and thus perpetuated the large-list system. In 1950 Chamoun joined forces with Kamal Junblatt and the deputies from the National Bloc to reform the electoral law. New legislation was consequently passed by the Chamber increasing the number of deputies from 55 to 77 and dividing North Lebanon and Mount Lebanon into smaller constituencies, but leaving the Biqa' and South Lebanon with their large constituencies. A new Chamber was elected under this law in April, 1951. Although they felt it was an improvement on the previous law, the reformers could see that the new legislation still allowed feudal lords in the Biqa' and the south to control elections in these regions.

Soon after his election to the presidency in September, 1952—following the forced resignation of el-Khouri—Chamoun called for further electoral reforms. With powers from the Chamber to rule by legislative decree for six months, the new Cabinet ordered the introduction of the small constituency everywhere, the reduction of the number of deputies from 77 to 44, and the enfranchisement of women. Elections were called in July, 1953, and the results satisfied the President, for it appeared to him that the powers of the feudal lords were somewhat curbed. It was now possible for the first time since independence to elect a man to the presidency of the Chamber whom the regime considered a liberal, Adel Osseiran from the south. Previously, that important office had been monopolized by two feudal lords: Sabri Hamade of the Hermel, who had occupied it from 1943 until 1951, except in 1945–1946, and Ahmad al-Asaad, feudal lord from the south, who had occupied it from 1951 until 1953.

Though they satisfied the President, the electoral changes

were criticized by many politicians. First, they were initiated through legislative decree and had never been sanctioned by the previous Chamber. Then it was argued, and rightly so, that the President, who already enjoyed extensive powers under the constitution, could easily control a small Chamber of 44 if a large enough Cabinet was drawn from it. Agitation by dissatisfied politicians led to the adoption of the 1957 electoral law. But it was largely a loyalist Chamber, itself elected through the application of a legislative decree, that had adopted this law. As already indicated, both the law and the elections of 1957 were condemned by the Opposition. It was now obvious to Chamoun's opponents that the limitation of the new Chamber to 66—instead of 88— deputies, the perpetuation of the small-list system, the gerrymandering of certain constituencies, and pre-election pressures and propaganda by the Government had all been part of a plot to eliminate effective opposition from the Chamber to a regime and a President intent on allying themselves through the Eisenhower Doctrine with the West against both Egypt and Syria. It was obvious too, that the President had also intended to rid the Chamber at the same time of his own personal adversaries so that he could realize his own ambitions for a second term and continue to frustrate them in their own ambitions.

That the President had intended to strike at his enemies was later admitted by his own supporters. Whether it was intended to pave the way for the President's renewal or not, one writer stated, the electoral law was legal, democratic, and modern. It had broken the back of feudalism and strengthened popular representation by providing for the one-man constituency, and where that was not possible for the small-list constituency.[14]

The Opposition, of course, did not see the electoral law in that light. As the returns from the first phases of the elections came in, it became more apparent to the Opposition that the law had been intended to put all effective control of the country into the hands of one man—the President. In Beirut, the division of the city into two smaller constituencies had separated Saeb Salam and Abdallah al-Yafi from some of their traditional supporters and contributed to their defeat. In the *mohafazat* of South Lebanon, use of the small constituency had also contributed to the failure of Ahmad al-Asaad. There the Shi'i leader had been impelled to leave the Shi'i seat for Marjeyoun, his traditional stamping ground, to be contested by his son Kamel, and to seek one of the two seats assigned to his sect in the town of Tyre. But this was the stronghold of his opponent, Kathem al-Khalil, who carried himself and his teammate to victory.

In Mount Lebanon, the feudal leader Kamal Junblatt attributed his failure in his native Chouf both to gerrymandering and to unfair solicitation of voter good will by the opposing Government-sponsored slate of Naim Moghabghab. Junblatt accused the Government of having deliberately detached part of the electorate of the Deir el-Kamar area from the administrative district of the Chouf and replaced it by another electorate from the administrative district of Aley. If the boundaries of his constituency had followed those of the Chouf, he said, he and his teammates would have been unbeatable.[15]

It was after the defeat of al-Yafi, Salam, al-Asaad, and Junblatt that the Beiruti dignitary Henri Pharaon, who had been counseling moderation to both sides, stepped in to support Sabri Hamade's Opposition slate in the forthcoming elections in the Biqa' *mohafazat*. It was necessary, he later stated, to allow opposition to be exercised within the legal framework of the Chamber. He went on to explain:

> I really think an Opposition is necessary, but I also consider that this Opposition must be moderate in order to play an effective role. If this Opposition were to continue to be exasperated, which it has not ceased to be for some time, if all its members were to find themselves outside the Chamber, this would result in a troubled political climate which would bring very serious injuries to Lebanon.[16]

What Pharaon had hoped to avoid appeared to be unavoidable. Though technically representative of the whole nation, the new Chamber could no longer be the place for communal conciliation as the legislature was intended to be. For the important Opposition leaders who were left outside it, as well as those who managed to get elected, enjoyed substantial popular support. If they could tolerate neither the President's foreign policy nor his own ambitions, they felt sufficiently strong to challenge him. Opposition continued to be exercised outside the Chamber. Even Kamal Junblatt, who had been moderately critical of the Lebanese-American communiqué of March 16 and seemed ready to accept it upon its further clarification, now joined the ranks of the all-out critics. He had become convinced after the elections that Chamoun had accepted the Eisenhower Doctrine as a means of strengthening his regime in the face of growing domestic unrest and as a show of "American support" for the expected renewal of his presidential mandate.[17]

There was, indeed a growing restlessness and a growing sense of anxiety among the Lebanese people. These frustrations were divisive rather than unifying. The Christians, on the whole, feared the growing admiration for Gamal Abdel Nasser among their Muslim compatriots and the threat that this might pose to Lebanese viability and sovereignty. With encouragement from the regime, they turned to President Chamoun as the man who could and would safeguard Lebanese sovereignty against any attempts to subvert it. To enable him to do so, they supported a second presidential term for him and continued to favor his pro-Western foreign policy, namely the Lebanese-American communiqué of March 16, 1957. Thus Chamoun was emerging as the *za'im* of the Christians and the symbol of Lebanese rights and integrity.

The Muslim community, however, generally feared the exact opposite of what the Christians feared. Muslims worried that

Lebanese acceptance of the Eisenhower Doctrine was alienating their country from the general stream of Arab thought and feeling and isolating them from both Syria and Egypt. This had not been the object of the National Pact of 1943 and they resented it. The confusions and fears of the people in the postelection months were further compounded by conflicting pronouncements from their respective political leaders and by outside interests and pressures. On the one side stood the Opposition politicians, the Damascus and Cairo regimes, and the Soviet Union, all condemning Lebanese acceptance of the Eisenhower Doctrine. On the other side stood Chamoun and his Government as well as Britain, France, and the United States, all fearful of the possible extension of Egyptian hegemony over the entire Arab Middle East. The three Western powers thus supported the Chamoun regime. It was one way, they felt, of checking the rampant ambitions of Gamal Abdel Nasser.

MEN AND POLITICS
IN THE CHAMBER OF 1957-1958

Against this background of growing ill will, emphasized by an increase in domestic disturbances, the new 66-man Chamber of Deputies held two extraordinary and two ordinary sessions between August 12, 1957, and May 8, 1958, when it was forced to adjourn before the legal termination of the session at the end of the month by the outbreak of the revolution. During the many meetings held between August and May the lawmakers were engaged in lengthy debates over the Government's domestic, regional, and foreign policies. The discussions were provoked by the old-time Opposition leaders who had managed to get re-elected, by their few new colleagues who shared their views, and sometimes by a few deputies who considered themselves independents. The Government was often called on to explain

and justify its domestic and foreign policies. But there was no
compromise, no conciliation. Both sides were moving toward a
deadlock.

Behind the scenes, on the personal level, there was more at
stake for the Opposition leadership than the loss of good relations with Egypt and Syria alone. Sabri Hamade, lord of the
Hermel, for instance, aspired to the presidency of the Chamber,
an honor reserved for a Shi'i deputy and the position of the highest prestige and influence that a Shi'i could attain within the
state. He tried for the office when the new Chamber first convened in extraordinary session in August, and when it again convened in ordinary session in October. And although he received
strong support, both times he lost to his rival Adel Osseiran, a
loyalist deputy from the south who carried off the presidency
with about twice as many votes. In fact, Osseiran had held the
presidency since 1953—almost since the beginning of the Chamoun regime. In previous parliaments, it appeared, Osseiran's
main rival for the presidency had been Hamade's father-in-law,
Ahmad al-Asaad, a well-known leader of the south.

Hamade's and al-Asaad's repeated failure to capture the presidency of the Chamber during the Chamoun regime was not a
mere coincidence. Since independence, the President of the Republic and the Cabinet had always been interested in having the
"right" person occupy that office, for he was a key man with
power to help or block the Cabinet's legislative program. With
the President enjoying so much power in his office, there were
always enough loyalist deputies who could be induced to elect
his own chosen candidate for the presidency of the Chamber.
Thus it was that Chamoun was held responsible for blocking
Hamade's and al-Asaad's way to that high office and promoting
to it instead the more cooperative Osseiran. The repeated ob-
structions of Chamoun rankled as much with Kamel el-Asaad,
who was again a member of the Chamber, as they did with his
father Ahmad.

The interests of Hamid Frangieh, Maronite deputy from Zgharta, were of another kind. He hoped to succeed Camille Chamoun to the presidency of the Republic when the latter's six-year term in office expired in September, 1958. He would thus be especially antagonistic to any move the Chamber might make to allow Chamoun to succeed himself. Frangieh's presidential ambitions came to public attention as early as September, 1952, when, following the forced resignation of President el-Khouri, he and Chamoun emerged as the two contenders for his office. At that time, Chamoun enjoyed more public backing, for he had already made a name for himself as the capable defender of Arab interests in international diplomacy. Frangieh withdrew his candidacy so that Chamoun could be elected unanimously by the Chamber, but cherished the hope that he would be the next President. When later the traditional feud between the Frangieh-Mouawad and the Doueihy-Karam clans erupted in open strife, it was felt by Frangieh's backers that Chamoun had instigated his enemies against him in order to weaken this leading citizen of Zgharta and eliminate him as a competitor for the presidency. It was thus with a special zeal that the Frangieh-Mouawad team campaigned against the Government-endorsed Doueihy-Karam team in the June parliamentary elections. For by tradition the Maronite President was elected from within the Chamber, and the time for the selection of the next one, by the deputies, was fast approaching.

A new mandate for President Chamoun also seemed to be against the interests of Rachid Karame, Sunni deputy from Tripoli. Now that he had gone on record as a sharp critic of Lebanon's acceptance of the Eisenhower Doctrine and of the regime's attitude toward Syria and Lebanon, he could not hope to be called upon by the President to occupy, as he had done in the past, that most prestigious position a Sunni could aspire to —the premiership.

It was obvious, of course, that a presidential renewal for Chamoun would be distasteful to all the Opposition deputies. But how were they to prevent it? They and the other deputies who had collaborated with them during the electoral campaign were altogether less than one-third of the whole legislature. They could not alone prevent a constitutional amendment that would permit the President to succeed himself, for there would probably be plenty of votes to pass it by a two-thirds majority, as required, in plenary session. Still, it was not a foregone conclusion that such an amendment would be passed, for among both the independents and the loyal Maronite deputies there were those who were suspected of having presidential ambitions of their own or perhaps considered others as worthy of the office.

Frustrated and fearful, the legislative Opposition doggedly continued the attacks of the pre-election period on the Government's foreign and domestic policies. The Cabinet that it now faced had been slightly reshuffled, but still included most of the old faces. What was important was that Sami es-Solh was Prime Minister again and Charles Malik was Minister of Foreign Affairs—an indication that the President would pursue the same foreign policy. Malik was even in a more advantageous position than in the spring, for he was now also a deputy.[18] Seeking a vote of confidence, the new Cabinet on August 29 presented to the Chamber its postelection statement of policy, and emphasized, as before, its domestic program for social and economic development and for administrative reorganization, Lebanon's friendship for all Arab nations alike on a basis of complete equality, and Lebanon's policy of cooperation with all nations, also on the basis of complete equality. The Lebanese-American communiqué of March 16, 1957, the statement stressed, in no way impinged on Lebanese independence and sovereignty.

As expected, Opposition deputies criticized the Government for its handling of both domestic and foreign policies. But this time there were also attacks from new quarters. Emile Bustani, an independent, took the Government to task for its inability to maintain domestic security and for its failure so far to acquire worthwhile economic aid from the United States under the Eisenhower Doctrine. Joseph Chader, a member of the Political Bureau of the *Kataeb* party, was likewise critical of the paucity of American aid and of the Government's failure to initiate the necessary domestic development projects. Speaking for himself and for the three other members of the National Bloc (Raymond Edde, Pierre Edde, and Nouhad Bouiez), Edward Honein lambasted the Government's inertia at home, but approved its foreign policy. The Bloc, however, was in time to join those who criticized American aid as being too meager and therefore not worth the trouble. When at the end of the meeting the Chamber voted on the Government's policy statement, the National Bloc deputies and Chader of the *Kataeb* joined the Opposition, though for different reasons, in withholding their confidence. Bustani, who had threatened to withhold his confidence, abstained. Government policy nevertheless was approved by a vote of 38 against 17, a more than two to one majority.

On November 26–27 the Government was again called upon by the Chamber to give an accounting of both its domestic and foreign policies. After a long, heated debate it won the confidence of the legislature with 37 votes for it, 13 against it, and three abstentions. This time, Bustani joined the National Bloc in voting against the Government because of the meagerness of American aid under the Eisenhower Doctrine. Joseph Chader of the *Kataeb* abstained as an indication of continued disapproval by his party of the Government's inability to maintain domestic security.

The meeting of November 26–27 reflected, more than that of August 29, the widening split between the Christian and Muslim communities, the growing alienation between Lebanon, on the one hand, and Syria and Egypt, on the other, and the consequent intensification of domestic political disturbances. The debates on these issues were most acrimonious. Premier es-Solh blamed bomb explosions at home, riots, and other disturbances on "foreign agents," hinting that these were the agents of Syria and Egypt, which were at the time conducting a press and radio campaign against Lebanese acceptance of the Eisenhower Doctrine. Opposition deputies, on their part, charged that Lebanon had become a center of foreign, i.e., Western, intrigue against the sister Arab countries, Syria and Egypt. But loyalist deputies countercharged that Syria and Egypt were in fact intriguing against Lebanon, and claimed that arms were being smuggled into Lebanon to be used against the legally constituted authorities. To this the Opposition replied that the Government was arming its partisans against the people and curtailing the rights and freedoms of the public.

In an attempt to placate the Opposition, Foreign Minister Malik read into the record an exchange of letters between himself and U.S. Secretary of State Dulles which reiterated that the Lebanese-American communiqué of March 16, 1957, based on the Eisenhower Doctrine, was neither a military pact nor a political treaty. But Opposition deputies would not be propitiated, and charged that American aid was in fact accomplishing the exact opposite of its purpose by drawing Communist attention to Lebanon and exposing it to the possibility of Communist aggression. To this the loyalists countered that the Communist danger already existed and there could be no Lebanese neutrality where Communism was concerned. Behind these peripheral arguments lay the basic issues: whether to go the way of Cairo and Damascus and declare for "positive neutralism," as the Opposition and vocal Muslim groups demanded, or to maintain the official alliance with the American anti-Communist policy, as the loyalists and vocal Christian groups wished.

Subsequent meetings of the Chamber were devoted to the same tug of war, but now the Opposition also conducted an all-out campaign to obtain the resignation of Charles Malik as Foreign Minister and to force the regime to replace the Cabinet with a "Government of National Union," representing both the Opposition and the loyalists. Both efforts failed and a vote on the Government's domestic policy taken on January 28, 1958, indicated the usual line of division: 36 votes for the Government and 15 against, with one abstention.

It was during the February recess of the Chamber that Egypt and Syria merged into the United Arab Republic. For Lebanon, the event served only to drive a deeper wedge between the Christian and Muslim communities. As already stated, there was great rejoicing within Muslim quarters and demonstrations of support. Many popular delegations went to Damascus to meet and congratulate its distinguished visitor, President Gamal Abdel Nasser. Within certain Muslim groups there was a general air of hopeful expectancy that Lebanon would be next to join the union. But this very idea was anathema to the Christians. They felt that it must be avoided at all costs, for union would convert them into a minority group in a predominantly Muslim nation and would lead to the loss of their rights and privileges.

It was now necessary to calm the apprehensions of the Christian community by drawing the attention of the enthusiastic supporters of the U.A.R. to their responsibilities to their own state. This was the task of the Christian leadership within the Opposition camp. Thus in March Nassib al-Matni, editor of the leftist Arabic daily *al-Talegraph* and a sharp critic of the Chamoun regime, counseled the Muslim community in these words:

> Of those who go to Damascus we ask that they not think of anything but the independence of Lebanon and act accordingly. If they will furnish proof of their attachment to Lebanon, the *Christians will no longer have any fear* and will be disposed themselves to serve Arabism and the Arabs.
> To those who organize pro-Arab manifestations in Beirut itself, we say that it is indispensable *that they reaffirm their faith in their fatherland.*
> *Some of the Christians are disturbed; you must hasten to give them all the assurances to which they are entitled* and must not

give in to the intrigues of a few politicians who deliberately strive to exploit this sentiment of fear.

All that the Christians, who are anxious, wish for, is to be told that the independence and sovereignty of Lebanon are beyond dispute, and then the present climate of apprehension and mistrust will disappear immediately.[19]

But to the politicians who were personally locked in a power struggle with President Chamoun this was no time to counsel moderation to their followers. They made one last attempt to achieve through legal means a reversal of Lebanese foreign policy and to prevent an extension of Chamoun's term in office. Both objectives had to be attained at the same time because, they felt, if the President were to continue in office for another six years he would surely pursue his deviationist foreign policy, and if he were allowed to continue this policy he would have sufficient strength to perpetuate himself on the country for another term. The Chamber of Deputies convoked a new session in March, and the Opposition deputies prepared themselves for the fight, for in the next two to three months the legislature would have to pass the necessary constitutional amendment if Chamoun were to succeed himself in September.

The regime itself was also prepared for the fight. When the Chamber reconvened, a new Government was waiting to receive its vote of confidence. But this was a fourteen-member Cabinet, exceeding the former by six. Sami es-Solh and Charles Malik both reappeared as Prime Minister and Foreign Minister respectively. Two ministers from the old Cabinet had been dropped, and eight new ministers had been chosen from the Chamber. Some of the newcomers were former critics of the Government but not opponents of the regime. They included Pierre Edde of the National Bloc and Joseph Chader, the only *Kataeb* deputy. The larger Cabinet meant of course that the regime could now muster even greater support for its policies within the Chamber.

In presenting the new Government's policy statement to the Chamber on March 25, Prime Minister es-Solh explained that the Cabinet had been enlarged for two purposes: (1) to provide each ministry with its own full-time minister because of the pressure of work that needed to be done; (2) to strengthen the bonds of national unity in accordance with the principles of the National Pact of 1943. He then stressed Lebanon's attachment to complete independence and its intolerance of any foreign interference in its domestic affairs. This was an obvious warning to the newly established United Arab Republic. But the statement did not go unchallenged, and there followed an exchange of accusations between loyalists and Opposition with regard to the disturbed state of the nation and its deteriorating relations with the U.A.R.

To the Opposition, furthermore, the new Cabinet was unacceptable because it was not the "Government of National Union" it had been calling for. Voicing what others had only implied, Sabri Hamade on March 26 charged that the Cabinet had actually been enlarged to accomplish one "known objective." Selim Lahhoud had been replaced by Pierre Edde to win the Government four votes from within the Chamber, he stated, and Jamil Mekkawi had been replaced by Bachir al-Othman to win another four votes. For three years now, Hamade went on, one person had been leading the Chamber on a merry-go-round with regard to domestic and external matters so as to strengthen his position for ruling Lebanon. The only purpose of this large Cabinet, the deputy concluded, was to guarantee a two-thirds vote in the Chamber to assure the continuance in power of the person who had drawn the outline of this Government's foreign policy.

The loud protests and table thumping that ensued meant that everyone knew President Chamoun was the object of this attack. Though Hamade's charges went into the record, they did not prevent the Government from receiving an overwhelming vote of confidence: 38 votes for it and only 15 against it.

To a group of loyalist deputies, this vote of confidence indicated that the way was now fully open to the President to renew his mandate. They prepared to submit a proposal to the Chamber to pass the required constitutional amendment to make this possible. But the country was divided on the matter. Outside the Chamber the division was reflected in the battle of words that raged between the loyalist and the Opposition press. The latter looked upon renewal as a step toward dictatorship and a measure that would lead to a national crisis. Parliament, it cautioned, did not have the final word. On April 3 the pro-Egyptian Christian editor Sa'id Freyha warned President Chamoun in the Arabic weekly *as-Sayyad* that he was no longer as popular as he used to be before the Suez Canal war. Freyha continued: "But now, where do you stand, your Excellency? Where are you in relation to Damascus and Cairo and the Arab peoples?"[20]

It was partly such talk as this that made the loyalist press call for a second term for the President. Only renewal, it was felt, could safeguard Lebanese viability and sovereignty.

Wiser counsel tried to prevail against the fears of both sides. For some time now, former Foreign Minister Henri Pharaon had been trying to avert the crisis that he foresaw by advocating moderation and conciliation in statements to the press. In the spring of 1958 he emerged as the leader of a group calling itself "the Third Force." Its members included leading citizens and former deputies and ministers, and its purpose was to bring the extremists on both sides back to their senses. Using the columns of *L'Orient* and *al-Jarida* to disseminate its views, the Third Force advocated nonrenewal for Chamoun and the election of a new President, to take office in September, who enjoyed the confidence and respect of both the loyalists and the Opposition. On April 11 Georges Naccache, a member of the Third Force and editor-publisher of *L'Orient,* advised in his paper that it was not worth bargaining away the nation's future for a constitutional revision which would allow Chamoun to succeed himself and thus imperil Lebanon's institutional equilibrium—the whole system of the balance of powers. He added: "A presidential election could, if necessary, become the object of a battle. It is conceivable that it may not be unanimous. A REELECTION IS NOT CONCEIVABLE UNLESS IT IS UNANIMOUS. But we know today THAT IT COULD NOT BE."[21]

Within the Chamber, the loyalist deputies who had contemplated introducing the constitutional amendment that would allow the President to succeed himself were, for the time being, diverted from their purpose. Opposition deputies kept them engaged in a series of debates over the deteriorating domestic situation. There had been bloody incidents in Tyre between demonstrators and the gendarmerie, precipitated by public celebrations in the south of the Syro-Egyptian union. Similar clashes were now taking place between the gendarmerie and groups of armed citizens in other parts of the country. On April 15 Maarouf Saad, Sunni deputy from Sidon, warned the Government of an unavoidable popular insurrection if the sponsors of renewal did not give up the idea. He demanded the dissolution of the Chamber and the holding of new elections as the only way of avoiding the insurrection.

The insurrection was, in fact, ready to erupt at any moment. Preparations for it had been going on for some time under the direction of the leading opponents of the Chamoun regime. Large amounts of arms and ammunition had already been smuggled into the country. If the Opposition could not attain its demands legally, it would use arms to do so. The Chamber seemed deadlocked, it was time to resort to arms. What was needed was an incident to spark the revolution and give it the appearance of spontaneity.

The opportunity came when on the night of May 7 Nassib al-Matni, editor of the leftist daily *al-Talegraph* and a critic of Chamoun, was murdered in the streets of Beirut. The assassin was never found, and the Opposition blamed his death on the regime. The Chamber met the following day to discuss the crime, and loyalist deputies claimed the innocence of the regime. But the meeting soon broke up when several other deputies walked out of the Chamber, advising the Government to attend to the disturbed state of affairs and find a solution. This was the last meeting of the legislature before the revolution.

CHAPTER 8

The Revolution of 1958:
A Power Struggle among the Politicians
and an Ideological Split among the People

The revolution of 1958 broke out with rioting in Tripoli on May 8, followed by clashes in the north between the Jaafar tribe and the gendarmerie in the Akkar region and between the people of Zgharta and the gendarmerie. In Beirut, the Opposition, calling itself now the United National Opposition Front, decreed on May 8 the closing of all shops and the press announced a three-day strike from May 10 to 13 in protest against the murder of Nassib al-Matni, editor of *al-Talegraph*. The newspaper strike delayed dissemination in the capital of news of the riots and clashes in the north, and the city remained calm until May 12. On that day barricades were set up in the Muslim quarter of the Basta, signaling the beginning of the insurrection in Beirut.

It was declared by the United National Opposition Front that the purpose of the "strike" was to obtain the resignation of President Chamoun, and that it would remain in force until he had actually vacated his office. He was again accused of oppression at home and of deviation in his foreign policy. On his part, the President categorically refused to resign and charged in turn that the troubles at home were inspired not by internal motives but by massive external interference in the affairs of Lebanon, calculated to destroy its independence and sovereignty. He put the blame on the United Arab Republic and accused the Opposition leaders of acting as its agents. The President and his opponents were deadlocked; the fighting continued, sometimes sporadically, sometimes more seriously.

LINEUP OF OPPONENTS AND SUPPORTERS OF THE REGIME

Within the camp of the United National Opposition Front, Chamoun's major opponents directed their operations against the regime from their respective strongholds. They operated on several main fronts, as follows:

1. In Beirut, former deputies and former Prime Ministers Saeb Salam, Abdallah al-Yafi, and Hussein Oueini were in effective control of the Basta, an all-Muslim quarter of Beirut. Salam and al-Yafi, it may be recalled, had lost the parliamentary elections in 1957. They now had their own armed supporters patrol the streets of the Basta and engage any attackers from the Government side. Supporting the revolution from the Basta, too, was Adnan al-Hakim, head of the *Najjadah*, the Muslim youth organization with unionist aspirations. All four leaders here were Sunnis.

2. In Tripoli, Rashid Karame, Sunni deputy and former Premier, held the core of the city, which is predominantly Sunni Muslim, with the consent and armed support of its people. By sharply criticizing the regime's acceptance of the Eisenhower Doctrine and its alienation of Lebanon from Syria and Egypt, he had excluded himself from playing any role in the Government while Chamoun was still in power.

3. In Zgharta, Maronite deputy Hamid Frangieh was in control of the Opposition forces. These, in fact, were his own followers from the Frangieh and Mouawad clans living in the city and its environs. For him the revolution had an especial meaning: it was to get rid of a President who was bent on renewing his term in office and leaving him, Frangieh, disappointed once

again. For the Zgharta notable had aspired to the presidency ever since Chamoun beat him to it in 1952.

4. In the Hermel mountains close to the Syrian border, Sabri Hamade held sway, supported by a larger following of armed Shi'i tribesmen. The Shi'i deputy from that area, he had continuously been frustrated by Chamoun in his attempts to get elected to the presidency of the Chamber—most recently, during the sessions of 1957-1958.

5. In the village of Rachaya and its environs, Druze tribal leader Chebli al-Aryan and his tribesmen were in complete command. A defeated candidate for the Chamber in the elections of 1957, al-Aryan was a less significant member of the Opposition. Yet the area he controlled was of major importance because it bordered on Syria, from where men and arms could flow without Government interference.

6. In the south the most significant leader of the revolution was Ahmad al-Asaad, Shi'i feudal lord who had been defeated in the 1957 elections and who had earlier been frustrated by the regime in his attempt to occupy the presidency of the Chamber. He was supported by his son, Kamel al-Asaad, an Opposition deputy, and by their tribal following. In the town of Sidon, Maarouf Saad, Sunni Opposition deputy from that city, was in control. He was enthusiastically backed by the predominantly Sunni population.

7. In Mount Lebanon, Druze feudal leader Kamal Junblatt was ensconced in his native town of Moukhtara in the Chouf district, directing his tribal followers, as well as Druze reinforcements from the Hauran and Jabal Druze in Syria, against all comers. Junblatt had also lost in the parliamentary elections of 1957.

Supporting the top Opposition leadership were a number of Christian and Muslim politicians who had either won or lost the elections on Opposition tickets. Among them were Philippe

Takla, Greek Catholic, chairman of the parliamentary Foreign
Affairs Committee; Fuad Ammoun, a Maronite presidential as-
pirant who had lost in the Chouf on Kamal Junblatt's ticket; Nassim al-Majdalani, Greek Orthodox deputy from Beirut; Abdallah Machnouk, Sunni editor of the pro-Egyptian daily *Beirut
al-Masa* and a loser in the elections; Takieddine es-Solh, Sunni
deputy from the town of Zahle in the Biqaʻ; and Ali Bazzi, Shiʻi
deputy from the town of Bint Jbeil in the south. Though predominantly Muslim, the United National Opposition Front thus
enjoyed intersectarian support at the highest level.

Two ideological groups gave their support to the revolution
against the regime: the Communist party and the Baath Socialist party. The former was of course completely opposed to Chamoun's pro-Western policy, but it was disclaimed by the Opposition leadership, who, rightly, did not see the movement against
the regime as Communist-inspired or Communist-directed.
Thus, despite the Government's charge of extensive Communist
participation in the revolution, the small but well-organized
Communist party of Lebanon could only exploit public dissatisfaction and its role remained insignificant.

Of Syrian origin and leadership, the Baath Socialist party was
impelled to support the revolution by other considerations.
Though a minority party in Lebanon, which had played no significant role in Lebanese politics in the past, it was informed by
a secular Arab nationalism and worked for the unification of the
Arab world. It was the Baath in Syria which had precipitated
union with Egypt a few months before. Now, both the Syrian
and the Lebanese branches of the party looked upon President
Chamoun's acceptance of the Eisenhower Doctrine as a step
toward the alienation of Lebanon from the Arab world. Still in a
controlling position in politics and in the army in Syria, the
northern province of the U.A.R., at the time of the Lebanese
revolution, the Syrian Baath became the object of Lebanese
Government accusations of "official interference" by the U.A.R.

in the affairs of Lebanon. There was no "official intervention" in the sense of an armed contingent of the Syrian army crossing into Lebanon to fight on the side of the rebels. However, with the obvious blessing if not assistance of the authorities in Syria, there was a flow of arms, money, and men from the Syrian border into the neighboring areas of Lebanon, which were held almost exclusively by rebel factions.

Within Lebanon itself, the great majority of Muslims, who constituted almost half of the population, sympathized with and supported the objectives of the revolution. The other half of the population, the Christians, however, were overwhelmingly in favor of the regime and of its position. Partisans of the regime included the following groups:

1. The *Kataeb* party under the leadership of Pierre Gemayel. Though it had not been happy with the regime's record of reform and internal development, the party stood firmly by Chamoun. It had always feared Lebanese engulfment in an upsurge of Arab nationalism, and now saw the revolution as an effort to scuttle Lebanese sovereignty and unite Lebanon with the U.A.R.

2. The Social Nationalist party, under the leadership of its President, Asad al-Ashkar, Maronite deputy for the Northern Metn in Mount Lebanon. The party fully supported the Chamoun regime with a strong, well-trained fighting force because it was hostile to Egyptian politics, to the establishment of the U.A.R., and to any attempt to extend Baath-Egyptian influence into Lebanese territory. The National Socialists were not committed to the preservation of Lebanese independence, but now felt forced to defend it because they also saw in the revolution an attempt to unite Lebanon with Egypt and Syria. In their own scheme for a Greater Syria there was no place for Egypt.

3. Prime Minister Sami es-Solh, of course, and a small minority of Beiruti Muslims who constituted his personal following.

4. The Lebanese branch of *Tashnak* (Armenian Revolutionary Federation), an international anti-Communist party. Leba-

non also has a local branch of an international leftist Armenian organization called *Hunchak* (the Social Democratic *Hunchak* party). Within Lebanon, both parties have limited membership, although *Tashnak* is the larger of the two. Both are traditional rivals, and during the crisis they concentrated mainly on fighting each other and settling old scores, although *Hunchak* also supported the Communists. But the Armenian community as a whole lent public support to the Chamoun regime, not out of partiality but because it has been the community's policy to support the regime that happens to be in power as an investment in its own security and continued well-being.

5. Naim Moghabghab, Greek Catholic deputy from the Chouf, and his own personal following. A loyalist, Moghabghab had headed the pro-Government ticket that defeated the ticket of Kamal Junblatt in the parliamentary elections of 1957. He and Junblatt were enemies.

6. Majid Arslan, Druze feudal lord from Aley, a deputy, and a perennial minister in old and new Cabinets. He was also a traditional rival of Junblatt, and at the outbreak of hostilities had pitched his Druze followers in a common effort with Naim Moghabghab's Christian fighters against Junblatt's Druze tribesmen. The bonds of religion, however, proved to be stronger than political differences, and Arslan soon concluded a truce with Junblatt and withdrew his men from the field, leaving Moghabghab's men to go it alone against his rival's supporters.

ATTITUDES OF PUBLIC AND RELIGIOUS PERSONALITIES

The deadlock between the regime and the Opposition produced a flurry of activity by third parties in search of a solution, and afforded public personalities and interest groups an opportunity to indicate their position in relation to the two embattled camps. Within the Christian community, two influential men identified themselves with the Opposition: ex-President Bishara el-Khouri and the Maronite Patriarch, Mgr. Paul Meouchy. Though members of his own Constitutional Bloc, such as Philippe Takla, were publicly allied with the United National Opposition Front, el-Khouri himself generally remained in the background. He did, however, take a public stand when on July 17 he protested to President Eisenhower and U.N. Secretary General Dag Hammarskjold the landing of American marines in Lebanon two days earlier as a flagrant violation of Lebanese independence and sovereignty. But the landings apart, his hostility to the Chamoun regime was attributed partly to his own presidential ambitions. During the early mediation efforts, his name was mentioned as a possible successor to Chamoun. It was felt, especially by the rival National Bloc, that the Constitutionalists were against another term for Chamoun because they hoped to replace him by their own chief, el-Khouri.[1]

Mgr. Meouchy, the religious head of all Maronites, had from the beginning taken the side of the Opposition. On April 20, before the outbreak of hostilities, he was quoted in the Lebanese press as saying that Lebanon needed new men in office so that it could resolve its differences with its neighbors, and that it was not by dividing the Lebanese against each other that the country could be saved. He then accused the Chamoun regime of having failed in both its internal and external policies.[2] It was, however, Meouchy's press conference on May 30, held after the regime had complained to the Arab League and the United Nations Security Council of U.A.R. interference, which earned him the wrath of his own community and the praises of the Opposition. He told representatives of the foreign press that the Lebanese crisis was a domestic one and should not have been taken to either the regional or the world organization, that President Abdel Nasser had given his reassurances for Lebanese independence, and that the only solution for the crisis was for the President to take a trip abroad.

Reproduced widely in the Lebanese press, Meouchy's statement to the foreign correspondents helped harden the attitude of the Opposition leadership against the Chamoun regime. But at the same time there was general agreement that the Patriarch's intention was to strengthen the Christian character of the Opposition front and to avoid a possible sectarian war, since on the popular level the Muslims were ranged on the side of the rebels, and the Christians on the side of the regime.

Identifying themselves also with the Opposition were the religious heads of the three Muslim communities: Sunni, Shi'i, and Druze. Separately and collectively, they issued statements to the press protesting the Government's arming of its partisans, sent messages to the United Nations condemning the Government's complaint against the U.A.R., and later messages to President Eisenhower, the U.S. Congress, and the U.N. Secretary General censuring the landing of American marines in Lebanon. On June 6, using the authority of their religious office, twenty-eight Muslim *muftis* and jurists issued a canonical edict accusing Prime Minister es-Solh of ruling over the people against their unanimous will, of creating religious strife and acting against the interests of the Muslim community. They added: "We therefore call upon the people to disclaim and disown him for he has renounced the ethics of Islam and has followed a different course to that of the faithful."[3] The edict was in effect an excommunication of the Prime Minister for having continuously refused to resign. Had he done so, it was felt that he would have precipitated the collapse of the regime, since no other Sunni politician seemed ready to accept the premiership.

MEDIATION EFFORTS BY THIRD PARTIES

Among the mediators, the Third Force of Henri Pharaon played an active role. Since the elections of 1957 this group had continued to counsel moderation to both Government and Opposition. It now saw the crisis in essentially domestic terms:

it was traceable to those very elections and to the consequent Opposition-loyalist debate over the future exercise of the presidential mandate. Thus, the crisis could abate only with the election of a new President to take office in September who would enjoy the confidence of both loyalists and Opposition alike, and who would play the role of arbiter among all political factions. In the meantime, on May 24, Third Force spokesmen Henri Pharaon and Charles Helou, who like Pharaon was also a former minister, proposed that General Fuad Chehab, commander of the Lebanese Army, "be charged with the formation of a Government of National Salvation to stop the spilling of blood, to assure the return of security and unity, as well as to safeguard, on both the economic and political levels, the integrity of Lebanon."[4] The plan appealed to Mgr. Meouchy and to Raymond Edde, leader of the National Bloc, and both joined in the effort to get it accepted by the disputants.

To the mediators, General Chehab appeared to be a happy choice to solve the crisis, for though a Maronite, he was an apolitical soldier who enjoyed the respect and confidence of Muslims and Christians alike. Thus it would be possible to deviate temporarily from the tradition of appointing a Sunni as Premier and to ask him instead to fill the office. He had once before come to the rescue of Lebanon when President Bishara el-Khouri temporarily left the reins of government in his hands before resigning in September, 1952. Unwilling at first to get into politics, General Chehab was reported to have finally agreed to form a new Government provided this was acceptable to both the regime and the Opposition. However, the Opposition continued to insist on the immediate resignation of the President, while Chamoun himself at first appeared to have consented to the arrangement but changed his mind within a few hours. His Prime Minister, Sami es-Solh, supported him by refusing to resign.

Besides Pharaon and Helou, members of the Third Force included Georges Naccache, Joseph Salem, Gabriel Murr, Dr. Joseph Hitti, Bahige Takieddine, Ghassan Tueni, Negib Salha, and Mohammed Shoukair. Naccache was an influential newspaper publisher-editor. The others were all well-known personalities on the Lebanese political scene, and had all previously participated in government as either deputies or ministers. The Maronites among them, Helou and Dr. Hitti, were presidential possibilities whose names had been mentioned in the past, as they were again being mentioned now, in connection with the supreme magistracy of the state. But it was the contention of all Third Force members, Maronites and others alike, that a second term for Chamoun was out of the question. The man was too controversial; he had tried to monopolize all sources of power, and thus threatened to upset the sectarian balance within the state. (It was also reported that he cramped his adversaries in their business affairs, among them Joseph Salem of the Third Force.) Pharaon himself was opposed to a renewal of Chamoun's presidential mandate on principle: any tampering with the constitution might lead to the destruction of the political and confessional equilibrium through which Lebanon maintained its independence and sovereignty. On that basis, Pharaon had already fought against a renewal for his own brother-in-law, Bishara el-Khouri, and even now disagreed with Opposition proposals to have the latter returned to the presidency. Still, the Third Force wished to see Chamoun complete his legal term in office, but also warned that this might not be possible if he and the Opposition continued to turn down its proposals for conciliation.

Meanwhile, efforts at reconciliation were continued in the last week of May by Deputy Raymond Edde of the National Bloc. He presented to Government and Opposition the following plan:

1. The Prime Minister would make a declaration to the nation in the name of the Government committing it (a) to present no

proposal for amendment of the constitution; (b) not to call the Chamber of Deputies into special session for amendment of the constitution; (c) to request the President of the Chamber to hold an early session beginning July 23, 1958, to elect a new President of the Republic.

2. After a period of forty-eight hours, if the Opposition decided to continue the strike, the Government would proclaim a state of emergency.[5]

The Opposition turned down the plan, but the Government was willing to adopt those portions of it which called for non-amendment of the constitution. And on May 27 Premier es-Solh, in the absence of a parliamentary quorum to hear him out, broadcast an official statement in which he promised that the Government would never present a plan for amendment of the constitution to permit the reelection of the President.

The Third Force, however, had felt all along that it was necessary for the President himself, if he wished to terminate the crisis, to publicly declare that he would not seek a second term in office. But the President refused to make such a public statement on the ground that he could not deny what he had never proclaimed.

While Government and Opposition remained deadlocked, individual deputies tried their hand at peacemaking, but the Chamber as a whole took an unannounced holiday. Between its last meeting on May 8 and July 31, when it met to elect General Fuad Chehab as President of the Republic, it could not convene for want of a quorum. Though a majority of the deputies were loyalists, the crisis, it appeared, had immobilized them. Since few of them were guided by party doctrine or by clear-cut political principles, it seemed best to wait and see how the issues would be resolved outside the Chamber. Thus when agreement was finally reached that the revolution would end with "no victor, no vanquished" and that the next President would be General Fuad Chehab, the duly elected representatives of the people met to give their consent to a formula that had been worked out outside the legislature.

GENERAL CHEHAB KEEPS ARMY OUT OF POLITICS

In sharp contrast to the hesitancy of the Chamber, General Fuad Chehab, commander-in-chief of the Lebanese army, knew his mind and acted independently, despite the demands of the Chamoun regime to put down the rebellion forthwith. For it appeared to him that the fighting was a protest by a mass of the citizenry against a presidential renewal and not an attempt to subvert Lebanese independence. This was a political problem for which a political solution must be found without implicating the army. Thus he would not use it to launch attacks on the rebels but limited its use to resisting their attacks, patrolling the streets of the capital, preventing clashes between the Christian and Muslim quarters of Beirut, and preventing the rebels from acquiring positions of strength outside their respective strongholds. This was possible because the army was completely loyal to him, and he continued to ignore orders from the President and Prime Minister to crush the rebel centers.

But there was another reason why General Chehab was so careful in the use of his 6,000-man army, whose only plausible reason for existence, it seemed, was to maintain internal security. First, although about three-quarters of the soldiers were Christian and only about one-quarter were Muslim, the army was popular with all the Lebanese. Then, since the rebel forces were overwhelmingly Muslim and the volunteer fighters of the regime were overwhelmingly Christian, use of the army to crush the rebels might ruin its reputation for impartiality, and would probably cause a split within its ranks. Should either possibility be allowed to develop, the army would lose its usefulness.

Criticism was of course directed at the General for "wanting to save the army at the expense of the country." Yet a more forceful stand against the rebels by the army might itself have led to the disintegration of the Lebanese entity. A close observer of the revolution put the problem this way:

Solutions by force are impossible in a country like this, founded on compromise and the need for mutual tolerance. If the Army moved against the rebels, it would have little difficulty in reestablishing order, even without the tanks and other equipment which the United States continues to supply with what seems needless generosity. But if it cleared the Moslem quarters of Beirut and Tripoli, knocking down a few houses in the process, the Army—which is predominantly Christian—would in fact be destroying the structure of the Lebanon as a political entity. The memories of 1860, when the Druze massacred the Christians and the Moslems joined in, are still alive today, dimly amid the vulgar cosmopolitanism of Beirut, but vividly in the mountain villages beyond. The present opposition is principally, though not entirely, Moslem, especially in its lower ranks. If it were to be suppressed by force, the memories of 1958 would still be green in fifty years' time, and the Lebanon would have ceased to exist.[6]

COMPLAINTS TO THE ARAB LEAGUE
AND THE UNITED NATIONS

As mediators trudged back and forth between Government and Opposition headquarters seeking a compromise that would bring peace back to their embattled country, the regime itself kept insisting that the revolution was of more than domestic proportions. It now claimed that it had "innumerable proofs, formal and irrefutable" of the interference of the United Arab Republic in the internal affairs of Lebanon, "interference which has taken the character of an aggression."[7] Thus on May 21 the Government submitted a complaint against the U.A.R. to the Arab League Council, and on May 27 it carried the same complaint to the United Nations Security Council. The charges were: (1) intervention of the U.A.R. in Lebanese affairs through infiltration of armed bands from Syria; (2) destruction of Lebanese life and property through this intervention; (3) participation in terrorism and rebellion; (4) supply of arms to individuals in rebellion against the legal government of Lebanon; (5) violent press and radio campaigns conducted by the U.A.R. against the government of Lebanon.

By submitting its case against the U.A.R. to the Arab League and the United Nations, the Lebanese Government now expected a regional or an international solution. Voices within the Opposition camp decried this move, and protested especially to the world organization that the crisis was an entirely domestic matter and that the U.A.R. had nothing to do with it. One thing was obvious. The U.A.R. was indeed conducting a concerted press and radio campaign against the Chamoun regime and against Lebanese foreign policy, which it considered hostile to Cairo. It was inciting the rebels to topple the regime. But was "aggression" by propaganda to be considered a justifiable cause for action by the regional or international body? If so, then most of the members of both organizations stood in danger of being accused and censured for similar "aggression." But the problem was more complicated than that. Radio and press propaganda was merely a manifestation of the fact that the internal struggle for power in Lebanon had long been joined through Lebanese foreign policy with the regional struggle for power, that is between the Damascus-Cairo entente and Western policy in the Middle East, which favored the rival Baghdad-Amman entente. Thus over the past year and a half the Opposition had depicted President Chamoun as a man who had followed a deviationist, anti-Arab policy by accepting the Eisenhower Doctrine, who had accepted the Eisenhower Doctrine as a means of pressuring the nation into granting him a second term in office, who had rigged the 1957 elections to obtain a docile Chamber that would assure him his second term, and who also wanted this second term so as to continue saddling the nation with his deviationist, anti-Arab policy. On its part, the regime charged the Opposition with attempting to destroy Lebanon's traditional neutrality among its Arab neighbors and with attempting to compromise its sovereignty and to make it a satellite of Cairo. This, the regime stated, it would never allow.

The mediators themselves had their differences as to the cause of the revolution. Third Force leader Henri Pharaon was of the opinion that the U.A.R. aided the rebels only to help them get rid of a regime that had become deviationist in its regional policy and unfriendly to Egypt. Raymond Edde of the National Bloc, however, felt that the Syrian authorities were aiding the rebels with the definite objective of uniting Lebanon with the U.A.R. Abdel Nasser had fallen in with the plan, Edde stated, at the urging of the Syrian nationalists. Edde believed that despite some interference, the 1957 elections had been generally fair; but Pharaon thought that the Chamoun regime had supported some candidates against others and had obtained the election results that it had wanted.

What was more important was that the appeals of Gamal Abdel Nasser for Arab unity and for a liberated Arab policy had fallen on willing ears in Lebanon, and despite the public pronouncements of the Egyptian leader during the crisis that his government respected the independence and integrity of Lebanon, there was a noticeable expectation among some of the Muslim rank and file that the revolution would lead to union with the U.A.R. Would there be a unification move from the Syrian border? The partisans of the regime, composed largely of young men from the National Socialist Party and from the *Kataeb*, fought especially hard to discourage any such possibility.

Although the hate campaign against the Chamoun regime was continued by the Egyptian and Syrian press and radio, the U.A.R. again denied involvement in the Lebanese revolution when the Arab League Council met the first week in June in

Benghazi, Libya, to take up the charges of the Chamoun regime. The latter wished to obtain an official censure of "U.A.R. intervention" and received strong support from both Iraq and Jordan. But the League was generally disposed to attempt a reconciliation, and both Iraq and Jordan joined Libya, Saudi Arabia, and the Sudan in sponsoring a compromise resolution that was conciliatory to the U.A.R. Lebanon rejected it, and turned to the U.N. Security Council for more satisfactory action. On June 11 the Security Council authorized Secretary General Dag Hammarskjold to set up an Observation Group in Lebanon to ensure that there was no illegal infiltration of personnel or smuggling of arms or other material from across the Lebanese borders (i.e. from Syria).

In its several reports to the U.N. Secretary General between July 1 and September 25, the Observation Group failed to agree with the es-Solh Government that there was massive intervention by the U.A.R. in the internal affairs of Lebanon. The Group's reports indicated that the U.N. observers were unable to detect the presence of Syrian and other infiltrators among the rebels, and could only concede the possibility of a limited smuggling of arms from Syria into certain areas of Lebanon. Furthermore, the Group failed to implicate the U.A.R. authorities in the Lebanese revolution. The Chamoun regime was furious. It accused the observers of making no attempt to determine the origin of rebel arms and of being incapable of determining the national character of rebel forces. The regime stood by its former point-by-point charges against the U.A.R., but the Opposition leadership welcomed the Group's reports as proof that the revolution was an entirely domestic affair.

That there had been a lively traffic in arms and ammunition from across the Syrian border as well as an infiltration of Druze tribesmen and other Syrians was common knowledge in Lebanon. But most of that activity had taken place before the arrival of the U.N. observers and before their admittance to the rebel-held areas, most of which were adjacent to the Syrian border. The number of infiltrators was variously estimated at between 1,000 and 3,000, and these were joined by some Syrians with work permits in Lebanon, who avoided deportation by taking up arms with the rebels. But the Syrians were indistinguishable from the Lebanese, especially to visitors from outside the Arab world. Furthermore, the infiltrators and other Syrians did not represent an official military intervention and could not implicate the U.A.R.; nor could the arms smuggled from Syria, for these could have been bought by the rebels themselves from private Syrian sources.

Still, the presence of the United Nations in Lebanon began to have a calming effect on the situation, for it provided the Secretary General with the opportunity to press for an understanding between Cairo and Beirut and consequently to clear the air for a domestic solution. But before his efforts could produce definite results they were interrupted by the landing of American marines in Lebanon on July 15. Faced with the Iraqi revolution that had taken place the previous day, the United States had acted independently of the United Nations and answered President Chamoun's request for American troops to protect his life and to prevent a possible *Anschluss* from the Syrian border. The measure was in accordance with the Lebanese-American communiqué, which was based on the Eisenhower Doctrine. The *Anschluss*, of course, never came, but President Chamoun felt that was due only to timely American aid. "If I had not accepted the Eisenhower Doctrine in July 1958," he later stated, "Lebanon would have been taken over by Nasser."[8]

But was it not perhaps partly due to his original acceptance of the Eisenhower Doctrine that Lebanon had faced this dangerous possibility? Earlier, on May 28, deputy Emile Bustani, who had been one of the more enthusiastic supporters of the Lebanese-American communiqué of March 16, 1957, had this to say in a press conference:

I admit that the Lebanese government agreed with the Americans on the Malik-Richards statement, in the belief that this agreement would be in the interests of the Arabs in general and the Lebanese in particular. Finally, American policy aimed at isolating Egypt and Abdul Nasser from the Arab bloc, and the material profits of the Eisenhower Doctrine to Lebanon were not huge. This is why I have previously asked, and repeat now, that we should decide that our relations with the United Arab Republic and the Arab Union [of Iraq and Jordan] are more important than our relations with the United States.[9]

Thus if Lebanon was to interpose itself between the conflicting policies of Egypt and the United States it was bound to get hurt, especially since the sympathies of half its population were with Egypt. But Mr. Bustani did not fail to lay the rest of the blame where it belonged. He noted that some of the Opposition politicians, but not all, had exploited popular feelings and had incited the present disturbances. As a solution to the crisis, he called for the resignation of the Cabinet, especially of Premier Sami es-Solh and Foreign Minister Charles Malik, and the assumption of powers by a new Government committed to the principles of: (1) reestablishment of law and order; (2) no amendment of the constitution; (3) noninvolvement in the East-West conflict; (4) nonalignment with either of the two conflicting Arab camps.

The President of the Republic, however, was to continue in office until his legal term ended.

Ironically, after the landing of the marines it was the United States which took over from the United Nations the role of peacemaker between the regime and the Opposition. Peace would come when the Lebanese had agreed among themselves on the principles that Mr. Bustani had outlined in May. The question of how and why the United States had come to accept the third principle—noninvolvement in the East-West conflict— is reserved for discussion in the next chapter. Here it may be said that President Eisenhower's special envoy, Robert D.

Murphy, through his patience and diplomacy, helped smooth the way for a political compromise which the two warring camps arrived at without any outside pressure.

THE COMPROMISE

When the Chamoun regime realized that there was not going to be either a coup d'etat or an invasion from Syria after the revolution in Iraq, and when the Opposition in turn understood that the United States had not come in with its marines to impose a puppet government on them, both sides were ready to talk business. Since the regime had loudly proclaimed during the crisis that there would be no renewal for Chamoun and since the Opposition had insisted that all it wanted was the removal of Chamoun, the first point of discussion was the presidency. The only man who was deemed worthy by both sides of occupying the office was General Fuad Chehab, the apolitical soldier who had maintained his neutrality from the beginning of the revolution. After he was persuaded to accept the presidency, the Chamber of Deputies was convened into special session on July 31 to elect him officially. His term would begin September 24. As a further gesture of conciliation, both sides also agreed that the motto of the new regime would be "no victor, no vanquished," which meant, of course, that neither major community had lost its rights to the other.

Technically the revolution and the strike continued because of the Opposition's previous pronouncement that the "general strike" would remain in effect until Chamoun resigned. Practically, however, hostilities were gradually subsiding as the President's term approached its end. But they temporarily flared up again following Chehab's installment as President. This time it was the *Kataeb* party which declared, in the interests of the Christian community, a general strike that rapidly paralyzed the whole country. The strike started as a protest against the abduction of a *Kataeb* newspaperman, Fuad Haddad, by unknown assailants. If such a thing could happen now, the party argued, then the new Government which was in the process of being formed under a former Opposition leader, Rachid Karame, from independent and neutral elements, would be incapable of preventing further acts of vengeance against the Christian community. After the Government assumed its duties on September 24, the *Kataeb* also protested that it had not given the expected guarantees for the independence and integrity of Lebanon.

The counterrevolution, as the strike called by the *Kataeb* was known, revealed a concern for the preservation of Christian interests vis-à-vis Muslim interests, which had already been secured through the revolution. Thus there was no overtone this time of a personal struggle for power between politicians. The strike was maintained in effect until another Cabinet was formed which satisfied the needs of the Christian community by representing a perfect numerical equilibrium between Christians and Muslims. There were two Muslims, Prime Minister Rachid Karame and Hussein Ouieni, and two Christians, Pierre Gemayel, chief of the *Kataeb*, and Raymond Edde, chief of the National Bloc. Each minister assumed several portfolios. Furthermore, the two Muslims were from the Sunni community, the largest Muslim community and the most devoted to Arab nationalism; the two Christians were from the Maronite community, the largest Christian community and the chief repository of Lebanese nationalism.

On October 17 the Cabinet of four appeared before the Chamber of Deputies and received a vote of confidence. Prime Minister Karame stated that his Government was a "Government of National Salvation" which would act in keeping with the National Pact of 1943. But what did this mean in terms of the post-crisis compromise? He explained to the Chamber:

> Finally, the Government wants to assert once again, to prevent any misinterpretation or ambiguity, that it is committed to

safeguarding the sovereignty of Lebanon and to defending its independence so that Lebanon will remain for all of us what it is today, an Arab country, free, proud and independent.[10]

As in 1943, a formula was found in 1958 for satisfying the conflicting aspirations of the Christian and Muslim communities by declaring Lebanon to be "independent" and "Arab" at the same time.

On the international scene, similar guarantees for Lebanese independence had already been assured. Since neither the U.N. Security Council nor the General Assembly, which convened in special session August 8-21 to discuss the landing of American troops, could resolve the issue of "massive intervention" to the satisfaction of both the Chamoun regime and the U.A.R., the question was tossed back into the lap of the Arab League. The Arabs would have to find their own solution. They finally did so by circumventing Lebanon's charges against the U.A.R. Thus on August 21 the General Assembly was able to adopt unanimously a resolution presented by the ten members of the Arab League which emphasized mutual respect for the independence and sovereignty of one another. Lebanon's Christians could take comfort in the clause which stated that "each member State shall respect the systems of government established in the other member States and regard them as exclusive concerns of these States, and that each shall pledge to abstain from any action calculated to change established systems of government."[11]

POLITICS BACK TO NORMAL

After reestablishing the equilibrium between Lebanon's Christian and Muslim communities, the Karame Government proceeded to bring the country back to its traditional policy of neutrality among its Arab neighbors. This step was the necessary counterpart of the Arab League resolution voted in the United Nations as a guarantee for Lebanese sovereignty and integrity. It was also the necessary assurance that would set the mind of the Muslim community, in turn, at rest. Thus the Government forthwith declared the Eisenhower Doctrine, which had counterposed Lebanon against Egypt and Syria, no longer applicable to the country. On December 10 the Prime Minister officially communicated this decision to the United States in an interview with Assistant Secretary of State William Roundtree. Washington itself, however, had already decided to abandon the Doctrine as a policy for the Middle East. But as an indication of continued friendship for Lebanon, it offered it an outright grant of $10 million to help normalize its strained economy.

Gradually, as the months went by, the old pattern of personal and clan rivalries returned to the political scene. Ideology, though still important, was no longer a divisive issue. Politicians now clamored for a much larger Chamber of Deputies as more representative of the country. Since new elections were scheduled for the summer of 1960, the old Chamber of 66 passed an electoral law increasing the number of deputies to 99 before it resigned in the spring of that year. The elections returned to office most of the *za'ims* and feudal leaders who had been enemies during the crisis of 1958, but it also resulted in the election of newcomers to politics. Still, as in the past, the legislature was dominated by regional and confessional interests rather than by political doctrine. Since these were multiplied with the enlargement of the Chamber, it was going to be difficult for any Government to obtain its vote of confidence and to elicit its cooperation. The deputy commissioned to form the new Government was Saeb Salam of Beirut, a leading spokesman for the Opposition during the 1958 crisis. Finally, after much hard work, he formed a Cabinet of eighteen ministers which represented most of the factions within the Chamber. It won the latter's confidence, but it presented Salam with a new problem: how to get all eighteen ministers to agree to Government policy.

Another indication that Lebanese politics had returned to its former groove was the breakup of old-time alliances and the appearance of new ones. For example, Saeb Salam and Abdallah al-Yafi, who had collaborated closely as leaders of the Opposition during the revolution, fell out shortly before election time in 1960, although they were running on the same ticket. To the public, the reason for their quarrel was all too obvious. As Sunni *za'ims* of the revolution, each would be a likely candidate for the premiership should he win the elections. So when Salam won and al-Yafi lost, the former was accused of dumping the latter in order to improve his own chances for the premiership. Al-Yafi himself complained of having been "stabbed in the back" by Salam. In fact, as in previous elections, accusations of unfair play were freely exchanged between candidates. What was important, however, was that a balance of power was maintained in the Chamber of 99 among a sufficient number of big-name politicians who enjoyed the confidence of their respective sects.

After al-Yafi lost the elections, Salam had only one important rival for the premiership. He was Rachid Karame, Sunni deputy from Tripoli who had been the leader of the revolution there. Karame soon declared his opposition to the Government. However, since most factions in the Chamber were represented in the eighteen-man Cabinet, the coalition which formed the Opposition was necessarily weak, and Karame could only hope for an irreparable split within the Cabinet for a chance to head a new Government himself.

There was, however, one new element on the political scene. The new President, Fuad Chehab, though enjoying the vast powers and influence of his office, used both more as an umpire than a player in the game of politics. He had accepted the presidency out of patriotic duty, and his noninvolvement transferred political patronage to a lower level. Chehab's withdrawing attitude also allowed the Sunni Prime Minister much greater freedom of action than in the past. Thus there could be no room now for the old-time complaint that the Muslim community, which was almost as large as the Christian community, was dominated by the latter at the highest level of political power.

CHAPTER 9

The Eisenhower Doctrine:
A Balance Sheet

The landing of American marines in Lebanon on July 15, 1958, represented the fullest application of the Eisenhower Doctrine. It was in accordance with section 2 of the Joint Resolution, which stated in part: "the United States regards as vital to the national interest and world peace the preservation of the independence and integrity of the nations of the Middle East. To this end, if the President determines the necessity thereof, the United States is prepared to use armed forces to assist any such nation or group of such nations requesting assistance against armed aggression from any country controlled by international communism. . . ." So, according to the strict letter of the law, Lebanon had become a country threatened by armed aggression from another country controlled by international Communism, and the United States was fulfilling Lebanon's request to repel this aggression.

But was this, in fact, both the reason and purpose of the American landings? It was not. The two most immediate reasons were to prevent a possible Arab nationalist *Anschluss* from the Syrian border in the wake of the Iraqi coup d'etat, and to protect the life of President Chamoun. The Iraqi coup had taken both London and Washington by surprise, and fearing that the worst might befall the pro-Western regimes of Jordan and Lebanon, both governments acted with alacrity. London airlifted paratroops to Jordan, where indeed King Hussein was in danger of being overthrown, and Washington sent the marines to Lebanon. When no fighting developed, they remained for three and a half months as a symbol of American armed presence. During that time and with the help of American mediation, a new President acceptable to both loyalist and Opposition forces was elected by the Chamber of Deputies and installed in an orderly fashion, and a Government acceptable to both sides was set up. When the last of the marines left Lebanese soil late in October, the crisis was over and civil order had returned to Lebanon. With this final gesture, the United States abandoned the Eisenhower Doctrine as a policy for the Arab Middle East. Thus in less than two years this controversial policy for preventing a Communist takeover in the Middle East had been promulgated, applied, and found wanting. What caused its demise?

THE DOCTRINE ON TRIAL

To a large extent the end of the Eisenhower Doctrine was implicit in its beginning. As Chapter Six indicates, it was inspired by the wrong reasons and found tremendous resistance in the Middle East. And when Washington had occasion to apply it in the Jordanian crisis of April, 1957, and the Syrian crisis of August, 1957, it won no accolades for the United States in the Arab world, though in the first instance it did strengthen King Hussein's hand in foiling a Baathist-army plot to overthrow him. If at the end of the Syrian crisis policy-makers in Washington began to question the wisdom of the Eisenhower Doctrine, they had reason to subject it to a thorough review by the spring of 1958. For Gamal Abdel Nasser and the Baath party of Syria, erstwhile source of Washington's anxieties, had negotiated a union between their countries in February and eliminated the danger of a Communist takeover in Syria. By that time, too, Abdel Nasser had become somewhat disenchanted with his trade and aid relations with the Communist states and had also shown that he was not a malleable tool of the Soviets as Mr. Dulles had feared him to be. Both developments imposed on Washington a reappraisal of its Middle Eastern policy.

The United States received its first rebuff under the Eisenhower Doctrine on the very first occasion it sought to apply it. King Hussein of Jordan, who had earlier been forced by public opinion and the left-wing government of Suleiman al-Nabulsi to declare his solidarity with the Cairo-Damascus neutralist stand, uncovered in April a plot to unseat him. With encouragements from Cairo and Damascus, the plot had been hatched by his army chief of staff and the Jordanian Baath party, and he moved in to forestall it. Alarmed by the crisis, the United States announced under the Eisenhower Doctrine that it considered the integrity of Jordan as vital to its interests and let it be known that units of the Sixth Fleet were being dispatched for maneuvers in the Eastern Mediterranean. The threat to Hussein, however, was not one of direct aggression, but of subversion and a possible coup, against which this showing of military power could have no effect. When Hussein had the situation well in hand through his own efforts, he gladly accepted economic aid offered under the Eisenhower Doctrine, but still did not dare to associate himself publicly with it. In fact, his new conservative Government made a point of announcing that they did not consider the American aid that Jordan was now receiving as coming within the scope of the doctrine. Thus, even when Hussein was desperate for American aid, he could not afford to break with the anti-doctrine nationalist front of the Arab world, which saw the Sixth Fleet maneuvers as a threatening gesture not to the Communists but to Jordan's next-door neighbor, Syria. In other words, the Arabs on the whole saw the Eisenhower Doctrine as a divisive policy, and because of this Hussein could not break ranks and declare for it.

The Syrian crisis in the fall focused attention once again, and on a wider scale, on the unrewarding aspects of the doctrine. There were several elements involved in the crisis. Relations between the Syrian government and the Iraqi government during 1957 were strained, for the Syrians felt that Nuri es-Said, taking advantage of his membership in the Baghdad Pact, was making moves to unify Syria with Iraq under his Fertile Crescent plan. And Damascus was not in the mood for a union that would append Syria to what it felt was a reactionary monarchy subservient to the West. Apprehension increased in Damascus following the Jordanian crisis in April, for it now seemed to the Syrian government that with Hussein back in the Western camp, despite his declarations to the contrary, Syria was surrounded by three hostile Arab governments, those of Lebanon, Jordan, and Iraq; and Israel pressed threateningly against one border.

But Washington saw the situation in a different light. Early in August, the Soviet government agreed to extend extensive economic aid to Syria. Washington's dismay caused resentment in Damascus, which claimed American interference in Syrian affairs and expelled officials of the American embassy. Washington retaliated by expelling the Syrian ambassador, then voiced fears of a Communist coup in Syria when a few days later pro-Soviet elements in the Syrian army gained the upper hand. President Eisenhower's special envoy, Loy Henderson, was sent on a flying trip to the Middle East to consult with Syria's neighbors, while the Sixth Fleet again visited the Eastern Mediterranean. Upon Henderson's return to Washington, Secretary Dulles announced that there was deep concern in the Middle East about the growing Communist domination of Syria, and hoped that the Communists would not drive Syria into aggression against her neighbors. At the same time Washington announced the shipment of arms to Lebanon, Jordan, Iraq, and Saudi Arabia.

Reaction to the Dulles statement from the Middle East came fast. Contradicting Mr. Henderson's finding, the governments of

Lebanon, Iraq, and Jordan promptly announced that they did not entertain any fears of Syria and did not consider her a threat to their security. The American arms were accepted but the assumptions of the Eisenhower Doctrine were rejected once again. They were rejected a third time when the Syrian affair developed into a dispute with neighboring Turkey. Soon after Mr. Henderson's visit to the Middle East at the end of August, Turkish troops began concentrating along Turkey's frontier with Syria and conducting maneuvers there. To reassure the frightened Syrians, the Russian government protested the maneuvers and sent warships to visit Syrian ports while the Egyptian government landed troops at Latakia. Secretary Dulles, on the other hand, announced his readiness to guarantee Turkey, a NATO ally, against aggression by Syria or the Soviet Union. He did not say that the United States would also protect Syria from attack. But before this war of nerves was finally extinguished in the United Nations General Assembly in October, all the Arab governments, irrespective of foreign ties and orientations, had ranged themselves alongside Syria and against Mr. Dulles' assumptions that Syria constituted a military threat to her neighbors. Lebanon, Jordan, and Iraq, like Egypt and Saudi Arabia, declared that they considered an attack on Syria as an attack on all of them. When the chips were down, Arab governments allied with the West had to follow the lead of public opinion by expressing solidarity with a sister Arab state.

That there was growing, though not yet dominant, Soviet and Communist influence within the Syrian government no one doubted. But Washington had itself to blame for its inability to do anything effective either to limit or to reverse the trend. In the first place it had excluded itself from any advisory role in Syrian affairs (as in Egyptian affairs) by assuming a rigid posture under the Eisenhower Doctrine. Syria refused to abandon its fruitful neutralist policy for a declaration against international Communism, and when Washington attempted to ostracize Syria it was left out of the counsels of Damascus. Unable to stop the flow of Soviet arms and aid into Syria, Washington continued by issuing warnings about the dangerous situation that Syria was creating in the Middle East. This only helped to increase Soviet influence in Syria, where there was a marked feeling in government circles that in order for Syria to be able to continue with her policy of positive neutralism and follow her national aspirations, American attempts to dictate policy to the Middle Eastern countries must be countered with recognition of legitimate Soviet interests there.

In following its policy of counterposing the American presence in the Middle East with that of the Soviet Union, the Syrian government had allowed Communists and Communist sympathizers within the ranks of the National Front coalition of the Nationalist and Baath parties directing its affairs. The Communist party was also free and even had a member in the Chamber of Deputies, Khaled Bakdash. All parties, however, including the Communist, which did not dare go against public sentiment, supported Arab nationalism and the objective of Arab unity. The natural candidate for the first step toward Arab unity at that time was Egypt, which shared with Syria a mutual interest in Arab nationalism and in the policy of positive neutralism. There was much discussion of unification but little action until the power struggle within Syria threatened to push the Communists and their sympathizers within the ruling coalition into a dominant position. Baathist leaders and President Shukri al-Quwatli rushed to Cairo and pleaded with President Abdel Nasser for unification of their two countries. A merger was announced on February 1, 1958, in the name of the United Arab Republic, a unitary state headed by President Abdel Nasser. All political parties were dissolved, as in Egypt, including the Communist. The threat of a Communist takeover in Syria had passed.

The threat had passed not through any positive action under the Eisenhower Doctrine, but through the joint action of President Abdel Nasser and the socialist Baath party. As the U.A.R. President continued to maintain his crackdown on domestic Communists despite his economic relations with the Communist bloc, the United States began to think of a rapprochement with Cairo. The way to a rapprochement was opened when President Abdel Nasser decided not to rely so heavily on Soviet-bloc aid and trade, the quality and type of which did not always fulfill Egyptian needs. Washington realized, however, that any improvement of relations with Cairo would have to be undertaken outside the scope of the Eisenhower Doctrine.

THE MARINE LANDING:
DIFFICULT CHOICE FOR WASHINGTON

American-Egyptian relations had begun to improve early in 1958 when the Lebanese revolution broke out in May. This event put Washington in a difficult position. On the one hand, Washington was beginning to feel its way to a new approach in its Middle East policy; on the other, it was committed through the Eisenhower Doctrine to support Lebanon against armed aggression from any country controlled by international Communism. But now the Lebanese government was claiming that Lebanon's integrity and sovereignty were being endangered not by a country controlled by international Communism but by the newly formed United Arab Republic. On May 13 Foreign Minister Charles Malik charged that Egypt and Syria were trying to destroy Lebanon both by subversion and by frontal assault. What was the United States going to do now?

Though Secretary Dulles did not wish to absolve the Communists from interference in the Lebanese crisis, he concurred in the charges the Lebanese regime was making against the U.A.R. In the week following Malik's declaration, the United States began doubling its marine forces in the Mediterranean and airlifting arms to the Lebanese government. On May 17 the United

States announced that it would consider sending troops to Lebanon if requested, and on May 20 Secretary Dulles explained at a press conference in Washington the provision of the Eisenhower Doctrine under which the United States could come to the military assistance of Lebanon if called upon:

> . . . we do not consider under the present state of affairs that there is likely to be an attack, an armed attack, from a country which we would consider under the control of international communism. That doesn't mean, however, that there is nothing that can be done. There is the provision of the Middle East Resolution which says that the independence of these countries is vital to peace and the national interest of the United States. That is certainly a mandate to do something if we think that our peace and vital interests are endangered from any quarter.[1]

The Secretary went on to say, however, that "we are not anxious to have a situation which would be in any sense a pretext for introducing American forces into the area. We hope and believe that that will not be called for." Thus, if the need should arise, the United States stood ready under the broad authorization of the Eisenhower Doctrine to use American troops to defend Lebanese independence even against a non-Communist attack, presumably one that might be launched from the Syrian border. But at the same time it hoped that a solution to the crisis would be found without the use of American forces.

Other than the dangerous international situation that it might create, it was understandable why the United States wished to avoid using American troops as a last resort. The Lebanese crisis and the revolution started by the Opposition began to appear in a new light in Washington as time went by. Though it was true that the President of the U.A.R., by press and radio propaganda, was instigating Lebanese Muslims against the Chamoun regime because of the latter's close identification with United States policy, reports from Beirut kept indicating that the quarrel between Government and Opposition leaders was essentially a domestic one. During his presidency Camille Chamoun had alienated important Muslim leaders from the sources of power, then seized upon the Eisenhower Doctrine to perpetuate himself in office at their expense. These Muslim leaders seized the opportunity to attack the policy with which Chamoun was identified partly because they themselves objected to it, but also because this was a means of getting back the powers they had been denied and which they thought were rightfully theirs. Thus the issue of foreign policy was joined with a domestic power struggle in the Lebanese revolution.

Would the United States impose by force of arms a regime rejected by at least half the people of Lebanon? Though the United States had at first indicated its approval of a second term for President Chamoun, it could not now in all conscience support it. However it was still committed to two basic propositions: (1) that President Chamoun complete his legal term in office, despite Opposition demands that he resign immediately, and that there should be an orderly transfer of power to the next President; (2) that Lebanese independence and sovereignty should be protected against any attempts to destroy them.

For the first few weeks of the Lebanese crisis Washington was subjected to conflicting counsels and reports on the causes and objectives of the revolution. The Lebanese Government was insisting that there was massive infiltration of men and arms from Syria to join the rebel side. A United Nations Observation Group sent to investigate the Lebanese charges reported no evidence of massive infiltration of arms and men from the Syrian side of the border. The Lebanese Government took exception and suggested that the U.N. observers were not carrying out their task of investigating the rebel-held border areas where infiltration was actually taking place. Though inclined to discount the "massive infiltration" charges of the Lebanese Government, the United States could not discount infiltration altogether. Independent foreign observers in Lebanon supported the view that arms and aid were reaching the rebels from Syria, though most of the smuggling had probably taken place before the arrival of the United Nations Observation Group. And Washington was also aware of the continuous U.A.R. broadcasts inciting the Lebanese against their Government, which Mr. Dulles denounced as "indirect aggression."   •

Still, since Lebanon had internationalized the conflict by taking it to the United Nations, the United States wished to give the world organization time to find a solution. The matter was now in the capable hands of U.N. Secretary General Dag Hammarskjold, who was making observations on the spot and conducting a personal diplomacy at Beirut and Cairo. So, by the end of June, the United States was assuming a wait and see policy, staying the hand of Camille Chamoun, discouraging him for the time being from requesting United States troops.

U.N. efforts to end the fighting in Lebanon and find a solution acceptable to both Opposition and loyalist factions were making progress when the Iraqi army revolt broke out on July 14. This ended the negotiations. There was rejoicing and elation in the Opposition camp, but among the loyalists there was consternation and fear both for the life of President Chamoun and for the independence of Lebanon. Suspecting that Abdel Nasser had instigated the Iraqi coup, and was possibly planning new moves against the pro-West governments of Lebanon and Jordan, the United States acted sympathetically this time to Chamoun's request for American troops. The next day, the first contingent of U.S. marines was landed in Lebanon. In a statement to the nation, President Eisenhower said that Lebanon was the victim of "indirect aggression" and that the United States was sending in the marines to help her maintain her independence and integrity. Earlier, the President had declared that the assistance was given in accordance with article 51 of the United Nations Charter, which provided for collective self-defense by U.N. members pending action by the Security Council to maintain international peace and security.² At the United Nations Security Council, Ambassador Henry Cabot Lodge called upon the world organization to recruit a military force to defend Lebanese independence against subversion and infiltration by the United Arab Republic. He said that American troops would be withdrawn as soon as the U.N. assumed their responsibilities.

Lack of information about the true state of affairs regarding the Iraqi coup d'etat brought dormant fears and suspicions back to the fore. "We learn now . . . that with the outbreak of the revolt in Iraq," Ambassador Lodge told the Security Council, "the infiltrations of arms and personnel into Lebanon from the United Arab Republic in an effort to subvert the legally constituted government have suddenly become much more alarming. This development, coupled with persistent efforts over the past months to subvert the government of Jordan must be a cause of grave concern to us all. They place in jeopardy both the independence of Lebanon and that of any Middle Eastern state which seeks to maintain its national integrity free from outside influence and pressures."³

Britain, consulted previously on the American landing, was in agreement with this action to preserve the independence and integrity of Lebanon in what it called a "very uncertain situation." It was soon to airlift its own forces to Jordan, where there existed a very real danger of a coup against the Crown. But the American action was condemned not only by the U.A.R. government and the Soviet Union, but also by neutralist governments, by Sweden, and in the press of the West. Realizing that a risk of a major war was involved in its decision, the United States had taken its case to the United Nations to explain its good intentions, to insist on the legality of its action, to stall for time so that more marines could be rushed to the scene unhindered, and to lay the case before the world organization so that extended debate would in itself reduce the risk of a major war.

But the risk was inherent in the American landing, and although not a shot was fired, there were a few anxious hours when it was feared that the Lebanese army might engage the Americans in fighting and possibly spark a wider conflict. For the Lebanese troops, personally loyal to their commander, General Fuad Chehab, and not to President Chamoun, were inclined at first to consider the landing as a foreign intervention which they were honor bound to resist and repel. It was only through the resourcefulness and ingenuity of American Ambassador Robert McClintock and the good will and prestige of General Chehab that a clash was averted. Before the marine column made its entry into Beirut, it was broken up and interspersed with Lebanese jeeps; then the whole procession advanced with the Ambassador and General together in the lead. The Lebanese troops withheld their fire.[4]

Fortunately, too, no attempts were made by the marines to penetrate rebel strongholds; on instructions from their leaders, the rebels also wisely refrained from attacking the marines. Since neither a coup d'etat nor the much feared onslaught from the Syrian border materialized, the American troops, which in a few days were to increase to some 15,000 men, settled down to guard and patrol duties. It was time for American diplomacy to take over.

LOOKING BACK AND LOOKING AHEAD

As the United Nations struggled with proposals and counterproposals to make possible the replacement of American troops by an expanded U.N. observation force, there arrived in Beirut, almost on the heels of the American landing, Under Secretary of State Robert D. Murphy, President Eisenhower's special troubleshooter. Murphy made it clear that the United States considered this to be a Lebanese crisis and that it had no candidate for the presidency and would not intervene in the election. His mediation between Government and Opposition factions, however, helped the Lebanese to arrive at an acceptable compromise and the election by parliament on July 31 of General Fuad Chehab as the new President to succeed Mr. Chamoun on September 23. By this act of mediation, the United States finally came around to accept fully the fact of Arab neutrality and nonalignment. For out of the crisis that Mr. Murphy helped mediate, there emerged a new regime which, though friendly to the United States, repudiated the Eisenhower Doctrine and declared for a policy of neutralism.

The short but agonizing history of the Eisenhower Doctrine suggests its own conclusions. First, the implementation of the policy's most extreme provision, the use of American troops in Lebanon, was an indictment of the whole policy. The policy had failed to create the conditions which would have made it unnecessary to invoke the extreme provision. In fact, the policy itself became such a controversial issue in Lebanese domestic politics that it complicated the more elemental power struggle and made more difficult the reestablishment of the balance of communal interests within the governing institutions that is so essential to Lebanon's well-being.

As it divided Lebanon against herself, the doctrine divided Lebanon against her neighbors. The United States was sincerely interested in the maintenance of Lebanon's independence and integrity. It offered her a guarantee, a political alignment which, however, put her in the Western camp alongside the government of Iraq but in opposition to Egypt and Syria. It was a game that endangered Lebanon's traditional neutrality among the Arab states and earned her the hostility of the hinterland. But Lebanon must have good relations with all her Arab neighbors to maintain her independence and integrity, as well as her very vital commercial role as gateway to the interior. By the same token, the United States could not benefit from the friendship of Lebanon if all around the Arabs were uniformly hostile.

On the international plane, the great risk that the United States was taking of starting a major war with its armed intervention brought it face to face with a reality that it had refused to face when it formulated the Eisenhower Doctrine: the Middle East was not a closed area, was not the backyard of any one power. It had become an open area when Britain lost her firm hold and the Soviet Union extended her influence through the sale of arms to the Arab countries and the support of the Arab cause in international politics. With this came the realization that the Arabs no more wanted Soviet domination than they wanted British, French, or American domination. They sincerely wanted a neutralist policy through which they could trade and work with all comers. That Syrian and Egyptian positive neutralism seemed to work in favor of the Soviet bloc was due largely to United States refusal to have anything to do with that neutralism. The United States reaped no rewards from its negative approach.

On the regional level the doctrine policy also failed in its attempt to isolate the "suspect" governments of Egypt and Syria from the rest of the Arab world. It failed because in Lebanon, Iraq, and Jordan—whose regimes were acceptable to the United States—there was tremendous public sympathy and identification with Syria and Egypt. The United States had overlooked the fact that Arab nationalism, though often parochial, closes ranks and transcends national boundaries when it feels it is threatened by an outside danger. Furthermore, when the chips were down, U.S. policy was bound to disappoint its Arab friends because it had identified them too closely with its own interests, as it had done in the case of Lebanon. Lebanese supporters of the Eisenhower Doctrine felt bitter and angry when American mediation after the marine landing did not reward their hitherto pro-West stand but helped bring into power men dedicated to a policy of nonalignment. In his memoirs,[5] former President Camille Cha-

moun expresses bewilderment and dismay about what appeared
to him was America's about-face in the midst of carrying out her
commitment under the Eisenhower Doctrine.

Though it appeared perfidious to some at the time, the American role of mediating the crisis turned out to be in the best interests of both the United States and Lebanon. Having taken the
risk of landing the marines, and having assured the security of
the legal government, the United States needed to show while
its forces were still there that its intentions were good and
proper. It acted as an impartial mediator and thus took the first
step to redeem itself in the eyes of the Arab nationalists. It was
a bid for accommodation with the Arab world. At the same
time, by its impartiality, it indicated that it was releasing Lebanon from the tight embrace that had estranged her from some
of her sister states. Lebanon would not be suspect, now that she
had retrieved her independent identity. She was free from the
tug of war between Washington and Cairo, and could now be
more useful as a friend and as a neighbor. And this also suited
her own interests best.

With the termination of the Lebanese revolution, the United
States seriously launched on a policy that it should have embarked on at the close of the Suez Canal war: accommodation
with Arab nationalism and its concomitant attitude of positive
neutralism. Putting aside the Eisenhower Doctrine, and leaving
behind all thoughts about military or political pacts, it probed
into the possibility of making positive neutralism also work for
American interests in the Middle East, which essentially were
the same as Arab interests: peace and stability, free trade, keeping open the area's land, sea, and air routes between Asia, Africa,
and Europe, keeping the oil flowing to the West, and of course
keeping national governments free from foreign domination. The
new approach implicitly recognized the right of all nations, including the Soviets, to pursue their trade with the area, and it
put aside all thought of pitting one Arab nation against another

or trying to isolate any one of them from the Arab family. American policy would hence employ a quiet diplomacy, a flexible diplomacy, approaching each country individually, trying to build those links of mutuality which in the end are much more durable than formal alliances that do not serve mutual interests. With its new freedom, the United States found that it could also address itself patiently and quietly—though perhaps it must do so for a long time to come—to the difficult task of finding a peaceful solution to the Palestine problem. For as had been repeatedly pointed out and as the United States realized at the end of the Lebanese crisis, genuine peace and stability could not be brought to the Arab world as long as the Palestine question remained unsolved.

The failure of the Eisenhower Doctrine emphasized another home truth—that stability within nations, as among nations, can be maintained only when the avenues are open for the expression and balancing of justified interests. In the now free and open marketplace of the Arab world, the United States has much more to gain than the Soviet Union. For though the Arabs are still rebelling against what they deem to be the injustices of the West, they are by culture, economic interests, and beliefs oriented toward the West.

CHAPTER 10

Political Power and Authority in Lebanon

This study was undertaken primarily to find the causes of the 1958 crisis and revolution in Lebanon, as well as the reasons behind the conflicting contentions of the two opposing political camps involved. At that time, the regime of Camille Chamoun complained of "massive intervention" in Lebanon's domestic affairs by the United Arab Republic, claiming that Lebanon was in danger of being absorbed by the U.A.R. The United National Opposition Front maintained that the issues between it and the regime were entirely domestic and that the U.A.R. had nothing to do with them. The Front declared that its purpose was to obtain the immediate resignation of President Chamoun and to put an end to the "deviationist" foreign policy that he was following.

Charges and countercharges revealed that the 1958 conflict was not merely a superficial quarrel of the moment between two rival political cliques. Personal interests of rival politicians were very much involved, but these were grafted on and received sustenance from the traditional fears and apprehensions of the now divided population. Thus a historical study was indicated; its object was to trace the origins and development of the controlling factors in present-day Lebanese politics. These, it appeared, have been both internal and external.

EVOLUTION OF THE STATE AND OF
ITS POWER STRUCTURE—THE HIGHLIGHTS

In the nineteenth century, external pressures and influences resulted successively in the curtailment of Lebanese autonomy, the division of Mount Lebanon into two governorates and the loss of its coastal holdings, then in the reunification of the Mountain and the restoration of its full autonomy under international guarantees. But this last step was possible only because the autonomous state remained small and consisted mainly of Maronites and Druze. Under such conditions it enjoyed fifty years of relative peace, but limited prosperity.

In the twentieth century, the situation changed again. An enlarged state under French mandate was subjected to an internal-external irredentism and was held together only through the presence of the mandatory. It achieved its independence and continued to be viable only as a result of a timely compromise between the state's Christian and Muslim communities. But some fifteen years later, the undue influence of external pressures on domestic politics threatened the confessional balance within the state, a balance which was the bedrock of Lebanese viability and independence.

The tragedy of 1958 was caused by a disregard for the lessons that have been repeated throughout Lebanon's long history because of the inescapable realities of its geography and topography. For our purpose, however, it is sufficient to note that from the 1830's on Lebanon's geographical position led to an invasion from the south (by Mohammed Ali's Egyptian army), to interference from the west (by the European powers), and later to irredentist agitation from the east (the Syrian hinterland). The country's topography had another effect. Its high peaks and deep valleys, which were difficult to negotiate, made it for centuries the refuge of Christian and Muslim heretic sects and thus determined its social composition. Feudally organized for self-preservation, these religious communities kept their autonomy so long as they cooperated in common defense and so long as their feudal lords maintained their neutrality in regional politics. Feudalism was then the mainstay of Lebanese autonomy.

It was Emir Bechir II, princely ruler of the mountain ranges, who inadvertently invited the destruction of Lebanon's feudal institutions and the consequent undermining of its autonomy when in the 1830's he collaborated with Mohammed Ali of Egypt against his Ottoman suzerain. The withdrawal of Egyptian authority from Lebanon in 1840 brought in its wake the active interference of European powers on behalf of various religious communities, as well as attempts by the Sublime Porte to coerce the population into accepting direct Ottoman rule. Thus between the 1840's and the 1860's the feudal institutions of the past were dealt a heavy blow and a new element was introduced from the outside into Lebanese politics: confessionalism. This new system of government was first consecrated in the 1840's, when Mount Lebanon was divided into a Druze governorate and a Christian governorate and representation in the political institutions of each was put on a sectarian basis. Confessionalism was established on a firmer foundation by the statutes of 1861 and 1864, the organic law of the *Mutasarrifyya* regime, which lasted until the outbreak of World War I.

The institutionalization of confessionalism in the autonomous state of Mount Lebanon gave the people the opportunity to familiarize themselves with representative government, but at the same time limited the competition of economic and social interests to a sectarian framework. Emerging to take advantage of confessionalism were two important socio-political groups, the clergy and the feudal lords. The former used the system to cash in on the advantages they had gained as champions of the peasantry during the twenty years of social revolution that preceded the 1860's; the latter seized upon it to revive their political power and to protect their class interests. To the people, the system was a guarantee against a repetition of the upheavals and massacres of the recent past, but at the same time it was a reminder of this past.

It was inevitable that political feudalism and sectarian antagonism should continue to flourish in mandated Lebanon, for the mandatory power had established the new government on a confessional basis. Furthermore, both political feudalism and sectarian antagonism were now stronger than before because of the establishment in 1920 of Greater Lebanon. This arrangement attached to the mountainous core, populated mainly by Maronites and Druze, areas inhabited largely by people who were unwilling to belong to the new state. It also reduced the Maronite community from a dominant majority to one-third of the whole population and introduced as its major rival the Sunni community, which was now the second largest. The Sunnis' most cherished hope was union with Syria, an aspiration that ran counter to the Maronites' determination to maintain the status quo. Sharing the Sunnis' hope, but with less determination and more fluctuation, were smaller numbers of the newly included Shi'is of the Biqa' and of the south.

In an effort to reconcile both these communities to the existence of Lebanon within its enlarged borders, a system was gradually evolved whereby the premiership became the right of the Sunni community and the presidency of the Chamber the right of the Shi'i community. The presidency of the Republic became the prerogative of the Maronites not only because they were the largest community, but also because they were thus reassured that a Maronite President would use his powers to safeguard the independence of Lebanon within its existing boundaries. This arrangement for the top three offices of the state was consecrated by the National Pact of 1943, which spelled out the conditions for the common achievement and maintenance of

Lebanese independence as well as for the assurance of a Christian-Muslim balance of power within the governing institutions of the state.

In the postindependence period political feudalism continued to operate through the confessional institutions of the state. But the system was democratic nonetheless because it assured representation for all the sects, none of which was a majority in itself, although the Christians and Muslims were about equal in numbers. There was, however, one aspect of government that was undemocratic: under the constitution, the President of the Republic was endowed with vast powers which were subject to only limited controls by either the Chamber or the Cabinet. Other than the amendments introduced in 1943 in conformity with Lebanon's new status as an independent nation, and a few more amendments in 1947, the constitution was the same one that was adopted in 1926 and revised in 1927 and 1929 under the watchful eye of the mandatory power. Although France was charged with preparing the country for self-government and eventual independence, it had sought the mandate as a guise for establishing its influence in Lebanon and maintaining its control over it indefinitely. The best way this could be done was through the constitution, and so, when that instrument came to be written, France saw to it that the executive was made much stronger than the legislature, and that all the important powers were vested in the President. For it was easier to control the actions of one man than the actions of many. All the High Commissioner had to do, since he alone enjoyed greater power than the President, was to direct the latter according to the interests of the mandatory. But when Lebanon became independent and struck out all constitutional references to the mandatory, the powers of the President remained unchecked with one exception: since all the seats in the Chamber of Deputies became elective, he could no longer make a certain number of appointments to the legislature as in previous years.

THE PRESIDENT'S CONSTITUTIONAL POWERS

In independent Lebanon, the President of the Republic has continued to hold the following constitutional powers:

1. He appoints ministers and can also dismiss them at will. Although the ministers are also jointly and individually responsible to the Chamber of Deputies and must receive its vote of confidence to remain in office, to date Cabinets have not failed to obtain this vote because they are generally representative of the majority interests within the legislature. Usually, when the Chamber wishes to express disapproval of a minister, it does so before a Cabinet is formed. It is thus the President who has the final say about how long a Cabinet is to remain in office.

But it is the threat of removal rather than the actual exercise of the dismissal power that keeps the President's Cabinet in line with his policies. In fact, the presidential right of dismissal was exercised only once during the constitutional history of Lebanon,[1] but because it exists the President exerts considerable influence on the composition of the Cabinet and later on its attitude. Thus a Premier who finds himself unable to follow the policy of the President is forced to resign. It was Sami es-Solh, long-time Premier under the Chamoun regime, who aptly pointed out that whereas the Chief of State remains in office for six years, the Prime Minister can legally be removed from office after he has occupied it for as little as twenty-four hours.[2]

Furthermore, as head of the executive branch of the government, it is the President and not the Prime Minister who presides at Cabinet meetings, and thus determines the climate of its debates. But it is the Premier who must shoulder the responsibility of Government action.

It has been argued that the President is not altogether powerful as far as the Cabinet is concerned. For, it is pointed out, legislative programs and acts initiated by the President—other than the appointment of Cabinet members and their indirect dismissal through forced resignation—must be countersigned by the minister or ministers concerned.

It remains true, however, that the power of dismissal that the President holds over the Cabinet is an important factor in obtaining the cooperation of recalcitrant ministers who nevertheless wish to remain in office.

A second argument claims that the tradition of selecting a Prime Minister from among the Sunni deputies gives their community authority to exercise some restraint on the presidential powers. For, it is stated, the President must be on good terms with the Sunni community so that one of its deputies could accept his invitation to form a Cabinet. This statement is true enough, and perhaps it was best proved by a situation that was the exception to the rule. It was during the 1958 crisis that the Sunni community, angered by President Chamoun's policies, urged his Prime Minister, Sami es-Solh, to resign because it knew that no other Sunni politician would be willing to replace him, and it could thus force the President's own resignation. But es-Solh resisted his community's pressures, and was duly censured and renounced by it and by its religious leaders. He remained in power as an unaccepted "representative" of his community, and thus enabled the President to complete his legal term in office.

2. Constitutionally, the President, with the approval of the Cabinet, can dissolve the Chamber of Deputies before the legal expiration of its mandate. In practice, however, "approval of the Cabinet" becomes meaningless in view of the President's legal power to dismiss ministers. Furthermore, without the necessity of Cabinet approval, he can adjourn the Chamber for one month or less, but not more than once during the same session.

3. An important constitutional amendment of 1927 empowers the President to issue a decree, with the approval of the Cabinet, to bring into operation any bill which had been submitted to the

Chamber as an "urgent bill" but on which the legislature had not acted within forty days of its receipt. In practice, the amendment endows the President with the power to execute the budget and carry out projects still unapproved by the Chamber.

4. Another constitutional amendment of 1927 gives the President the opportunity to try to defeat a new bill he does not like. Within the time he is allowed to promulgate a law, he may request, but not more than once, for a further discussion of the law, and the Chamber may not refuse him. Adoption of the law a second time by an absolute majority of the Chamber, meeting in plenary session, is necessary before the President is required to promulgate it.

5. The President is constitutionally empowered to negotiate treaties. But he is also authorized to ratify them, and given the prerogative of bringing them to the knowledge of the Chamber "as soon as the interest and safety of the State permit." The Chamber, however, retains the right to indicate, by adoption or rejection, as either binding or not binding on the state treaties involving financial commitments by Lebanon, commercial treaties, and in general treaties which cannot be renounced at the end of a year.

6. Finally, the President has the power of pardon, which is enjoyed by all heads of state, and the right to make all appointments which have not been determined by law.

There appears to be a certain gray area between the respective powers of the President and of the Chamber of Deputies with regard to one question of vital interest to the nation: which of the two has final authority over a request for foreign military aid? The constitution is silent on the subject, but it became a matter for hot debate when American troops were landed in Lebanon on July 15, 1958, at the request of President Chamoun. Assuming the right to act unilaterally, the President told the nation at the time that he had invoked article 51 of the United Nations Charter[3] only after the Arab League and the U.N. observers had failed to put a stop to U.A.R. interference. He later explained that he had acted within his constitutional rights when he called for American military aid, for this was a responsibility of the legal government, that is, the executive branch, with no authorization from the Chamber of Deputies necessary.[4]

A contrary view was held by spokesmen for the United National Opposition Front and by Muslim religious leaders, all of whom termed the American landing a violation of Lebanese sovereignty. Their view was shared by Adel Osseiran, president of the Chamber, and theretofore a warm supporter of President Chamoun. Protesting the landing of the American troops to the United States and to the United Nations, Osseiran stated that the only authority representing the Lebanese people was the Chamber of Deputies.[5] He later claimed that the President should have first secured the Chamber's approval before requesting the troops, for it was within the Chamber's legal right to authorize requests for foreign military aid.[6]

Be that as it may, the President did secure on his own initiative the landing of American troops for a nation that was divided about equally for and against his action.

THE PRESIDENCY: AN OFFICE OF VAST INFLUENCE

Existing side by side with Lebanon's democratic tradition is another which had preceded it and had managed to survive even as the country was building its representative institutions. It is the tradition of the strong ruler. In predemocratic days, Emir Bechir II played off the lesser feudal lords against each other and thus managed to concentrate more power in his own hands. Later, during the *Mutasarrifyya* regime, successive Governors General augmented their vast executive powers at the expense of the confessionalized and divided Central Council. Some of them exercised strong pressure on the voters to obtain the election of their own partisans to the Council. Others arbitrarily pursued their political adversaries before the courts and pressured the judges into passing judgment against them.[7]

Occupying the most prestigious office in the nation, the President of the Republic who is so inclined can similarly, but with greater finesse, use his vast constitutional and administrative powers to help his friends and confound his enemies. In fact, because of his commanding position, he can exploit more than any other politician Lebanon's system of confessional representation to make of his office a center of special privilege and power. The presidencies of both Bishara el-Khouri and Camille Chamoun are reported to have been strongholds of privilege and power. President el-Khouri is said to have allowed his friends and relatives to use the machinery of the state for personal advantage and enrichment. And during his first term in office there was a great deal of corruption, traffic in influence, interference with the courts, and irregular dealings by both the administration and its friends.[8] Still, this state of affairs did not at first arouse sufficient public indignation to prevent the Chamber of Deputies in 1948 from amending the constitution to allow el-Khouri to succeed himself for a second term. But by 1952 the nation was too angry at all the corruption to allow the regime to continue in power. Thus in September a four-day general strike was declared in Beirut and other cities which forced the President to resign.

Chamoun's conduct in office was somewhat different. The President, it appears, started out on a policy of gradually excluding the important politicians from the sources of executive power, and from their previous role of informal advisers to the presidency on matters of policy.[9] Seized with the desire to break the back of political feudalism, which flourished during the el-Khouri regime, he further took advantage of the decree powers granted him by the Chamber in 1952 to push through electoral reforms calculated to curtail the power of the feudal lords over the elections by reducing the size of the constituencies and therefore also the size of the tickets they could control. At the same time, he decreed that the size of the Chamber be reduced by 33 members. The new legislature elected in July, 1953, consisted of only 44 members, and was the smallest one the country had had since independence. Then, using his influence over the Chamber, Chamoun also managed to exclude from the presidency of that body two of its former occupants, Shi'i feudal lords Sabri Hamade and Ahmad al-Asaad. Instead he secured the repeated election to that office of a man he favored, Adel Osseiran.

In 1957 the Chamoun regime secured the adoption by the Chamber of 44 of an electoral law which the supporters of the President later claimed was intended to reduce the influence of the mountain lords and city *za'ims* within the legislature, and to bring in more democratic elements. But those who lost the elections that summer, and those who won but were still frustrated in their ambitions, concluded that the purpose of the law had been both to limit the size of the Chamber to 66 deputies (instead of 88) and to fill it with a majority of loyalists who would ensure Chamoun's election to a second term and assure the continuation of what was now in effect his one-man rule.

That President Chamoun should aspire to a second term and then have a predominantly loyalist Chamber amend the constitution to grant him his wish was nothing new. It had been done before by Bishara el-Khouri. But the postelection situation in 1957 was markedly different from the situation in 1949, when el-Khouri was returned to office. In 1949 the prominent politicians were not excluded from the sources of power, nor was Lebanese foreign policy an issue of domestic politics. In 1957 both these conditions obtained. By then Chamoun had made too many enemies, both political and personal, had concentrated too much power in his own hands, and was preparing to maintain the status quo for another six years. Furthermore, by accepting the Eisenhower Doctrine, he had launched the country on a foreign policy that was not acceptable to the majority of Muslims, who constituted about half the population, and whose real spokesmen came to be the small Opposition minority in parliament as well as those very *za'ims* and feudal leaders who were excluded from the Chamber by the 1957 elections. By not discouraging his supporters in the legislature from making preparations for his reelection, even though he had not publicly declared for it, Chamoun gave the impression that he was planning to continue to deny the Muslim community an accommodation on foreign policy. For the men who felt they had been frustrated by him in their business or political affairs, he created the fear of an impending catastrophe.

How much must have been at stake for the President's personal and political adversaries was indicated by an observer writing at the beginning of the 1958 revolution:

> The President of the Republic has vast powers, which he uses to run the country; but he also uses them like all chiefs of feudal communities to favor his supporters, to help them find public employment and to help them in some way to succeed in their work and affairs.
>
> The adversaries founder, but they accept this manifest abuse of power in the hope that the next President will allow them to recuperate their losses and actually to make some gains. To renew the presidential mandate would be cheating at the game; this would cause the adversaries irreparable losses, both in money and influence, and would destroy all hope for redress.
>
> Conversely, the President in power is irresistibly tempted to have his mandate renewed so that there would be enough of a delay to assure the definite success of his clientele and the ruination of his adversaries.[10]

But the President's opponents of 1957–1958 were not willing to experience personal disaster. Many of them, too, viewed with apprehension his favoritism toward the Hashemites against the Cairo-Damascus camp, as well as his identification with American policy when that policy aimed at isolating Egypt and Syria from the Arab world unless they abandoned positive neutralism. Since the situation could not be rectified legally, and since it appeared by the spring of 1958 that the President's friends in parliament were about to put through the dreaded constitutional amendment that would allow him to succeed himself, his opponents decided then and there to settle the matter by force. And by now, they were in a position to use force. Many of them had their own armed partisans. There was also a call to arms among Muslims as well as assistance from Syrian volunteers. But not least of the opponents' assets was the general mood of the Muslim community. For months many of them had addressed it on the deviationism of the Chamoun regime and it had listened willingly, for it was already excited by Gamal Abdel Nasser's achievements for Arab unity, and many of its members now hoped for union with the U.A.R.

This mood made the Muslim community hostile to the Chamoun regime. But it also struck fear in the hearts of the Christian community. Not only that, but acts of violence within the country, implicating at times Egyptian and Syrian nationals, the general state of restlessness, the high-geared Egyptian and Syrian propaganda for Arab unification and against "imperialist alliances" (the Baghdad Pact and the Eisenhower Doctrine), all combined to give the Christians the impression that Lebanese sovereignty and independence were in danger. With much encouragement from the regime, a great many of them saw in President Chamoun the man of the hour: he must be kept at the helm of the state to safeguard its independence. They also looked to the Eisenhower Doctrine as a continued guarantee of Lebanese sovereignty.

Thus by the time the revolution broke out in May, the struggle for power between Chamoun and his opponents had merged into the larger issue of Lebanon's direction and future. In retrospect, this appears to have been inevitable. For in alienating those termed "feudal lords" and "*za'ims*" from the sources of power, the President was in fact unbalancing the Christian-Muslim equilibrium within the organs of the state because these leaders represented the interests of the majority of the Muslim population. In fact he helped to establish a closer identification between Muslim leaders and followers by subscribing to the Eisenhower Doctrine, which was directed against Egypt and Syria. Not only was it necessary for these leaders to get back into power for personal reasons, but also in the interest of re-establishing the internal balance of power so that they could also reestablish the external balance—return Lebanon to its neutrality in Arab politics. Other politicians who had also been antagonized by Chamoun, but were not so concerned over these matters, joined in the general resistance.

That the regime itself had a genuine cause for concern cannot be denied. After the Suez Canal crisis there was indeed much talk of Arab unity by Gamal Abdel Nasser, which moved many Muslims within Lebanon. For the regime, this should have been a time for binding the nation together, as wise Maronite leadership had attempted to do in the twenties and thirties when the Arab nationalist spirit was also at a peak. It should have been a time, in fact, to observe closely the spirit and the terms of the National Pact of 1943: neutrality in Arab affairs, a sectarian balance within the state. Instead, the regime proceeded to upset the sectarian balance and to abandon its neutrality. Then it sought to perpetuate both conditions through another term for the President. It was called to a halt before this could happen, but it did manage to alienate the Muslim community and to contribute by its actions and pronouncements to the growth of their Arab nationalist zeal.

The settlement of the 1958 crisis reestablished the balance of power between Christians and Muslims and recommitted Lebanon to her traditional neutrality among her Arab neighbors. It also disassociated Lebanon from the Eisenhower Doctrine and from its divisive influences on the Arab Middle East. By then, of course, the United States had also decided to abandon the doctrine.

Thus it was proved in 1958 as in 1943 that only by compromise and moderation, as represented in the National Pact, could Lebanon's disparate aspirations find accommodation within her sovereign borders. Without compromise and moderation on the part of both Christians and Muslims, each community must contemplate a frightening alternative to Lebanese viability. To the Christians it is the possibility that nonaccommodation with the Muslims might precipitate the absorption of Lebanon by the Syrian hinterland and the consequent loss of their rights and identity. Yet to the Muslims—of both Syria and Lebanon—unification would not be an unmixed blessing, for it would leave in their midst a large dissatisfied Christian minority that would become a source of constant trouble. But the really unacceptable alternative to Lebanese viability to the Muslims is the possibility that nonaccommodation with the Christians might lead to the partition of the country and the establishment in the midst of the Arab heartland of a *Mutasarrifyya*-type Christian state protected by the arms of the West, and used as a base for foreign interference in the affairs of the Arab world.

A viable Lebanon, therefore, is in the best interests of both Lebanon and her Arab neighbors. What she now needs is continued prosperity as well as genuine economic and social progress for all sectors of her population—all of which should help to turn gradually the disparate aspirations of her people into a common nationalist spirit.

APPENDIX

The Eisenhower Doctrine

JOINT RESOLUTION
TO PROMOTE PEACE AND STABILITY IN THE MIDDLE EAST

Resolved by the Senate and House of Representatives of the United States of America in Congress assembled, That the President be and hereby is authorized to cooperate with and assist any nation or group of nations in the general area of the Middle East desiring such assistance in the development of economic strength dedicated to the maintenance of national independence.

Sec. 2. The President is authorized to undertake, in the general area of the Middle East, military assistance programs with any nation or group of nations of that area desiring such assistance. Furthermore, the United States regards as vital to the national interest and world peace the preservation of the independence and integrity of the nations of the Middle East. To this end, if the President determines the necessity thereof, the United States is prepared to use armed forces to assist any nation or group of such nations requesting assistance against armed aggression from any country controlled by international communism: *Provided,* That such employment shall be consonant with the treaty obligations of the United States and with the Constitution of the United States.

Sec. 3. The President is hereby authorized to use during the balance of fiscal year 1957 for economic and military assistance under this joint resolution not to exceed $200,000,000 from any appropria-

H. J. Res. 117, March 9, 1957, from *United States Policy in the Middle East,* September 1956–June 1957, Department of State Publication 6505, Near and Middle Eastern Series 25, U.S. Government Printing Office, Washington, 1957, pp. 44–47.

tion now available for carrying out the provisions of the Mutual Security Act of 1954, as amended, in accord with the provisions of such Act: *Provided,* That, whenever the President determines it to be important to the security of the United States, such use may be under the authority of section 401 (a) of the Mutual Security Act of 1954, as amended (except that provisions of section 105 (a) thereof shall be waived), and without regard to the provisions of section 105 of the Mutual Security Appropriation Act, 1957: *Provided further,* That obligations incurred in carrying out the purpose of the first sentence of section 2 of this joint resolution shall be paid only out of appropriations for military assistance, and obligations incurred in carrying out the purposes of the first section of this joint resolution shall be paid only out of appropriations other than those for military assistance. This authorization is in addition to other existing authorizations with respect to the use of such appropriations. None of the additional authorization contained in this section shall be used until fifteen days after the Committee on Foreign Relations of the Senate, the Committee on Foreign Affairs of the House of Representatives, the Committees on Appropriations of the Senate and the House of Representatives and, when military assistance is involved, the Committees on Armed Services of the Senate and the House of Representatives have been furnished a report showing the object of the proposed use, the country for the benefit of which such use is intended, and the particular appropriation or appropriations for carrying out the provisions of the Mutual Security Act of 1954, as amended, from which the funds are proposed to be derived: *Provided,* That funds available under this section during the balance of fiscal year 1957 shall, in the case of any such report submitted during the last fifteen days of the fiscal year, remain available for use under this section for the purposes stated in such report for a period of twenty days following the date of submission of such report. Nothing contained in this joint resolution shall be construed as itself authorizing the appropriation of additional funds for the purpose of carrying out the provisions of the first section or of the first sentence of section 2 of this joint resolution.

Sec. 4. The President should continue to furnish facilities and military assistance, within the provisions of applicable law and established policies, to the United Nations Emergency Force in the Middle East, with a view to maintaining the truce in that region.

Sec. 5. The President shall within the months of January and July of each year report to the Congress his action hereunder.

Sec. 6. This joint resolution shall expire when the President shall determine that the peace and security of the nations in the general area of the Middle East are reasonably assured by international conditions created by action of the United Nations or otherwise except that it may be terminated earlier by a concurrent resolution of the two Houses of Congress.

Approved March 9, 1957

SELECT BIBLIOGRAPHY

Arabic Books

Titles marked ⁰ deal with the interpretations of various groups and individuals within Lebanon of the crisis of 1958, or with their recommendations for Lebanon's political future.

⁰Ammoun, Fuad. *Siyasat Lubnan al-kharijiya (Lebanon's Foreign Policy)*. Beirut: Dar an-nashr al-'arabiya, 1959.

Chamoun, Camille. *Marahil al-istiqlal (Stages of the Independence)*. Beirut: Maktabat Sader, 1949.

al-Hassan, Hassan. *al-Qanun ad-dusturi wad-dustur fi Lubnan (Constitutional Law and the Constitution in Lebanon)*. Beirut: Dar maktabat *al-Hayat*, 1959.

⁰al-Jisr, Basim. *Nahwa Lubnan jadid (Toward a New Lebanon)*. Beirut: al-Maktab at-tijari, 1959.

⁰Junblatt, Kamal. *Haqiqat ath-thawra al-lubnaniya (The Truth about the Lebanese Revolution)*. Beirut: Dar an-nashr al-'arabiya, 1959.

⁰Karame, Nadia and Nawwaf. *Waqi' ath-thawra al-lubnaniya (The Facts of the Lebanese Revolution)*. Beirut: Matba'at Karam, 1959.

el-Khouri, Bishara. *Haqa'iq lubnaniya (Lebanese Realities)*. (Memoirs of Bishara el-Khouri.) Beirut: Manshurat awraq lubnaniya, Part I, 1960.

⁰Majzoub, Mohammad, and Ma'rouf Saad. *'Indima qawamna (When We Resisted)*. Beirut: Dar al-'ilm lil-malayin, 1959.

Mokdessi, Toufic, and Lucien George. *Al-ahzab as-siyasiya fi Lubnan 'am 1959 (Political Parties in Lebanon in 1959)*. Beirut: al-Jarida and L'Orient Publications, 1959. (Information on the parties also appears in the same volume in French.)

⁰Mughaizal, Joseph. *Lubnan wal-qadiyya al-'arabiya (Lebanon and the Arab Question)*. Beirut: Manshurat 'Oueidat, 1959.

⁰Nijm, Antoun. *al-Wihda al-lubnaniya (Lebanese Unity)*. Beirut: Matba'at al-jihad, 1960.

ar-Riachi, Iskandar. *Qabl wa-ba'd (Before and After)*. (Memoirs of journalist ar-Riachi, 1918–1941.) Beirut: Maktabat al-'urfan, 1955.

Sayegh, Anis. *Lubnan at-ta'ifi (Sectarian Lebanon)*. Beirut: Dar assira' al-fikri, 1955.

Takieddine, Munir. *Wiladat istiqlal (Birth of Independence)*. Beirut: Dar al-'ilm lil-malayin, 1953.

Wahba, Tewfiq. *Lubnan fi haba'il as-siyasa (Lebanon in the Field of Politics)*. Beirut: Matabi' ad-dunia, 1953.

*az-Zaila', Na'im. *Chamoun yatakallam (Chamoun Speaks)*. Beirut: Matba'at al-jihad, n.d. (The book appeared on the Beirut market toward the end of 1959.)

English Books

ON LEBANON AND THE ARAB WORLD IN GENERAL

Antonius, George. *The Arab Awakening*. London: Hamish Hamilton, 1945.

Faris, Nabih Amin, and Mohammad Tewfik Husayn. *The Crescent in Crisis*. Lawrence: University of Kansas Press, 1955.

Grassmuck, George, and Kamal Salibi. *A Manual of Lebanese Administration*. Beirut: Public Administration Dept., American University of Beirut, 1955.

Hitti, Philip K. *Lebanon in History*. London and New York: Macmillan, 1957.

Hourani, Albert H. *Minorities in the Arab World*. London: Oxford University Press, 1946.

———. *Syria and Lebanon*. London: Oxford University Press, updated 3rd impression, 1954.

Kerr, Malcolm H. *Lebanon in the Last Years of Feudalism, 1840–1868:* "A Contemporary Account by Antun Dahir al-'Aqiqi and other Documents," translated with notes and commentary by Kerr. Beirut: American University, Faculty of Arts and Sciences, Oriental Series No. 33, 1959.

Longrigg, Stephen Hemsley. *Syria and Lebanon under French Mandate*. London: Oxford University Press, 1958.

Scheltema, J. F. *The Lebanon in Turmoil: Syria and the Powers in 1860.* "Book of the Marvels of the Time Concerning the Massacres in the Arab Country by Iskander Ibn Ya'qub Abkarius," translated with annotation and commentary by Scheltema. New Haven: Yale University Press, Yale Oriental Series, Vol. VII, 1920.

Smith, Wilfred Cantwell. *Islam in Modern History*. Princeton: Princeton University Press, 1957.

Zeine, Zeine N. *Arab-Turkish Relations and the Emergence of Arab Nationalism*. Beirut: Khayat's, 1958.

Ziadeh, Nicola A. *Syria and Lebanon*. London: Ernest Benn, 1957.

ON THE EISENHOWER DOCTRINE, AND ON REGIONAL AND INTER-
NATIONAL EVENTS AFFECTING THE LEBANESE CRISIS OF 1958

Banerji, *The Middle East in World Politics*. Calcutta: World Press
Private, 1960.
Beal, John Robinson. *John Foster Dulles:1888–1959*. New York: Har-
per, 1959 updated ed.
Council on Foreign Relations. *The United States in World Affairs,
1957*. Compiled by Richard P. Stebbins et al. New York: Harper,
1958.
————. *The United States in World Affairs, 1958*. Compiled by
Richard P. Stebbins et al. New York: Harper, 1959.
Drummond, Roscoe, and Gaston Coblentz. *Duel at the Brink: John
Foster Dulles' Command of American Power*. Garden City, N.Y.:
Doubleday, 1960.
Ellis, Harry B. *Challenge in the Middle East: Communist Influence
and American Policy*. New York: Ronald Press, 1960.
Heller, Deane and David. *John Foster Dulles: Soldier for Peace*. New
York: Holt, Rinehart and Winston, 1960.
Hourani, A. H. "The Middle East and the Crisis of 1956." *St. Antony's
Papers*, No. 4 (Middle Eastern Affairs, No. 1). New York: Praeger,
1959.
Humbaraci, Arslan. *Middle East Indictment*. London: Robert Hale,
1958.
Ionides, Michael. *Divide and Lose: The Arab Revolt of 1955–1958*.
London: Geoffrey Bles, 1960.
Partner, Peter. *A Short Political Guide to the Arab World*. New York:
Praeger, 1960.
Polk, William R. "A Decade of Discovery: America in the Middle
East, 1947–1958." *St. Antony's Papers*, No. 11, Albert Hourani, ed.
(Middle Eastern Affairs, No. 2). London: Chatto and Windus,
1961.
Strausz-Hupé, Robert, Alvin J. Cottrell, and James E. Dougherty, eds.
American-Asian Tensions. New York: Praeger, for Foreign Policy
Research Institute of the University of Pennsylvania, 1956.
Thayer, Charles W. *Diplomat*. New York: Harper, 1959.

French Books

Chamoun, Camille. *Crise au Moyen-Orient*. Paris: L'Air du Temps
179, Editions Gallimard, 1963. (Diary-type memoirs of the former
President of Lebanon.)

Chebli, Michel. *Une Histoire du Liban à l'époque des émirs (1635–1841)*. Beirut: Catholic Press, 1955.

Jouplain, M. *La Question du Liban*. Paris: Librairie Nouvelle de Droit et de Jurisprudence, 1908.

Pharaon, Henri. *Au Service du Liban et de son unité*. Beirut: Le Jour Press, 1959. (A collection of the public writings of the leader of the Third Force in Lebanon during 1957 and 1958.)

Rondot, Pierre. *Les Institutions politiques du Liban*. Paris: Institut d'Etudes de l'Orient Contemporain, 1947.

Tabbarah, Bahige B. "Les Forces politiques actuelles au Liban." Doct. diss., Faculté de Droit, Université de Grenoble, April, 1954. Mimeographed copy at the library of the American University at Beirut.

Pamphlets

al-Kataeb al-lubnaniya. (A collection of memoranda and open letters to the President of the Republic from the *Kataeb* party. Text in English, Arabic, and French.) Beirut: *Kataeb*, 1956.

al-Kataeb al-lubnaniya. (A report on the history, organization, creed, and objectives of the party in English and Arabic.) Beirut: *Kataeb*, 1958.

Minhaj al-kutlah al-wataniyah al-lubnaniya, 1943–1947–1951 (Program of the Lebanese National Bloc). Published by the Bloc in Beirut, n.d.

Najjadah Party. *Min qanunina al-asasi (From our Basic Law)*. (Report in Arabic on the party's program and objectives compiled by Ramadan Lawand, Secretary of the Committee on Party Doctrine.) Beirut: Muniymna Press, n.d.

Tueni, Ghassan. *al-Ayyam al-'asabiyah (The Critical Days)*. (Reprint of editorials by publisher-editor Tueni appearing in his Beirut Arabic daily *an-Nahar* May–August 1958.)

United Nations Observation Group in Lebanon—A Mission Completed. United Nations, New York, reprinted from *United Nations Review*, Vol. V, No. 7, January 1959.

23 Ans au Service du Liban. (Illustrated pamphlet on the *Kataeb's* accomplishments.) Beirut, *Kataeb*, n.d.

Conferences, Lectures, and Speeches

Asmar, Michel, ed. *Les Conférences du Cénacle*. (Arabic and French speeches on Lebanese history, politics, and society, and on Lebanese-Arab relations, delivered by various speakers at the public

meetings of Le Cénacle Libanais—of which Mr. Asmar is founder—
and published in issues of *Le Cénacle*, Beirut, from 1950 to 1960.)

Lebanon Indicts Nasser. (An address by Dr. Charles Malik, Lebanese
Minister for Foreign Affairs, at the Security Council of the United
Nations, Friday, June 6, 1958.) Detroit: Reprint by *The Lebanese
Gazette.*

President Gamal Abdel Nasser's Speeches and Press Interviews.
Cairo: Information Department, United Arab Republic, vols. for
1958, 1959, January–March 1960, and April–June 1960.

Sands, William, ed. *Middle East Report 1959: Nationalism, Neutralism, Communism—The Struggle for Power.* (A series of addresses
presented at the Thirteenth Annual Conference on Middle Eastern
Affairs, sponsored by the Middle East Institute, March 20–21,
1959. See especially Nabih Amin Faris, "Report on Lebanon," pp.
39–45.) Washington: The Middle East Institute, 1959.

Official Documents

Congressional Record, 85th Congress. Washington: U.S. Government
Printing Office, Vol. 103: Part I, Jan. 3–Feb. 1, 1957; Part II, Feb.
4–March, 1957; Part III, March 1–March 22, 1957. (These contain
the House and Senate debates leading to the adoption of the Eisenhower Doctrine. For a Senate debate on United States Middle East
policy see also Senator Fulbright's "Middle East Policy Inquiry,"
Vol. 103, Part XI, Aug. 9–Aug. 21, 1957, pp. 14701–14710.)

Davis, Helen Miller. "Constitution of the Lebanese Republic" and
"Pact of the League of Arab States" in *Constitutions, Electoral
Laws, Treaties of States in the Near and Middle East.* Durham,
N.C.: Duke University Press, 1953.

Documents on the Foreign Policy of Lebanon. (In English, Arabic,
and French.) Beirut: Republic of Lebanon, Publications of the
Ministry of Foreign Affairs and of Lebanese Abroad, January, 1958.

"Documents on the Present Situation in Lebanon." (Compiled by the
United National Opposition Front of Lebanon, August 10, 1958, in
Beirut, but unpublished. English translation courtesy of Prof.
Walid Khalidi, Department of Political Science and Public Admin-
istration, American University of Beirut.)

*Mahadir Majlis al-Nuwwab (Proceedings of the Chamber of Deputies
of Lebanon)* for 1957 (2 vols.), and for 1958 (1 vol.). Compiled by
the Office of the *Official Gazette,* Beirut.

*Report of the Committee on Foreign Relations and the Committee on
Armed Services on S. J. Res. 19 To Promote Peace and Stability
in the Middle East; Report No. 70,* U.S. Senate, 85th Cong., 1st
Sess. Washington: U.S. Government Printing Office, 1957.

United Nations Security Council documents on Lebanon's complaint: S/4007, S/4018, S/4022, S/4023, S/4029, S/4038, and S/4038/ Corr. 1. (These documents deal with the Lebanese case for May-June 1958.)

United Nations. *Security Council Official Records,* Thirteenth Year, Supplement for July, August and September 1958. New York.

United Nations. *Official Records of the General Assembly Third Emergency Special Session 8–21 August 1958.* Plenary Meetings and Annexes. New York.

United Nations. *Resolutions Adopted by the General Assembly during its Third Emergency Special Session from 8 to 21 August 1958.* U.N. General Assembly Official Records, Supplement No. 1 (A/3905). New York.

United States Policy in the Middle East, September 1956–June 1957. Department of State Publication 6505, Near and Middle Eastern Series 25. Washington: U.S. Government Printing Office, August, 1957.

Periodicals

Foreign Affairs, Council on Foreign Relations, New York.
Middle East Forum, Alumni Association, American University, Beirut.
Orient, Société d'Etudes et de Publications, Paris.

Interviews by the Author in Lebanon

Mr. Asad al-Ashkar, a former deputy from the Metn and a former president of the Social National party in Lebanon; in the village of Dik el-Mehdi, Sept. 1, 1960.

President Camille Chamoun, at his residence in Sa'diyat, Oct. 20, 1960.

Emir Maurice Chehab, curator of the Lebanese National Museum; in Beirut, June 3, 1960.

Mr. Raymond Edde, chief of the Lebanese National Bloc and traditional deputy from Jbeil, who has participated in several Cabinets; in Beirut, Aug. 4, 1960.

Sheikh Pierre Gemayel, chief of the Lebanese *Kataeb* party, and at the time of the interview a minister and a deputy from Beirut; in Beirut, Oct. 24, 1960.

Mr. Adnan al-Hakim, chief of the *Najjadah* party, who was elected to the Chamber of Deputies for the first time in the summer of 1960; in Beirut, May 10, 1960.

Mr. Rachid Karame, traditional deputy from Tripoli and participant in several Cabinets as Premier; in Beirut, Oct. 31, 1960.

Mr. Jibran al-Majdalani, at the time of the interview secretary of the Lebanese Baath Socialist party and editor of the party's weekly *as-Sahafa*; in Beirut, Nov. 2, 1960.

Mr. Nassim al-Majdalani, reelected in the summer of 1960 as deputy from Beirut, then appointed to the Cabinet; in Beirut, July 19, 1960.

Dr. Charles Malik, former Lebanese foreign minister and a former deputy; in Dhour Chweir, Sept. 20, 1960.

Mr. Adel Osseiran, at the time of the interview deputy from Zahrani; he is also a former president of the Lebanese Chamber of Deputies; in Dhour Chweir, Aug. 5, 1960.

Mr. Henri Pharaon, a former Lebanese foreign minister and leader of the Third Force during the crisis of 1957–1958; in Beirut, Aug. 17, 1960.

Mr. Saeb Salam, a former leader of the United National Opposition Front who was elected deputy from Beirut in the summer of 1960, then assumed the premiership; in Beirut, July 19, 1960.

Mr. Sami es-Solh, a former deputy from Beirut and a former Premier, who held that post at the time of the 1958 crisis; in Beirut, Aug. 1, 1960.

Dr. Abdallah al-Yafi, a former Premier and deputy who was one of the leaders of the former United National Opposition Front; in Beirut, July 27, 1960.

NOTES

1. The Introduction of Confessional Politics into Lebanese Society, 1830–1860

1. The last census in Lebanon was taken in 1932 when the country was still a French mandate. It revealed a slight Christian majority in a population of approximately 392,000 Christians and 383,000 Muslims. These figures were used in 1943 to fix a permanent parliamentary ratio of six Christian to five Muslim deputies. Since 1932 only official estimates of the population, based on records of births and deaths, have been made, and these have continued to indicate a slight majority of Christians over Muslims. A new census is not officially contemplated, for it would be bound to provoke a bitter argument between Christians and Muslims as to who should be included in it. From previous debates on this subject, it seems that the Christians would want to include in the census the Lebanese émigrés who have not acquired foreign citizenship, for most of them are Christian. The Muslims, on the other hand, would object to inclusion of the émigrés, but would want to include the Kurdish and Palestinian refugees in Lebanon, who are largely Muslim. In turn, the Christians would oppose consideration of any of the refugees. Furthermore, should these arguments somehow be miraculously resolved, the results of a new census might indicate the need for a new balance of power within the state, which would upset the conditions of its viability.

2. The Arabic word *mukate'ji* is derived from *mukata'a*, a feudal district. A *mukate'ji* was therefore a feudal district lord with the authority to collect taxes.

3. The Maronites are a Christian sect which originally held the Monothelete doctrine that Christ had two Natures but one Will. Although their church retained its Syriac liturgy, it gave up its doctrine and returned to the church of Rome in the twelfth century. The Druze are a heretic Muslim sect which originated in the eleventh century by splitting off from Isma'ilism, a heterodox sect of Islam practiced in Egypt under the Fatimid Caliphs. At that time a group of Isma'ilis

229

made the claim that the Fatimid Caliph Hakim was the last incarnation of the Deity. Persecuted for their beliefs, they fled to Syria, where they converted others to their religion, which in time came to have other doctrines and observances. Most of these, however, remain secret.

4. The Shi'is, commonly known in Lebanon as the Metawilis, split off from orthodox Islam in the seventh century in a struggle over the succession to the caliphate. They supported for the office Ali, son-in-law of the Prophet, against Mu'awiya, the candidate of the orthodox or Sunni Muslims. Mu'awiya won the caliphate, but the Shi'is continued to recognize only the hereditary successors of the Prophet, beginning with Ali, as the true Imams, or spiritual leaders of Islam. The Shi'is recognized altogether twelve Imams. The Sunni Muslims claim to be thé true exponents of the Koran, the Traditions of the Prophets and the theological works of the great Muslim thinkers.

The Greek Orthodox church broke off from the church of Rome in the eleventh century over differences regarding religious doctrine. In Syria and Lebanon, the liturgy of the Greek Orthodox church is Arabic and its spiritual head is the Patriarch of Antioch, who has been living in Damascus. The Greek Catholic church is a branch of the Greek Orthodox church that had given up certain doctrines unacceptable to the papacy and had returned to the Roman Catholic fold. For further details on religious minorities in Lebanon see A. H. Hourani, *Syria and Lebanon* (London: Oxford University Press, 1946), Chapter VII.

5. Michel Chebli, *Une Histoire du Liban à l'époque des émirs (1635–1841)* (Beirut: Catholic Press, 1955), pp. 250, 437.

6. Malcolm H. Kerr, *Lebanon in the Last Years of Feudalism, 1840–1868* ("A Contemporary Account by Antun Dahir al-'Aqiqi and other Documents," translated with notes and commentary by Kerr, Beirut: American University, Faculty of Arts and Sciences, Oriental Series No. 33, 1959), p. 1; see also Hourani, p. 27.

7. The period of the Egyptian occupation and the animosities it aroused between the Maronites and Druze are particularly well treated by M. Jouplain, *La Question du Liban* (Paris: Librairie Nouvelle de Droit et de Jurisprudence, 1908). Jouplain was a Christian Lebanese, Boulus Nujaim, who had used the assumed name to avoid possible persecution by the Ottomans for his criticism of their policies. For the effects of the Egyptian occupation on Lebanon see pp. 250–252, as well as Kerr, pp. 1–2; Anis Sayegh, *Lubnan at-ta'ifi (Sectarian Lebanon)* (Beirut: Dar as-sira' al-fikri, 1955), pp. 99–101; and Edward Honein, "at-ta'ifiya fi Lubnan" ("Sectarianism in Lebanon"), *Les Conférences du Cénacle*, Beirut, June 25, 1950, pp. 102–124.

8. Jouplain, p. 248, my translation.

9. For a detailed study of the *Hatti Cherif* of Gulhane, and of its application and effects on the peoples of the Ottoman empire, see Roderic H. Davison, *Reform in the Ottoman Empire 1856–1876* (Princeton: Princeton University Press, 1963), pp. 36-50, and Bernard Lewis, *The Emergence of Modern Turkey* (London: Oxford University Press, 1961), pp. 104-113 and pp. 329-330. See also Davison, pp. 10-13 and p. 65 on the organization of the religious minorities within the empire and the attitude of Turkish Muslims toward them, and see Lewis, pp. 348-350 for a further elaboration on the status of religious minorities within the Ottoman empire.

10. Kerr, p. 4.

11. The Arabic term *Abu-Tehine* means "father of flour," used here affectionately to denote the Emir's concern for the people.

12. Chebli, pp. 436–437, my translation.

13. Ibid., p. 437.

14. Jouplain, p. 266, my translation.

15. Kerr, p. 10.

16. For a full account of the 1860 massacres see J. F. Scheltema, *The Lebanon in Turmoil: Syria and the Powers in 1860* ("Book of the Marvels of the Time Concerning the Massacres in the Arab Country by Iskander Ibn Ya'qub Abkarius;" translated with annotation and commentary by Scheltema) (New Haven: Yale University Press, Yale Oriental Series, Vol. VII, 1920); see also Jouplain, Chapter IV, and Kerr, Chapter II. Sayegh, cited, deals with some of the causes of the massacres in Chapter VI.

2. *The Establishment of the* Mutasarrifyya *of Mount Lebanon, 1861*

1. For details of the jostling for advantages and privileges that took place among the European powers and Turkey during their drafting of the protocol for an autonomous regime in Lebanon, see J. F. Scheltema, *The Lebanon in Turmoil: Syria and the Powers in 1860* ("Book of the Marvels of the Time Concerning the Massacres in the Arab Country by Iskander Ibn Ya'qub Abkarius;" translated with annotation and commentary by Scheltema) (New Haven: Yale University Press, Yale Oriental Series, Vol. VII, 1920), pp. 159–170; and M. Jouplain, *La Question du Liban* (Paris: Librairie Nouvelle de Droit et de Jurisprudence, 1908), pp. 400–450.

2. I am indebted primarily to Jouplain, ibid., pp. 472–538 for details of the administrative organization of the *Mutasarrifyya,* its operation and politics, but also to other though less complete sources for corroborating or supplementary information on aspects of these questions. Among these sources are A. H. Hourani, *Syria and Lebanon*

(London: Oxford University Press, 1946), pp. 32–33; Bishara el-Khouri, *Haqa'iq lubnaniya* (*Lebanese Realities*, i.e. memoirs of Bishara el-Khouri) (Beirut: Manshurat *awraq lubnaniya*, Part I, 1960), pp. 24–59; Anis Sayegh, *Lubnan at-ta'ifi* (*Sectarian Lebanon*) (Beirut: Dar as-sira' al fikri, 1955), pp. 124–128; Stephen Hemsley Longrigg, *Syria and Lebanon under French Mandate* (London: Oxford University Press, 1958), pp. 21–24; and Scheltema, cited, p. 171 and passages in following pages.

3. El-Khouri, cited, relates on p. 28 that neither the decisions of the Central Council nor those of the courts could become effective without first being signed by the Governor General. Employees of the administration, el-Khouri adds, were also not authorized to affix their signatures to ordinary government transactions, but had to wait till the end of the day to have the Governor General sign and affix his seal to these transactions. But on occasion, the writer points out, the Governor General did allow a top official he could trust to use his seal in his presence after first learning the nature of the documents to be signed.

4. Jouplain, cited, pp. 507–508. On p. 532, Jouplain writes that the Maronite *qa'im maqams* and cantonal *moudirs* were generally chosen from among the members of the old noble families. On p. 30, el-Khouri, cited, comments that during the *Mutasarrifyya*, the important jobs, except in rare cases, were controlled by the influential families, owing to the continued practice of feudalism after it had been officially abolished as an institution.

3. *The Establishment of Greater Lebanon under French Mandate*

1. See, for example, Chapter IV of Zeine N. Zeine, *Arab-Turkish Relations and the Emergence of Arab Nationalism* (Beirut: Khayat's, 1958), where the author discusses the difference between Christian and Muslim anti-Turkish agitation in the last thirty years of the nineteenth century. He indicates that the Christians agitated for independence whereas the Muslims demanded only greater Arab autonomy within the Ottoman Empire. The earlier study by George Antonius, *The Arab Awakening* (London: Hamish Hamilton, 1938), which has received wide circulation, claims in Chapter V that the first organized Arab nationalist movement dates back to 1875, when a small secret society was organized in Beirut with the purpose of spreading anti-Turkish agitation. On pp. 56–57 Zeine refutes Antonius' contention by showing the differences between the self-identification of the Muslim masses with the Muslim Ottoman empire and the Christian communities' feeling of inferiority within that empire. Albert Hourani,

Minorities in the Arab World (London: Oxford University Press, 1947), indirectly supports Zeine's thesis by pointing to the early beginnings of the Arab nationalist movement after the Revolution of the Young Turks in 1908. The movement was encouraged, he says on p. 30, by the violent Turkish nationalism that the Young Turks displayed. Similarly, Nabih Amin Faris and Mohammed Tawfik Husayn, in *The Crescent in Crisis* (Lawrence: University of Kansas Press, 1955), report on p. 37 the appearance of a number of Arab parties and societies between 1909 and 1914 to promote the development of Arab nationalism.

2. Credit for the Central Council's motives is given by Nicola A. Ziadeh, *Syria and Lebanon* (London: Ernest Benn, 1957), p. 49. The man who claimed that the Council was bribed was Iskandar ar-Riachi, a Lebanese newspaperman who recorded his memoirs of Lebanese politics between 1918–1941 in *Qabl wa-ba'd* (*Before and After*) (Beirut: Maktabat al-'Urfan, 1955); see pp. 26–27 for the bribery charge.

3. For a detailed discussion of the position of the unionists, both Lebanese and Syrian, see George Dib, "The National Pact in Its Original Meaning Is a Progressive and Unifying Agreement," *an-Nahar* (Beirut Arabic daily), July 29, 1960, pp. 4 and 7.

4. The constitution of 1926 provided for a two-chamber legislative body, a Senate with nine elected and seven presidentially appointed members, and a Chamber of Deputies all of whose thirty members were elected. A constitutional amendment passed a year later abolished the upper house and increased the members of the Chamber to 45, 30 of whom were to be elected and 15 to be appointed by the President.

5. Ar-Riachi, p. 215, my translation.

6. For a detailed report on the identification of nationalism with Islam by the Arab Muslim masses, and indeed also by more educated groups, see Wilfred Cantwell Smith, *Islam in Modern History* (Princeton: Princeton University Press, 1957), Chapters II and III. As Smith also indicates, some Christian Arabs mistrust Arab nationalism because they fear that the Muslim Arabs cannot share it on a nonsectarian basis.

4. Political Groups in Lebanon's Confessional System

1. We have seen in Chapter Two how the feudal aristocracy under the *Mutasarrifyya* regime allied itself with the Governor and competed among itself and with the clergy for control of both the representative councils and the bureaucracy.

2. Nicola A. Ziadeh, *Syria and Lebanon* (London: Ernest Benn, 1957), p. 195.

3. Iskandar ar-Riachi, *Qabl wa-ba'd* (*Before and After*) (Beirut: Maktabat al-'Urfan, 1955), p. 124, my translation.

4. As quoted by Ziadeh, p. 199.

5. Details of the office-seeking activities of the Constitutional and the National Bloc are well presented by Bahige B. Tabbarah in his mimeographed dissertation, "Les Forces politiques actuelles au Liban" (Université de Grenoble, April, 1954), pp. 196–198. More insight into the personal motivations of members of both Blocs is given by ar-Riachi, Chapter 23: "The Second Republic and the Organization of the Constitutional Bloc."

6. Stephen Hemsley Longrigg, *Syria and Lebanon under French Mandate* (London: Oxford University Press, 1958), p. 219.

7. A. H. Hourani, *Syria and Lebanon* (London: Oxford University Press, 1946), p. 202.

8. George Dib, from his introduction to his own translation of "Selections from Riadh Solh's Speech in the Lebanese Assembly, Oct. [7,] 1943," *Middle East Forum*, Beirut, Jan. 1959, p. 6.

9. Upon their arrival in Lebanon, the Free French replaced the High Commissioner by a Delegate General in recognition of the new "independent" status of Lebanon.

10. An exception to this rule was made in 1945–1946 when Greek Orthodox Habib Abu-Chahlah replaced Shi'i Sabri Hamade as president of the Chamber.

11. George Dib, "Selections from Riadh Solh's Speech in the Lebanese Assembly," p. 7.

12. Ibid.

13. Ibid.

5. *Regional Developments and Lebanese Politics*

1. Of the 55 members of the Chamber three had deliberately kept away from this historic meeting, while two others, one of them Emile Edde, withdrew during the first stage of the discussions because the Chamber refused to submit the proposed amendments to a special committee for further study. See Munir Takieddine, *Wiladat istiqlal* (*Birth of an Independence*) (Beirut: Dar al-'Ilm lil-Malayin, 1953), pp. 52–53.

2. Stephen Hemsley Longrigg, *Syria and Lebanon under French Mandate* (London: Oxford University Press, 1958), p. 349.

3. Nicola A. Ziadeh, *Syria and Lebanon* (London: Ernest Benn, 1957), p. 277.

4. Francis Nour, "Particularisme libanais et nationalisme arabe,"

Orient, Paris, 3rd quarter, 1958, No. 7, affirms on p. 31 President Chamoun's deviation toward the Hashemites. The same is indicated by Walid Khalidi, "Nasser and the Arab World," *Middle East Forum,* Beirut, April, 1959, on p. 33: "In the meantime, Saudi Arabia had fallen in line with Egypt and Syria, for above all it was haunted by the Hashemite skull beneath the skin of the Baghdad Pact. As to Lebanon, the situation was that, as late as the spring of 1956, President Chamoun does not seem to have definitely crossed the Rubicon, although evidence released by the Baghdad trials indicates that he was already in effective liaison with the Baghdad Pact countries from 1955." In an interview with the author on February 18, 1960, the noted political columnist for the Beirut daily *L'Orient,* René Aggiouri, affirmed that President Chamoun had indeed supported the Hashemites against Gamal Abdel Nasser. Henri Pharaon, former Lebanese foreign minister and leader of the Third Force during the 1958 crisis, also told the author on August 17, 1960, that President Chamoun had attempted to strengthen the position of Iraq and Jordan vis-à-vis Egypt.

5. Interview by the author with President Camille Chamoun on October 20, 1960, at his residence in Sa'diyat near Beirut.

6. *Mahadir Majlis al-Nuwwab* (*Proceedings of the Chamber of Deputies*), Beirut, Vol. 2, 1957, p. 73.

7. Riad es-Solh was assassinated by members of the Syrian National Party (formerly known as the PPS—Partie Populaire Syrien) on July 16, 1951, as he was preparing to leave Jordan, where he had visited King Abdallah. His assassination was an act of revenge, for the Syrian Nationalists had held him responsible for the summary trial and execution of their leader Antoun Saadeh in 1949. At that time es-Solh was Prime Minister.

6. *The Eisenhower Doctrine versus Middle East Realities*

1. "Message to Congress by President Eisenhower, January 5, 1957," *United States Policy in the Middle East,* September 1956–June 1957, Department of State Publication 6505, Near and Middle Eastern Series 25, U.S. Government Printing Office, Washington, D.C., p. 19.

2. Deane and David Heller, *John Foster Dulles: Soldier for Peace,* (New York: Holt, Rinehart and Winston, 1960), p. 262.

3. Geoffrey Wheeler, "Russia and the Arab World," *Atlas* magazine, New York, Vol. 2, No. 5, Nov. 1961, p. 341.

4. *Hearings before the Committee on Foreign Affairs, House of Representatives, Eighty-Fifth Congress, First Session on H. J. Res.*

117, Jan. 7, 8, 9, 10, 15, 17, and 22, 1957, U. S. Government Printing Office, Washington, 1957, p. 68.

5. Ibid., p. 69.

6. *Hearings before the Committee on Foreign Relations and the Committee on Armed Services, United States Senate, Eighty-Fifth Congress, First Session on S. J. Res. 19 and H. J. Res. 117*, Part I, Jan. 14, 15, 24, 25, 28, 29, 30, and Feb. 1 and 4, 1957, U. S. Government Printing Office, Washington, 1957, p. 29.

7. Ibid., p. 429.

8. J. K. Banerji, *The Middle East in World Politics* (Calcutta: The World Press Private, 1960), as quoted by the author, p. 309.

9. Richard P. Stebbins, *The United States in World Affairs* (New York: Harper, 1958), as quoted on p. 176.

10. House of Representatives *Hearings on H. J. Res. 117*, pp. 67–68.

11. Tom Streithorst, "Face to Face with Camille Chamoun," *Middle East Forum*, Beirut, April, 1957, p. 7.

12. *Mahadir Majlis al-Nuwwab* (*Proceedings of the Chamber of Deputies*), Beirut, Vol. 1, 1957, p. 974. Members of the Government who are drawn from the Chamber are entitled to vote, but the president of the Chamber does not vote. Of the 44 deputies only 4 were absent from the April 5 meeting; a fifth, Kamal Junblatt, had resigned in February.

7. *Lebanon's Foreign Policy in Local Politics*

1. British and French institutions and diplomatic and consular representations in Lebanon were still in danger of acts of reprisal because of the Suez Canal attack. There were also some terrorist activities in Beirut, and the Government seized illicit arms with which Egyptian diplomatic personnel were implicated. Relations with Syria were very bad, and Syrian political refugees in Lebanon were being actively sought by agents of the Syrian Deuxième Bureau, the Army Secret Service.

2. During the Muslim month of *Ramadan*, devout Muslims fast all day and eat at night. *Iftar* is the first meal taken after sundown.

3. The *mohafazats* are North Lebanon, Mount Lebanon, South Lebanon, the Biqa', and the city of Beirut. Because the rather limited security forces must be used to keep order at the polls, the elections are held on four consecutive Sundays. Each *mohafazat* votes on a separate Sunday, except Beirut and South Lebanon, which vote on the same day.

4. Henri Pharaon, *Au Service du Liban et de son unité* (Beirut: Le Jour Press, 1959), pp. 19–22, my translation.

5. Article entitled "La sharq wala gharb" (Neither East nor West), *al-Hayat*, Beirut, March 23, 1957, my translation.

6. Article entitled "La ta'bidu rabbyin" (Don't Worship Two Gods), *al-Jarida*, Beirut, June 29, 1957.

7. Ibid., my translation.

8. The election of a new 99-man Chamber in the summer of 1960 indicated that a new trend might be developing. In the Baalback-Hermel constituency, only three of the seven candidates on the slate of Sabri Hamade, a feudal leader with a large Shi'i following, won the elections. Hamade was among them. The other four candidates lost to the opposing slate. There was also some less pronounced vote-splitting in other constituencies.

9. Because of the size of its population, Beirut was divided into two constituencies in 1957. In 1960 it was divided into three constituencies, since the enlargement of the Chamber entitled it to elect sixteen deputies—five more than in 1957.

10. A candidate can choose to run in any constituency, provided a member of his sect is to be elected there.

11. "Pharaon, Takla et Maalouf tirent la leçon du scrutin de Baalbeck," *L'Orient*, Beirut, June 25, 1957, my translation.

12. Ibid.

13. Iskander ar-Riarchi, *Qabl wa-ba'd (Before and After)* (Beirut: Maktabat al-'Urfan, 1955), p. 117.

14. Na'im al-Zaila', *Chamoun Yatakallam (Chamoun Speaks)* (Beirut: Matba'at al-Jihad, n.d.), pp. 33, and 35-36. The book appeared on the Beirut market toward the end of 1959.

15. Interview with Kamal Junblatt by reporter Lucien George entitled "Kamal Joumblatt: 'J'ai été battu? Oui! Par le Chef de l'Etat . . .'," *L'Orient*, Beirut, July 7, 1957.

16. "Pharaon, Takla et Maalouf tirent la leçon . . . ," my translation.

17. On April 16, 1957, the Beirut Arabic daily *al-Hayat* reported a press conference given by Junblatt in which he expressed the view that the Lebanese-American communiqué of March 16 was not a pact. He also stated that "positive neutralism" made no sense to anyone except to those who called for it as a policy for humoring the Communists. His later criticism of President Chamoun's acceptance of the Eisenhower Doctrine appears in his own book *Haqiqat ath-thawra al-Lubnaniya (The Truth about the Lebanese Revolution)* (Beirut: Dar an-nashr al-'arabiya, 1959), pp. 71-78

18. Feeling that it would strengthen his position as foreign minister if he could also be a member of the Chamber, the Chamoun regime had decided to sponsor Malik's candidacy for the Greek Orthodox seat of the Koura, a uninominal constituency in North

Lebanon. To ensure his election, however, it induced both Koura's traditional deputy, Fuad Ghosn, and the National Socialist Party candidate, Abdallah Saadeh, to withdraw their names from the race. Thus Malik's only opponent was left-winger Abdallah Hreike, who could muster only 276 votes.

19. As quoted by Francis Nour, "Particularisme libanais et nationalisme arabe," *Orient*, Paris, 3rd quarter, 1958, No. 7, pp. 37–38, my translation.

20. Freyha's editorial of the week, "The Last Open Letter to President Chamoun," *as-Sayyad*, April 3, 1958, my translation. *As-Sayyad* was known to have been subsidized by the Cairo regime.

21. Georges Naccache, "La Reconduction—cette aventure . . . ," *L'Orient,* Beirut, April 11, 1958, my translation.

8. *The Revolution of 1958*

1. From an interview by the author with Mr. Raymond Edde at his law office in Beirut on August 4, 1960.

2. Interview with Mgr. Paul Meouchy published in the Beirut dailies *al-Jarida* and *L'Orient* on April 20, 1958.

3. A Muslim canonical edict against Prime Minister Sami es-Solh issued June 6, 1958, and contained in a collection of documents of the United National Opposition Front.

4. Henri Pharaon, "Un Nouveau manifeste de la Troisième Force," *Au Service du Liban et de son unité* (Beirut: *Le Jour* Press, 1959), p. 100.

5. *L'Orient*, Beirut, May 26, 1958.

6. Michael Adams, "A Little Trip?" *The Spectator*, London, June 6, 1958, p. 721.

7. *L'Orient*, Beirut, May 22, 1958.

8. From an interview by the author with President Camille Chamoun on October 20, 1960, at his residence in Sa'diyat near Beirut.

9. *The Daily Star*, Beirut, May 29, 1958, p. 2.

10. *Mahadir Majlis al-Nuwwab* (*Proceedings of the Chamber of Deputies*), Beirut, 1958, p. 680.

11. *Resolutions Adopted by the General Assembly During Its Third Emergency Special Session from 8 to 21 August 1958*, U.N. General Assembly Official Records, Supplement No. 1 (A/3905), p. 1.

9. *The Eisenhower Doctrine: A Balance Sheet*

1. "Secretary Dulles' News Conference of May 20," The Department of State *Bulletin*, U.S. Government Printing Office, Washington, Vol. 38, No. 989, June 9, 1958, p. 945.

2. Article 51 of the United Nations Charter states: "Nothing in the present Charter shall impair the inherent right of individual or collective self-defense if an armed attack occurs against a Member of the United Nations, until the Security Council has taken the measures necessary to maintain international peace and security. Measures taken by Members in the exercise of this right of self-defense shall be immediately reported to the Security Council and shall not in any way affect the authority and responsibility of the Security Council under the present Charter to take at any time such action as it deems necessary in order to maintain or restore international peace and security."

3. Text of the statement on the Lebanese situation by Henry Cabot Lodge, United States ambassador to the United Nations, in the Security Council on July 15, 1958, *New York Herald Tribune*, European Edition, Rome, July 17, 1958, p. 8.

4. For the hour-by-hour drama of the landing operation see Charles W. Thayer, *Diplomat* (New York: Harper, 1959), Chapters 2 and 3. See also "U.S. Troops in Beirut Divide Lebanese Opinion," *The Times*, London, July 17, 1958, p. 10.

5. Camille Chamoun, *Crise au Moyen-Orient* (Paris: L'Air du Temps 179, Editions Gallimard, 1963), pp. 429–431. For another opinion on changing United States policy see pp. 359–360.

10. *Political Power and Authority in Lebanon*

1. Pierre Rondot, "Quelques réflexions sur les structures du Liban," *Orient*, Paris, 2nd quarter, 1958, No. 6, p. 31.

2. From an interview by the author with former Prime Minister Sami es-Solh at his law office in Beirut on August 1, 1960.

3. See note 2 of Chapter Nine.

4. From an interview by the author with President Camille Chamoun on October 20, 1960, at his residence in Sa'diyat near Beirut.

5. Identical telegrams sent by Mr. Osseiran on July 16, 1958, to President Eisenhower, the U.S. Secretary of State, the Speaker of the American Congress, the President of the U.N. Security Council, and the Secretary of the U.N. Security Council, contained in a collection of documents of the United National Opposition Front.

6. From an interview by the author with Mr. Osseiran on August 5, 1960, at his summer residence in Dhour Chweir.

7. See M. Jouplain, *La Question du Liban* (Paris: Librairie Nouvelle de Droit et de Jurisprudence, 1908), pp. 475–476, 506–509, and 527–528 for details on the legal and actual powers of the Governors General.

8. Nicola A. Ziadeh, *Syria and Lebanon* (London: Ernest Benn, 1957), deals briefly but pointedly with corruption in the el-Khouri regime in Chapter V.

9. Iskandar ar-Riachi, "Chamoun Entered the Presidency through the Wide Door" (translated title), *al-Hayat*, Beirut, October 16, 1960. This was No. 9 in a series of articles in *al-Hayat* by ar-Riachi on Lebanese heads of state, and it deals extensively with Chamoun's attitude toward other politicians.

10. Jean-Pierre Alem, "Troubles insurrectionnels au Liban," *Orient*, Paris, 2nd quarter, 1958, No. 6, my translation.

INDEX